HANDBOOK OF PSYCHIC DISCOVERIES

SHEILA OSTRANDER
and
LYNN SCHROEDER

A BERKLEY MEDALLION BOOK
published by
BERKLEY PUBLISHING CORPORATION

The Foley Agency
34 East 38th Street
New York, New York 10016

Library of Congress Catalog Card Number: 73-88532

SBN 425-02894-1

BERKLEY MEDALLION BOOKS are published by
Berkley Publishing Corporation
200 Madison Avenue
New York, N. Y. 10016

BERKLEY MEDALLION BOOK ® TM 757,375

Printed in the United States of America

Berkley Medallion Edition, JULY, 1975

Contents

Section One

Section Two

Section Three

Section Four

Section Five

Section Six

Photographs appear following p. 160

This book is dedicated to

Marjorie D. Kern
1896-1973
Author, and founder of the Southern California Society
for Psychical Research.

and

Ivan T. Sanderson
1911-1973
Author, artist, explorer, and founder of the Society for the
Investigation of the Unexplained.

1

Points of Departure

"I can't quite get it, I think it's MacBeth. Try again," urged the anxious young experimenter as a cluster of friends strained forward around him in silent suspense. All through the first few weeks of August 1876, a hodgepodge group of neighbors and relations from the countryside of Brantford, Ontario, had pitched in and worked hard to help with an experiment—one which certain other citizens asserted was the sheerest sort of fiddle-faddle.

That night, leaving a crowd of helpers at their post in Brantford, the young man had traveled to the town of Paris, nine miles distant. He was trying to connect with his cohorts in Brantford. "Try again," he urged. They did. They sent their experiment soaring into the history books on the wings of "Oh Dem Golden Slippers," "Auld Lang Syne," and "Do You Ken John Peel." Instead of MacBeth, now the young experimenter heard the clear resonant tones of his father, a world-famous elocutionist, asking "To be or not to be . . .''

And Alexander Graham Bell thought, "It is to be!"

Meanwhile the hour of the test had passed, but on and on and on they sang in Brantford. While in Paris, outside White's shoe store a crowd filled the sidewalk, and those lucky enough to be inside shouted, "I hear it! I hear it! It's 'Golden Slippers.' It's 'Auld Lang Syne.' '' And nobody minded a bit how late it grew, for they had succeeded in proving that human beings can communicate *long distance* over a wire. The telephone was to be more than "an electric toy."

As Bell, a speech instructor, and his group of amateurs strung miles of stovepipe wire, practiced songs, and built receivers, they got a firsthand feeling few could match for the new world of

1

communications in the making. Now, a hundred years later, we seem to be cycling around to another breakthrough into a different kind of communication. Just as the crowd at Brantford gained an inkling of what this discovery might mean to their lives, it may be the firsthanders today who get the clearest insight into where the discoveries of ESP will lead us. Bell made available a form of personal communication that has become an intimate part of everyone's life. Today we are still as much a part of the Bell experiment as the people who sang so doggedly over the first phone lines. Communications networks have become highly sophisticated, but it's still you who must do the talking.

Similarly the handful of explorers in psi are in the process of setting up some of the first primitive psychic communications systems for people to begin to "communicate" with other kingdoms, such as plants; to "communicate" with machines, with other dimensions of existence possibly, and with other people certainly.

This handbook is set up for people who would like to start making their own psi connections, and it maps a few of the various lines that have been opened via new instruments and techniques. Can we really begin to learn to connect in new ways with the visible and invisible world around us? Are there right numbers and wrong numbers? Can the growing and touted claims for psi connections be demonstrated objectively? Perhaps you can see see for yourself.

Among other ideas, this guide includes simplified, inexpensive adaptations of some of the devices, gadgets, and training techniques developed by recognized psi researchers and used in hallmark experiments. (There are details and patent summaries of sophisticated equipment for the technically minded.) There are devices that may enable you to talk to plants and have them answer back; ways to photograph auras of one kind or another and also the effect of your thoughts on plants and people; simple devices and special games that might prompt your telepathic ability; ways to explore "other" energies; ways to use your tape recorder to explore the paranormal. And there are gadgetless excursions into the paranormal—things as simple to do as planting a seed, lying back and relaxing, or playing bingo.

Though some of these new communications techniques and devices are still about the tin-can-and-wire stage of Bell's early telephone, to the people who've seen what they can do, they hold the same promise for the future that Bell's stovepipe wire experiments held a hundred years ago. This book invites the reader to exercise his or her own creative imagination; to explore, invent, accomplish; create new games, new ways of investigating. It asks more questions than it answers in the hope that you will come up with still more questions. You don't need a lot of money to do most of the things in the book. Experiments and games can be set up generally with household items or with inexpensive components.

For people already convinced that ESP exists, the methods and devices described may provide tangible demonstration of their ideas. They may prove a means of presenting convincing demonstration of psi to others. It is largely because technology has made possible clear demonstration of certain psi effects that what psychics have been claiming for centuries is at last being taken seriously. Is this labor of psychic and scientist bringing us more than a pot full of certified wonders? Right now the pot-pourri of things labeled psychic is a fashionable dish, serving up entertainment, increasingly providing tidbits for the original dissertation. But there seems to be something else growing below the winds of fashion.

A Change in Consciousness?

Bell and his contemporaries crossed the threshold to a new dimension of communication. A sudden splurge of understanding and innovation roared in. Telephone, telegraph, radio, movies, airplanes, all brought people closer together radically altering their view of the world and each other.

If even a part of the boom-time talk one hears about the opening of inner space is on target, it seems we are heading toward another genuine expansion in communication; perhaps toward a jump in understanding of how intimately connected we are with each other and the rest of the universe; perhaps toward a new kind of pragmatic science.

American Telephone & Telegraph has put plant communication on its research and development list. Researchers at Maimonides Medical Center in Brooklyn have established the reality of telepathy in dreams and pursue it now on a government grant. Others photograph and probe subtle energies in and around our bodies, some also working on government grants. US and Russian researchers are taking pictures of something more visible, more energetic than suggestion communicating between healers and patients. Top-level scientists in both these countries and in others are investigating women and men they say can move and twist matter at a distance, can influence film and magnetic tape from afar.

An Academy of Parapsychology and Medicine has been founded by doctors and is flourishing. So is an Academy of Psychical Research and Religion. An American astronaut, Dr. Edgar Mitchell, has founded the Institute of Noetic Sciences for the study of consciousness with the emphasis on psychic research; and anthropologist Carlos Castaneda has revealed his extraordinary transforming encounter with Don Juan, an Indian *brujo* (medicine man). In the pure sciences, too, there is a rapprochement at the top between science and Eastern philosophy in fields from physics to holography. Typical of this is the group of German scientists working with yogi Gopi Krishna at the Research Foundation for Eastern Wisdom and Western Science at Starnberg, Germany, headed by physicist Dr. C. F. von Weizäcker, a director of the famed Max Planck Institute.

American cyberneticist James Whitney suggests this confluence between Eastern philosophy and modern science may have a profound effect on art, too, and has turned to cybernetic cinema, to image changes of consciousness brought by his own yoga experiences—visualizations on film of such things as the *Akasha* or etheric energy.

This blending of art, science and Eastern thought has stirred a reexamining of psi. Defense engineer L. George Lawrence observes, ". . . the application of electronic instruments to this unique area has permitted dramatic experiments and brought forth a few stunning discoveries of excellent promise, which has prompted those most active in this field to predict that, in time, parapsychological methods might well rival the orthodox communications arts and sciences currently in use." (*Electronics World*, April, 1970.)

Psi (prounounced "sī"), the twenty-third letter of the Greek alphabet, the root of *psy*chology, *psy*chic—is a neutral term used now as an umbrella name covering all manner of the psychic, the unexplained. Today a growing number of people see psi or psychic research as simply part, though a very yeasty part, of a larger unfolding, the study of the nature of consciousness, a reexamination of the nature of the human being, of all of us.

So it appears psi is beginning to move into the mainstream. It is being taken seriously in established quarters. But the mainstream has many currents and there are others as strong. A remarkable number of people of every sort of education and background, all across America, are actively involved on their own with the psychic, the mystic, the occult and other psi-related realms. Overall it's as if an alarm clock had gone off in the collective unconscious signaling that now finally it is psi's turn to be that idea whose time has come. There is sense and nonsense afoot. To some extent the shapes this idea will take is up to everyone, not just the expert.

Is It Really New?

Occasionally, people say to us, "Those psi scientists aren't discovering anything new. We've known it all along!" Some people have. And in another sense, some contemporary psychic exploration appears to be a rediscovering of old knowledge. But there is a difference. Psi used to be a subjective event to both practitioner and researcher.

Today, instrumentation is making some paranormal events objective, bringing the possibility of understanding and use on a broad scale. Another major difference is who's doing it. Small dedicated groups of psychics and researchers are beginning to be joined in the investigation of the paranormal by powerful scientific centers—for instance, Stanford Research Institute and the Menninger Foundation. Governments of several countries have also begun putting money into the search for the secrets of psi.

Over the centuries, those who were psi-knowing opted heavily for keeping their knowledge secret. They feared misuse of the power. This fear is sometimes voiced today. Will the arrival of the public and particularly the technologist on the psi scene multiply the danger of misuse? Just as industrialization resulted in polluting the environment through ignorance, so could a too-narrow view lead to exploitation of a fragment of the psychic dimension without realization of the negative consequences. But could it not be that we've reached a day when ignorance of the totality of the psychic dimensions of ourselves and our world may prove as dangerous and costly to us as the misuse of it?

No doubt psi like intelligence, creativity, fire, steel or atomic energy can be used for good or ill. It may be worth noting that many leading psychics and esotericists of this century very much favored going public with information and research. Both the psychic Edgar Cayce and the metaphysician Alice Bailey, for instance, said that the exploration of the paranormal would start developing into a true science in the coming decades and that technological innovation would help bring in deeper understanding. Though cautioning about misuse, both saw this opening out as not only a benefit but also a necessity.

Psi may be one of those things that's too important to leave just to specialists or vested interests. The more people who understand a subject, perhaps the less likely it is to be misused on a wholesale basis and perhaps the better the social decisions that can eventually be made about it. Though only in its infancy, psi as an applied art and science is starting to give solutions to contemporary problems with promise of more to come. Here and there, psi is already an adjunct in crime detection, medical diagnosis, education, agriculture (water dowsing), geology, personnel selection—to name only a few areas. Application of ESP in one's own life is credited with increasing creativity, abundance, success, and meaningfulness, according to top business executives.

It may be a matter of enlightened self-interest to make some of these positive applications of psi better known, especially to the people who may make key decisions affecting your life and who may not be aware of some of these alternate solutions, which psi research has made available.

New Biology of Thinking

Why is psi research important to us all—and to all fields of knowledge? One major reason is that new scientific evidence is beginning to show that forms of energies as yet uncharted are involved with our thoughts and emotions—and thinking and feeling are hardly specialized activities. Many ancient texts, from the lore of poets and witches to the writings of Eastern religions, have described a methodology for modes of thinking capable of altering conditions in the material world, in effect manipulating energy. This way of thinking is described as creative, intuitive, prayerful, transcendental and is often said to be the method used to bring in new ideas and discoveries. It is a way of thinking common to poet, technologist, musician and businessman. The arts, religion, and science are linked by this dynamic and creative mode of thought.

Today we may be approaching a new *biology of thinking*. Through new instrumentation, new scientific techniques, we can now monitor and examine the way in which human thought and language interact with the energies of the universe around us. Contemporary technology may provide a means of transcending itself, a means of seeing how mind and matter are one continuum, how music and medicine are linked, how poet and technologist are connected through a similar operation of mind.

Making Your Own Psi Discoveries

The gist of this handbook is experience, explore, demonstrate, innovate, communicate. Where all the accelerating probing of psi may lead in a hundred years is probably as hard for us to project as it would have been for Graham Bell and his friends to quite imagine the content and feeling of life today. But they did have a feeling for what was happening in their own time. You can read, you can argue, you can say yes, never, maybe; but no matter what the subject, experience gives you an expanded view. It does make a difference if it's your telepathic experience or the picture you made of a sparkling corona around a leaf. It makes a difference too if you try out a claim and find it doesn't work for you.

We've tried to answer many how-to questions that people often ask us and, where possible, to supply fresh information, updating in areas that currently seem to be of cardinal interest to ad hoc experimenters. Some of the psi phenomena included, such as telepathy and PK, are well established. Others are highly controversial. Is a pyramid an energy generator? Is there truth to the claim that you can pick up paranormal voices during ordinary tape-recording? Yet every subject does have some basis in scientific work, a takeoff point, a certain measure of assurance that something unusual seems to be happening. And all are highly open ended, with much room for exploration. Recently the field has become so rich that we have only been able to cover some of the current routes to investigation. There are many more.

How you use this handbook is very much up to you and what your aim is for getting into psi firsthand. You can use it for family projects and entertainment, as some of Graham Bell's people used his experimenting, when after supper they headed out back to the barn to join in the fun with tin cans and stovepipe wire. Or, to go to the other end of the spectrum, information and technical details are presented in the technical section for serious researchers wishing to work strictly scientifically and explore psi within the context of their own specialities. Most of the projects can be adapted toward either of these poles with a lot of stop-off points in between. They can be converted into scientific experiments by simply applying general scientific methodology. In a field as new as psi there's plenty of room for coming up with your own form of expertise, the development of new techniques, the invention of new apparatus and systems. Even if that kind of innovation isn't your interest, you might simply be struck with a better idea. After all, Alexander Graham Bell was a speech teacher and the automatic dialing system for the phone was invented by an undertaker.

Inventions, technological advances, are often not produced by the experts in a field. As science writer Arthur C. Clarke remarks, "When an elderly and distinguished scientist tells you that something is impossible, he is almost certainly wrong. The experts can spot all the difficulties, but lack the imagination and vision to see how they can be overcome. The layman's ignorant optimism turns out, in the long run—and often in the short run—to be nearer the truth." This book provides a compendium of material drawn from a broad spectrum of sources often hard to find and from many countries. Psi researchers East and West have varying views on the topics that should be examined in the name of psi. Many Soviet-bloc workers lean toward the paraphysics approach, and many Westerners lean toward the psychology approach, though directions are changing, at least in the West. The controversy can lead to many fruitful and stimulating experiments. Ideally, both approaches could work in conjunction.

How to Use the Handbook

To give background on some of the equipment and on explorations you can do, we have given examples of how certain investigators have thought out and organized their projects. This book is in no sense intended as a survey of all the contemporary work going on East and West. Often, from a dozen or more people who have organized similar projects, all of them equally good and worthy of mention, we have had room to give only one or two examples and mention only one or two names. Source references are given in detail so those interested in a particular subject can catch up on all these different people and their explorations of psi.

In part, we have tried to answer some of the questions in the thousands of letters sent us by the readers of *Psychic Discoveries Behind The Iron Curtain*. (Because the title is quite a sentenceful, this book will be referred to in the text as *PDBIC*.) There grew to be so many requests for more data and specific information that it finally became—unfortunately but truthfully—impossible for us to answer individually everyone who wrote (though we really do like to hear from people). We hope you will find the answers to your questions here, and though not all answers could be crammed into this book, the "Where to Find It" sections were designed to put you on the trail of the sources of information you're looking for. We hope, too, that some of the very major topics omitted for lack of space can be covered elsewhere.

Here and there, this guide mentions products and commercial enterprises. This is in no way an endorsement or guarantee. Such references are added merely to help facilitate your finding certain items. Equally good alternate sources of supplies or services may be found in your own locale.

If a book or periodical is mentioned repeatedly in the text, publishing details of books and addresses of magazines will be found in Section Six. Where possible we've included prices for journal subscriptions, but in some cases where price may fluctuate (particularly with foreign exchange) they were omitted.

The handbook is structured in sections so that it can be dipped into at any point without having to be read consecutively.

Experiment-Experimenter Interactions

Concocting investigations, it's important to remember that with psi the observer and the observed are not quite as separated as in many other instances. Your thought and energy fields are part of the experiment—a reminder that our minds are not something apart from nature, but rather part of the whole. The point of many of the projects in this handbook is not to box psi into neat little compartments and wind up with so many cold eggs of objective truth. The point is rather to enhance human exploration by providing touchstones, reality checks to help keep on course in such largely uncharted territory. Your experiments can be touchstones, they can also be lodestones pointing to new discoveries, even new inventions.

Conclusion-leaping

Psi exploration requires somewhat of a balancing act on the way to a conclusion. It's vital not to have a mind so closed you can't see the significance of what's in front of you. On the other hand, it's important not to fasten on wrong conclusions on the basis of a few experiences. Humorist Maggie Grant pointed up this kind of conclusion hopscotch in her *Canadian Magazine* column. Question: It is true that department store escalators are run by the power generated by customers going through the revolving doors? Answer: If you will look into the store after the revolving doors have been closed and locked, you will see that the escalators have stopped running.

Some erroneous revolving-door conclusions come to mind—the researcher's jubilant find, a new mottled pattern flaring from fingertips in Kirlian photos. The mottling turned out to be bumps on the exposure plate. Then there was the man whose cat liked to lick hands. Because there are many acupuncture points on the hands, he concluded that cats like to lick acupuncture points and can detect them. (We haven't looked into this claim, but we suppose a statistical study could be done of how many cat licks are ''on point'' or ''off point.'') It's also important not to broadjump to conclusions on the basis of too few experiments.

Whatever experimental results you get—whether showing psi effects or not—it can be helpful to compare them with those of other researchers to see what the differing factors are or why a thing works on some days and not on others, or for some experimenters and not for others.

According to J. Benjamin Beal, a NASA research chief, a year or so before Bell secured his most famous patent, the following editorial appeared in an American paper.

A man was arrested yesterday, charged with attempting to obtain money under false pretenses. He claimed he was promoting a device whereby one person could talk to another several miles away, by means of a small apparatus and some wire. Without doubt this man is a fraud and an unscrupulous trickster and must be taught that the American public is too smart to be the victim of this and similar schemes. Even if this insane idea worked, it would have no practical value other than for circus sideshows.

When prospecting in the paranormal, we find it sometimes helps to remember the revolving-door effect while keeping in mind that we do on occasion talk along a wire all the way from New York to Los Angeles.

Frontier Map of the Paranormal

This is a do-it-yourself handbook in more ways than one, for it really is an unfinished map. Routes to the major jumping-off points are plotted. There are landmarks, pointers and finally trails that only go so far. The rest of the territory is waiting to be filled in. The explorers, and now the specialists and a lot of other people are on the move. It looks like the so-called frontier is open for homesteading all around.

Section One

2

Plants as a Paranormal Workshop

The time has come to talk of cabbages—and philodendrons. It seems the time has come to talk *to* many things—to all the soaring, creeping, sprouting, beautiful, bizarre, everyday, rooting, blooming members of the plant kingdom. Probably all of us know and probably all of us forget that without plants there wouldn't be any life on earth, and no way to convert solar energy to food. Plants are the basic life link. Right now, we seem to be verging into a time when plants may tell us more about the basics of life.

"Plants talk . . ." remarks *Pravda*, the official organ of the Communist Party in the Soviet Union.

"Plants have the ability to get emotionally involved," another Soviet paper, *Socialist Industry*, reported, referring to plant-communication research the Soviets have been doing for some time.

"Love, hate, joy . . . and countless other appropriate responses to stimuli are as universal in plants as in animals," Sir Jagadis Chandra Bose, the great Indian physicist and botanist, maintained.

"Staggering as it may be to contemplate, a life signal may connect all creation," says Cleve Backster, an international polygraph authority who has created lie-detector systems for the CIA and law-enforcement groups around the world. Backster, who still teaches classes of policemen, isn't the type one envisions at the bottom of the garden encouraging the petunias and commiserating with the tomatoes. Yet one evening in 1966, in what is beginning to look like a classic moment, Cleve Backster hooked up a polygraph to his office philodendron. He was wondering how long it would take the recently watered plant to soak up liquid. He didn't find out. He saw a tracing very similar to the line received when a human being experiences an emotion. Backster, of course, knew that

15

people react most strongly on the polygraph when their essential well-being is threatened. He began to wonder, "What would happen if I hurt the plant, if I burned it?" The pen recorder jumped. The plant, it seemed, had reacted to his thought. With that small movement, Backster was catapulted into a scientific research adventure that has obvious and enormous implications. He was not the first and is not the only scientist now to move into this unknown world all around us (AT&T has plans to explore plant communications), yet he remains the catalyst in the exploration of perception and communication in the plant kingdom.

A few years ago, in the very small hours of a New York night, we sat in Backster's lab with a NASA engineer. Earlier we'd looked at some of the plant experiments and one star philodendron remained hooked up to the recording machine. None of us had paid any attention to the system for probably half an hour. Conversation had veered far off, finally settling on the rapidly rising rents in New York. Backster has a fairly large establishment in the heart of the city. One of us said jokingly to Cleve, "If rents keep going up, you soon won't have enough left to feed your plants." Zip! The pen recorder shot up. Apparently, not four, but five of us were staying up late. The philodendron had gotten a word in. It was very funny, totally unscientific, and because it happened so unexpectedly, probably one of the more convincing demonstrations of plant perception for us personally.

Some of the recent claims by researchers of the green kingdom include: Plants react to thoughts about their well-being; they react to the death of living things and sympathize with those around them; they establish a communication bond with their owners that extends over hundreds of miles; they "faint" in moments of catastrophe, plants may have memory, and also might possibly be able to tell an observer whether you are thinking about your latest amour or a math problem. Plants can be used as sensors and detectors, as sort of "watch-plants"; they can be integrated into systems to help us turn on machines at a distance simply by thinking about them. Plants can be the key to unlocking new forms of energy. These are some of the ideas being put forth by researchers into plant perception. Are they right?

One of the nicest things about this psi adventure into the plant world is that you can try out the basic premises for yourself. Research isn't locked in a laboratory or wedded to complex machinery. It's as close as the package of beans on the supermarket shelf. We've found there's something very satisfying about working with plants. If nothing else, you cleanse your own perception and become more aware of the myriad life forms around you. But there is something else for almost everyone. Using a plant as your collaborator may be the easiest way to demonstrate for yourself the influence of your thoughts and emotions on living things—biocommunication in close quarters and sometimes over a distance. The field of plant perception hasn't been much trampled yet; you can be innovative, not just imitative, as you hunt communication and energetic interaction.

Backster named the effect he discovered with the use of the polygraph "primary perception." In a different sense, the plant kingdom can be looked at as a primary paranormal workshop—the transmission of thought, the effects of the human force of PK and healing, the play of life energies as seen in Kirlian photography and perhaps even the effect of a force resonating in a pyramidical shape—all these can converge in the plant workshop.

Perception in the vegetable kingdom—it's an idea broad enough to intrigue many besides just those interested in psi. Gardening buffs, certainly, would top the list, but beyond that, this emerging dimension in our relationship with the plant world may have something to say to philosophy, the humanities, ecology, religion, and even medicine. If any of these are your concern, working with plants could give you new insights; a plant experiment might provide tangible demonstrations of your theories and intuitions.

Basic Plant Experiments

You may, as described later, want to hook monitoring devices to your plants. But you can move right into plant perception without any equipment. You can begin to see if and how they respond to your thoughts and emotions. All you need have on hand are:

1. Six flowerpots, planting boxes, cake tins, or other suitable containers.

2. Seeds: barley, beans, and corn sprout quickly. Check the dried-bean section in your market. Seeds sold for food sprouts in health stores are excellent and reputedly have a high germination rate. Essentially any fruit, flower, or vegetable seed may be used.

3. Earth: with or without fertilizer or growing aids. Mix thoroughly. Each pot must receive exactly the same quality and quantity.

Remember, in any experiment, plants must be cared for equally, receiving the same amount of water, light, heat, etc. The only difference will be that designated plants receive your thoughts.

To begin, plant eight seeds in each of four pots at the same depth.

Determine by flipping a coin which two pots will get your thoughts. Mark "your" pots with a plus sign, the other two with a zero. Separate the plus pots from the controls by four feet. Determine how long your experiment will last, anywhere from two to five weeks depending on how much top growth you wish and on the growth rate of the particular seed used.

Communicating

Spend at least ten to fifteen minutes twice a day communicating with plus-marked plants. What to say? It seems to be a matter of temperament. Some like to pray for their plants; clergy often use formal blessings. Others evoke a universal life spirit. A great many get good results on an emotional frequency, beaming love, warmth, encouragement. They genuinely delight when sprouts appear and cheer on daily progress. Some people just give their plants positive pep talks and a few have even tried hypnotic commands to grow and flourish. Students of yoga, after breathing exercises, simply meditate holding the seeds in their thought. Communicate silently or talk out loud. Whatever, be positive, be assured; and if at all possible, visualize those plants growing, spreading out in space, green, vigorous, vital.

Almost everyone knows that Luther Burbank coaxed plants into unimagined combinations and abundance. Few seem aware of one of his cardinal techniques for success. Burbank always developed a mental model of what he wanted the plants to do. And he didn't keep it to himself, he told the plants. Once Burbank confided to the eminent swami, Paramahansa Yogananda, that when he was experimenting with cacti, he often tried to talk them out of their prickliness. " 'You have nothing to fear,' I would tell them. 'You don't need your defensive thorns. I will protect you.' Gradually the useful plant of the desert emerged in a thornless variety."

Burbank blended objective and subjective knowledge to achieve his extraordinary beneficial results. "The secret of improved plant breeding, apart from scientific knowledge," he said, "is love."

More recently, another innovative American, James Stegner, who has served at the Center of National Scientific Research in France and as Director of the University of Pittsburgh's Airglow Observatory, began suggesting improvements to an air plant. He wanted it to flower. After some months of intense conversation and suggestion, first one bud, then more, appeared, unfurling into lovely trumpetlike blossoms. "This variety of plant never has been known to produce blooms,'' Stegner reports.

There seems to be latitude in how you communicate with plants. Two rules, however, must be observed. You must give the plants daily treatment. You can't simply throw them a cursory thought or two and expect results. And, you must think that it is possible for you to influence a plant. If not, your thought will be limp, your conversation an exercise. It is best not to tell highly critical people what you are doing until you have gained some success and assurance. If you have a green thumb, it's a good bet you'll get excellent results because you've probably been communicating with your flowers all along. Experiments will give you some objective evidence to show your less well-connected friends.

Measuring Results

1. Note down when sprouts break ground. Take photos when possible.

2. At the end of the experiment, measure plants in millimeters; check for overall fullness and appearance; take a comparison photo of the four pots.

3. If you wish, plants may be carefully dug and soaked from the earth. Measure root system, weigh, and again make a comparison picture.

For a more controlled venture, have someone who doesn't know which you've selected for communication plant and tend the seeds. Of course, to prove much you will have to do this experiment more than once. Reverend Franklin Loehr, a Congregational minister with a master's degree in chemistry, was one of the first in the late fifties to try to show on a scientific level that humans can channel life-giving influence to plants. Loehr used 150 volunteers drawn mainly from church groups trained in disciplined prayer to beam attention to 27,000 seeds. The group made more than 100,000 measurements to document that their prayers and feelings strikingly affected plant growth. "Hurry Up and Grow," the female lead sings emphatically to her plants in Alan Jay Lerner's musical, *On a Clear Day You Can See Forever*. Reverend Loehr received tickets for the show, he once told us, because Lerner knew of his work and drew some inspiration from it.

For at-home experiments, one parapsychologist, Dr. Robert Brier, suggests planting five seeds in each of ten pots, five to chat up and the others as controls. Do this whole experiment ten times. If your seeds outgrow controls eight out of ten times, you can consider that you've made contact.

Belittling Thoughts

There's a place in the sun of psi research for "brown thumbs," too, the people whose ivy wilts and geraniums droop no matter how they try. Brown thumbs may have a special talent for retarding growth. Green thumbs can also join in, by switching their bond with plants from positive to negative. You may get highly dramatic evidence of the power of your thought. Plant six sets of seeds; two to be encouraged, two to be cursed, and two to ignore. Keep the sets well separated with controls in between. Pots may be marked plus, zero, minus. Treat and measure plants as in the basic experiment.

Be as withering and scornful as possible to the seeds and sprouts in the negative pots. (But be sure that their everyday care matches that of the others.) If you have it in you, treat them as something loathesome, command them not to grow, and if they do, *order them to stop.*

The Delawarr Laboratories in Oxford, England, asked the far-flung members of its Radionic Association to attempt such plant experiments. One South African surgeon found he didn't have to be an outright hater to stop his seeds, he just had to feed them a steady, overwhelming stream of discouragement. He planted pots of beans in his office during the winter. "It's too cold to grow, there isn't any sun," he told the beans in the negative pots. "It's no use trying to germinate, you'll be sorry if you do." The beans he had encouraged grew demonstrably better than the controls. "I was surprised to find that I appear to be the devil's right-hand man, re: the cursed group . . ." he reported. None of the discouraged seeds broke ground. Only three of eight ventured to put forth a tiny root under the earth.

Some people can't bring themselves to genuinely go after a barley sprout. Yet it can be a wholesome experience for you, if not for the plant, to see on the windowsill blunt evidence of how concretely belittling your thoughts can be to living things. Clergy involved with plant work usually point out that Jesus cursed the fig tree and it shriveled on the spot. Beyond demonstrating the potential of thought, as Reverend Loehr stressed, there are things we don't want to grow. He suggested that people who repeatedly demonstrate ability to halt plant growth be studied under close scientific supervision for any possible ability to halt unwanted growth in the body.

Biology students might try to slow or halt elementary plant life, such a fungus. Use a strain that exhibits a fairly clear boundary line. Cultivate ten petrie dishes, five for growth-retarding thought five for controls. Spend at least fifteen to thirty minutes trying to stop the fungus. This can be a single-session experiment or longer if you wish. French parapsychologist Dr. Jean Barry found in one series of tests with fungus that subjects could slow growth in twenty-seven out of twenty-eight cases. One wonders what they might do with athlete's foot.

Is a Tomato a Pushover?

Experiment with varieties of plants to see whether some are more susceptible to your encouragement than others. A professor of natural science at California's Blake College, Dr. Paul Blondel, claims he has found tomatoes, cabbages, and potatoes most influenced by loving attention and flattery. People who see so-called auras generally claim they can read plant emotions just as they do human emotions from changes in the light surround. The outstanding psychic Eileen Garrett once told us that while visiting Backster's lab she could "see" plants reacting to his concern and also twinges of jealousy when his attention shifted from one to another. Are there levels of "emotional" stability among plants with some more prey to outside influence than others? Keep records of the percentage of growth difference between treated and control plants. Compare for various species.

If you've succeeded in stunting plant growth, try to determine whether some plants are more resistant to negative thoughts than others. Reverend Loehr's group found it more difficult to stunt wheat. Was this a fluke, does it imply an added vitality, an extra jolt of "life force" in the staff of life?

Outdoor Gardens

Of course you can transplant positive and control plants outside, continue to treat and check progress. You can also go to work on your garden. If you're not as much interested in proof as you are in finding a way to make your flowers more lush and your vegetables plumper, simply select one part of the garden for encouragement and leave the rest as controls. For something more in the nature of an experiment, stake out a plot eight feet by eight feet. Remove topsoil, sieve and mix thoroughly so quality is even, and replace. Have a no-man's-land about a foot wide down the middle of the plot. Plant or seed, designating one side as positive and one as control. As always, tend both plots equally.

Thought for Food?

Pick two similar-looking leaves from the same bush or plant. Indoors, put one aside. Ensconce the other in a separate room. Encourage it, love it, talk to it, admire it, as often as you can. Remind yourself that all elements necessary for life are in the atmosphere. See whether you can help the leaf maintain itself. Compare leaves in one week, two weeks, a month. If you find some success, try the same approach with cut flowers. Some apartment dwellers say they can get flowers to last longer with a bit of love and good conversation. Others say the color of the room affects the vitality of flowers. Is there anything to this? It is known that different colored lights, i.e., varied frequencies, greatly influence plants.

Tuning in to Plants at a Distance

Using polygraph monitoring machines and carefully synchronizing time, Backster finds that plants tune in to their owners over fairly good distances—several hundred miles in one case. Plants pick up thoughts sent to them; they also seem to have a sympathetic reaction when their owner runs into an emotional snag of his own. For distance experiments:

1. Take two sets of seeds. Choose one group to receive your thoughts. Hold them in your hand, think about them, visualize them growing—make friends, so to speak. Plant both sets. Put the pots somewhere you rarely go, preferably have someone else tend them. If you wish, take them to a friend's house. Just be sure you can visualize how and where they are positioned. Label pots A and B, but don't tell your assistant which will receive your thoughts. Proceed as usual, remembering to really give the treatments.

2. Take two slips of plants, ivy or chrysanthemum for instance. Or two pots of seeds allowed to sprout normally. Label them A and B. Again send your thoughts from another room or house. But this time attempt to stunt the growth of one.

Precise evidence that plants can indeed be influenced at a distance was charted by Dr. Robert Miller, formerly professor of chemical engineering at Georgia Tech. Dr. Miller, research director for a chapter of the Spiritual Frontiers Fellowship, a national association of clergy and laymen, sought objective proof of prayer. He asked the respected healers Olga Worrall and her husband Ambrose Worrall, an aeronautics engineer, to include a rye plant in their nine P.M. nightly prayer session. The rye seedling grew in

Atlanta, the Worralls lived in Baltimore, 600 miles away. At nine o'clock, Miller's equipment locked inside an atmosphere-controlled lab recorded a sudden spurt in growth. By eight the next morning, the rye showed a growth rate of 840 percent above normal.

Measuring Plant Growth Rate

Dr. Miller employed a measuring system developed by the US Department of Agriculture that involves a rotary transducer hooked to a strip-chart recorder. A counterbalanced lever arm is connected to the transducer. The tiniest motion of the arm is converted to an electrical signal, which in turn moves the pen of the recorder. One end of an inch or so of scotch tape is attached to the tip of the lever, the other end to the top of a growing plant spear. Dr. Miller found rye an excellent subject as growth occurs at the bottom of the spear and not at the top, which can negate measurement. (For further details, see *Psychic*, April, 1972.)

Music and Plants

As the morning sun brightened southern India, every day for weeks a violinist began to play a traditional air. The highly sensitive audience found his music to their liking and doubled their usual growth. They were mimosa and their violinist was Dr. T.C.N. Singh, Chairman of the Botany Department of Annanalai University. Starting with a tuning fork, Dr. Singh determined that plant protoplasm, normally sluggish around dawn and dusk, could be activated by rhythmic sound waves, by music and dance. In 1958, he informed a meeting of the International Horticulture Society in France that violins, flutes, and human song quicken the growth, increase size and yield of petunias, onions, tapioca, and pepper plants. Some plants supposedly also pass along their new traits to succeeding generations. Music, Singh claimed, could bring about chromosomal changes.

Since then, formal and informal experiments seem to agree that some music—particularly classical (Bach and Brahms for example), as well as ballads by the Beatles—enhances plants. Acid rock reportedly withers the vine. One scientist found that his bryophyllum curled up its leaves in the dark, but when he played the *William Tell Overture*, dark or not, they rolled out for reveille.

Experiment with various types of music to see what your flowers like. You might even sing or play it yourself to add the personal thought to stimulate the plants. If you've taken to striking up the band at dawn in your garden, you may assuage your neighbors by doing a dance. Dr. Singh's assistant, Stella Ponniah, executed an Indian dance, the Bharata Natyam, every morning for a host of marigolds—they shot up 60 percent higher than controls. This is not quite as floaty as it sounds. Dancing was part of experiments on transmitting rhythmic sound through earth instead of air to plants. It works well, too, Singh maintains. Unfortunately, we don't have the steps to the Bharata Natyam.

The energetic gardener might try to find out if American dance steps do anything for plants. Miss Ponniah danced six feet from the marigolds for fifteen minutes each morning. In some tests, plants were potted and positioned on a low stone platform. It just might be intriguing to see if specific folk dances and American Indian dances traditionally done at planting time have any influence on plants, stimulating them by transmitting sound wave patterns through the earth.

Traditionally structured sound other than music may also affect plants. Yogis of the Sivananda Yoga Ashram in Val Morin, Quebec, joined Backster in experiments and observed specific plant reactions while chanting yoga mantras.

Plants and Water

Another interesting experiment is to attempt to influence the solution used to water plants. Have two sealed bottles of tap water, spring water or any solution you like to feed your greenery, just be sure the contents are identical. Hold one jar in your hands for fifteen to thirty minutes. Think in a positive vein, visualize the luxurious growth this water will stimulate, pray over or bless it if you wish. Try to direct a joyful, upbeat feeling or energy to the water. Use this to nourish the seeds planted in positive pots. Controls are watered from the untreated jar. If you run out of liquid before the end of the experiment, use tap water for both sets of plants.

The obvious basis for this approach comes from holy water and the belief that water can carry blessing or goodness. Canon William V. Rauscher, former President of Spiritual Frontiers Fellowship and rector of the Christ Episcopal Church in Woodbury, New Jersey, reportedly has seven-foot canna plants flourishing beside his church. For six years they've grown untended—except they receive holy water used in baptisms and other rites. Other canna, planted at the same time in the church flowerbed, stand only a foot and a half high.

Some scientific basis for the idea of influencing plants through water comes from the work of Dr. Bernard Grad of McGill University in Montreal. In tightly controlled, repeated experiments, Dr. Grad asked a well-known healer, Colonel Oskar Estabany, to hold a sealed beaker of weak saline solution in his hands. Plants watered with the solution treated by Estabany clearly outgrew those fed with identical, but unheld solution.

Grad conducted other tests less often mentioned. Mental patients held sealed flasks of water. Results suggest that if a person is severely depressed when he holds the bottle, plants will not fare well. It's as if the disturbance of a person can somehow communicate to the plant. As with so many ventures into psi, Grad's findings have ricocheting implications. What do we radiate to the living things about us? It's an advertising saw that mother's cooking tasted best because it was done with love. What happens when the cook is as boiling as the soup? More seriously, if our state of mind can be transmitted by liquid, can influence growth, would this ever have any effect on lab and medical tests, or on human health?

Dr. Grad from his many years of exploration asserts that an energy, a kind of vital force is active in all human interaction. "I believe it happens when food is blessed by grace before meals. . . . What is new in my work is that we have shown this energy to be something real and verifiable." Dr. Grad's research, more than most, seems to call for further investigation with an eye to practical application.

Orphan Plants

J. I. Rodale, organic pioneer and later founder-editor of *Prevention* magazine, some years ago visited the Delawarr Labs in England. There he heard of what he frankly called some unbelievable experiments. If a young plant's mother dies, the story went, it doesn't fare as well in the world as a slip whose mother remains hale and hearty. Rodale never was the sort to dismiss the officially unbelievable without a trial. Eventually, he reported what happened to slips taken from two coleus plants at his Pennsylvania farm. Rodale went to planned extremes, destroying one mother plant. The coleus, along with the potted earth it grew in, were consumed by fire, obliterating as far as possible all trace of organic material. Even the broken pieces of the plant's pot were buried some miles from the test site. What happened?

The four orphan slips grew poorly. The four coleus slips that retained their mother grew sturdily. Did the thought of the experimenters play a part or is some energy involved? Is the cut-away part, the slip, still part of the energy gestalt of the whole, its parent? How long would it take to establish its own individual identity and cease being affected by its parent? Anyone can try to duplicate this odd experiment—if it works—ask some questions and form some theories of his own.

Synthesizers

If you like to put things together, if you think that seemingly extraneous parts once in a while click into an unexpected whole, there are a number of facts, bits and pieces of research and knowledge that might be related to plant explorations.

Plants harmonize obviously with the seasons. They are less obviously affected perhaps by magnetic weather, daily fluctuations in the geomagnetic field, the circling of the moon, sun, and perhaps the planets. The late Dr. Harold Burr, professor of neurophysiology at Yale, spent a lifetime uncovering the electrical fields around living things. He found—to mention just one of many discoveries— that the life field of a tree is intimately bound to the monthly path of the moon. Burr's recent *Blueprint for Immortality, the Electric Patterns of Life* sums up his long years of work. How do Burr's findings and those of Backster and other plant researchers relate? Is there common ground? Will knowledge of one enhance the other? Another new field of study, bioclocks and periodicity—an examination of the symphony of biorhythms playing through living systems, might also have some relevance to plant reaction and interaction.

Solid research is showing that earth life including vegetation is much more linked to the movement of heavenly bodies than science has in recent times supposed. (See astrobiology section of *Natural Birth Control*, Bantam, 1973.) What twentieth-century science wouldn't imagine, country people have perhaps understood empirically over the millennia. Planting and moon guides put out by various astrology publications or the *Farmer's Almanac* can provide necessary data that might be correlated with or tested against plant work. Is it easier to influence plants at a specific phase of the moon? Can you stunt or enhance them more successfully at certain times? Is this only because of different growing conditions? A very simple example of this approach would be to determine whether it is easier to retard growth in seeds planted in winter, outside their normal cycle. Plant perception studies begin to imply that life is a constantly moving web of connectedness. Astrobiology is coming to the same view from a different direction. Sleuthing links, if any, between the two might be rewarding.

The moon may shine down in another way on plant research. US and Soviet bloc studies suggest that telepathy between humans occurs most easily at full moon. Does this affect your ability to influence a plant, to communicate with it over a distance? How does the great, round moon affect the plant itself? Are there shifts in its perception and "emotional" reactions?

There is a "green fuse," to crib Dylan Thomas, in all the world's literature and art. To our ancestors, the resonances between the plant and human kingdoms was more than an artistic insight. It was an everyday awareness. They moved easily in the green realm of Pan, of wood nymph and tree sprite, of Daphne and Narcissus. Orpheus, the legendary poet, was said to enthrall not only wild beasts but all growing things with his singing. Tree alphabets were used and the archetypal tree of life rooted in every tradition, changing its symbols with the seasons of culture. Tree and grove, vine and bush were sacred, protective, destructive, oracular. Generations of people took care to fashion their implements and decorations from the traditionally prescribed wood and plant. They thought it made a difference.

T.G. Lethbridge, the longtime director of excavations for the University Museum of Archaeology and Ethnology at Cambridge, is a man with developed dowsing ability. He uses it in his digs and he also claims that, dowsing, he found energy fields associated with trees and shrubs. Lethbridge suggests calling these "dryad fields," using the Greek name for wood nymphs or spirits of the forest.

Certainly the many and fabulous beliefs the ancient people held about the green kingdom were shaped by the curlicues and urgencies of a particular time and particular way of understanding the world. Such beliefs had a very real power in a mythic sense. Beyond that, did some have a touch of something else? Is there a psychophysical basis to pieces of the old mythology that we may come to understand in our own terms?

A student of the humanities interested in relating perceptive-plant investigation with literary and cultural studies might make a start by following the leads in Elizabeth Sewell's *The Orphic Voice*, Torch, 1971; and Robert Graves' *The White Goddess*, Noonday, 1966. Those who view psi research as a part of a much broader investigation, the expanding study of the nature and evolution of consciousness, might start with Rilke's question, "Nature, is not this what you wish: to become invisible in us?" As J.B. Leishman remarks of Rilke's vision, "Nature (including all the visible works of man) thus becomes a kind of externalized and visible consciousness, and consciousness a kind of internalized and invisible nature.''

Plant Energies

Ventures into the plant kingdom seem to have broken through to two new vistas: the possibility of communication with plants and the idea of plants as part of a subtle, shifting network of energies linking all life. Thought and energies—perhaps we are looking at the same thing from two perspectives, as physicists view light now as particles, now as waves.

Foliage may be concerned with more forms of energy than we realized. If some Soviets are right, doctors may one day send their patients roses on prescription. Dr. Nikolai Yurchenko has researched the influence of plants on human health for two decades at the Sukhumi Sanitorium on the Black Sea. He claims that particular flowers and trees—willows, birches, oaks, roses—have a healing effect on particular ailments. Roses, deep red blooms, supposedly aid nervous diseases. According to Dr. Yurchenko patients naturally gravitate to foliage and flowers that will be most beneficial to them. Another Soviet scientist, Akaki Kereselidze of the Georgian Institute of Subtropical Farming, proposes health parks designed not just for ''idle beauty'' but filled with selected greenery chosen to help revitalize and strengthen parts of the body. We're not suggesting you design a gallstone garden or hypertension trellis—at least not yet.

Soviet Kirlian photography does show highly individualized energy patterns emanating from various plants. Beyond that, with a thousand years of lore from very diverse folk, it's not surprising that while their colleagues seek yet more drugs from leaf and bark, some researchers are looking into the old folk idea that there are curative emanations as well as potions to be had from plants.

Psychic lore in the West holds that the energy fields of some trees may be noxious, but that you can draw healthy energy from others. Pine trees, for example, are supposed to be literally invigorating. One esoteric student, Joseph Weed, president of Weed Television, Inc., and of Van Drenthem International Ltd, suggests putting the balls of the thumb and first two fingers on the tips of pine needles, hold them there a few minutes and think of drawing energy from the tree. Can anyone figure out a way to test this old supposition objectively?

To experience some pleasant if not curative emanations you might try a technique proposed by Dr. Marcel Vogel, an IBM chemist who devotes his spare time to work similar to Backster's. Vogel maintains that you can learn to sense and interact with a field from a plant by holding your hand four or five inches above it. He suggests choosing a highly fragrant, aromatic plant. Oscillate your hand slowly above it. You'll be rewarded, he says, by a burst of scent.

If you are into serious investigation of plant energies and emanations, a key body of experimental data is that done by the Russian Dr. Alexander Gurvich, who declared flatly, "*All living cells produce an invisible radiation.*" He claimed to have found rays—what he termed mitogenetic radiation—coming from certain plants. Gurvich concocted an alluring experiment—the onion cannon. Supposedly, radiation from the tip of an onion root bombarded the side of another onion root causing a one-fourth increase in cell growth. This strange radiation increased the growth of yeast and bacteria, too. The energy reaction was halted by glass, but passed through quartz. Gurvich found mitogenetic rays coming from people as well as plants and discovered that illness altered it. A sick person need only hold a yeast culture for a few minutes to kill the vigorous yeast cells. Such yeast experiments were also conducted by Dr. Otto Rahn at Cornell University.

Famous in its day, Gurvich's work appeared to hold great promise for medicine, but it faded, basically because he lacked a theory. He could not explain the mechanism behind his supposed radiation. Currently, Soviet biophysicists exploring Kirlian phenomena and ultrafaint bioluminescence have undertaken a highly positive reassessment of Gurvich. For an overall view, an easily accessible source is "Radiation and Life—Russian Plant Research," *Harper's*, July, 1934. For German readers there is Gurvich's book, *Die Mitogenetische Strahlung*, Berlin: Springer, 1932. Also pertinent to this area is Otto Rahn's *Invisible Radiations of Organisms*, Ann Arbor: Edwards Bros., 1944.

Energy of some sort is clearly implied by one of Backster's first and most interesting discoveries. This experiment was totally automated, carried out inside a locked and peopleless lab. At random moments, minute brine shrimp plunged to their deaths in boiling water. As the tiny deaths occurred, philodendron—two, four, and five rooms away, monitored by polygraphs—reacted sharply. Since then, Backster and others have found that plants take note of the end of any life within their vicinity, a specific signal goes out apparently whenever life converts to death. Eulogizing Yeats, W.H. Auden wrote, "The death of the poet was kept from his poems." One wonders if it was kept from his plants.

Botanists at the Soviet Institute of Plant Research suggest an energy involved with life may circulate among plants. They put a growing cornstalk inside a glass container, placing it near other corn growing normally. The prisoner received no water. Yet as weeks went by it continued to flourish. The Soviet scientists feel that in some unknown way water was sent from the healthy plants to their captive fellow. It sounds rather romantic, particularly for dialectical materialists. Yet, as we are supposedly not so materialistic, it might be worth trying to duplicate and study.

Other communists, among them a team led by Moscow psychologist Dr. V. M. Pushkin, are following Backster's path. Instead of using the polygraph, plant leaves and a human are attached to an electroencephalograph—the EEG, generally used to record brain waves. According to the Russians, when the hypnotized subject experienced a surge of sorrow, the plant showed a similar "emotion"—an electrical change as charted by instruments.

Backster now also works with a four-channel EEG charting shifts in electrical potential. Test subjects include bacteria culture and animal life in his completely programmed and automated experiments.

Technology has jumped our comprehension of the plant world to a new level. To a greater or lesser degree, you can join in these instrumented "conversations" with plants.

3

How You Can Talk to Your Plants
and Have Them Answer Back

In 1969, F.L. Kunz, editor of *Main Currents*, an influential journal of contemporary thought, wrote, "At rare intervals, some empirical item, loaded with philosophical significance, comes forward in science, particularly biology." He was speaking of Backster's uncovering of plant perception. Kunz concluded, "Now that we know that plants are sentient, and that they respond (in some appropriate but as yet unknown way) to emotions, both beneficial and menacing, delivered from without, the way is open to establish the existence of a life force-field. What is that particular force?"

The idea of primary perception and communication with the plant world can have shattering implications for the way we view life. Yet to many people the philosophical speculations about plant research seem abstract and out of the way. Sometimes the actual experience of seeing a plant react to you and your thoughts can be worth a thousand abstractions.

Obviously for most of us it is too difficult to try to duplicate the level of Cleve Backster's research with polygraphs, sophisticated electronic lab equipment, and the carefully controlled conditions of a laboratory. But is there any simple device you could use to pick up your plants' reactions? we wondered. Investigating, we discovered that quite a few people were going on adventures with their own plants, using simple and inexpensive devices that measure changes in electrical resistance known as the psychogalvanic reflex or the galvanic skin response.

One of our fellow speakers at the 1971 Washington Conference of the Association for Humanistic Psychology, Dr. Marcel Vogel of California, IBM chemist and recognized scientific expert in the field of liquid crystals, explained how he started monitoring plants.

31

Dr. Vogel had initially been very skeptical of Cleve Backster's claim that plants reacted to thoughts and emotions. Just to see, he got a simple resistance-measuring device, the Psych-Analyzer, and hooked it up to a plant in his living room.

To Dr. Vogel's surprise, his plant really *did* react to his thoughts. Soon he had embarked on his own path into the plant world (which is detailed later). Vogel showed a series of slides at the conference and when the audience saw some of the things his plants had been up to, as shown on monitoring charts from the meter, they applauded the plants with delight. If nothing else, it's a captivating idea.

Despite all this evidence of the things plants could do, one of the authors of this handbook still could not summon up much interest in foliage, and in fact on several occasions had even been known to mistake a real plant for a plastic one. "Could plants really say anything that was all that interesting?" We decided to try a couple of the resistance-detecting devices. And eventually one of us had to reverse her opinion of plants. Plants seemed to have quite a bit to say, but that's something you may find out for yourself if you'd like to try talking to plants with instruments.

Instruments for Plant Talk

The most simple ready-made devices that might lead to plant talk can be obtained from Edmund Scientific (300 Edscorp Bldg., Great Barrington, New Jersey 08007). One of these, the Emotion Meter (#41,422) is sold for under $20.00 to be used as a party-game lie detector and also to pick up responses from plants and pets. Reactions are registered by a needle on a numbered dial. The electrodes on this small device are attached to a plastic bar. For a quick, simple test with plants, you can attach the bar to the topside of a leaf with a C-clamp. Generally, however, researchers work with an electrode on either side of a leaf. The Emotion Meter's electrodes can easily be slid off the plastic bar and converted to plant use. Battery run, this meter can be used indoors and out.

Another psychogalvanic device from Edmund Scientific is the so-called Hang Up Meter (#71,738), which sells for just under $30.00. (As with any devices mentioned in this handbook, several people might like to pool resources to get one instrument they share on a revolving basis.) This instrument is an audio-resistance meter, with it your plants can squawk if not talk to you. Audio registration allows for an easy way of gathering permanent records with a tape recorder. The finger-cup electrodes on this meter have to be converted for plant use.

Probably the best bet in the way of a simple, inexpensive device to monitor your plants is the Psych-Analyzer devised by Robert Devine as a homemade lie detector. This is a do-it-yourself project, if you're skilled in electronics or know someone who is. Often an electronic supply store can direct you to someone in your neighborhood who will put the equipment together for you for a small fee. Diagrams and complete instructions for building your Psych-Analyzer are in *Popular Electronics*, February, 1969, and in *The Electronic Experimenter's Handbook*, spring, 1970 (1 Park Avenue, New York, New York).

A somewhat more complex system, but one copied and used by many people, is that developed by defense engineer L. George Lawrence specifically for plant perception research and published for the home experimenter in *Popular Electronics*. With Lawrence's response detector you can both see plant reactions on a meter and hear them through a loudspeaker. He provides instructions on how to build the device and use it with plants in "More Experiments in Electroculture," *Popular Electronics*, June, 1971.

For extended experiments, permanent records are important and investigators use a strip-chart recorder. Such recorders are fairly costly to buy, but here again is something you might make on your own. You can find instructions for constructing a chart recorder in "The Amateur Scientist," *Scientific American*, March, 1972 (415 Madison Avenue, New York, N.Y.). Back issues of both *Scientific American* and *Popular Electronics* are usually held in libraries.

You may however get a lot of entertainment, and maybe even a little enlightenment, experimenting without chart recording. For an unusual, interesting record of your work, you might on occasion want to take movies of your plants as they perform.

The Psych-Analyzer and Lawrence's system are designed with the right sort of electrodes. To convert other systems for plant connections, use any good conductive metal for electrodes (avoid aluminum). A couple of researchers as a quick expedient have used silver dimes as electrodes and claim they give results. The classic setup involves two stainless-steel electrodes placed on either side of a leaf over a vein. Many investigators put a paste or gel of agar-agar with one percent salt added between electrode and leaf to enhance contact. Agar-agar is sold in hobby shops and scientific supply houses. Some people use medical jelly, the sort employed with EEG and EKG electrodes. Lawrence recommends ECG Kontax (Cat. No. 391, Birtcher Corp., Los Angeles, California 90032).

Using a gel if you wish, place the leaf securely but gently between the electrodes. A C-clamp, obtainable in any hardware store, holds

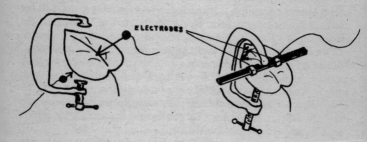

ELECTRODES

the electrodes in place. To insulate, put a piece of plastic between electrode and clamp. It is convenient to attach the C-clamp to a rod on a stand—you can use electrician's tape in a pinch. The stand avoids pulling on the leaf and enables you to use the setup for leaves at different heights. (See Figure 1.)

Most people start with philodendron or similar plants with leaves large enough and tough enough to support the system with ease. Try not to overtax the plant and clean it up after a test. No matter what device you're using, always be sure you have a base-line reading before attempting to stimulate your plant. In other words, let the plant settle down until you get a steady recording. What follows is a kind of conversation guide for your journey to the plant world.

Registering Primary Perception

If your plant is new, establish rapport. Touch the plant, talk to it, welcome it to your home more or less as you would a new pet. Let it get accustomed to you for several days. When you begin checking for reactions, you may find that some plants take a while to get used to the equipment. For some time they will show no movement from base, no matter what the stimulus. Or they will show a continually shifting line that never settles down. Establishing a bond with the plant seems to be a major factor in getting it to react to you and not other things in the environment. Vogel calls this "charging" the plant and continues working at it until a good steady base-line recording appears. We found that a healthy, domesticated plant, one used to you or at least to other people, gives by far the best results. Generally, we had difficulty rousing a reaction in a wild plant, in a park or garden. Difficulty probably also sprang from the variable conditions and from our own apprehensions—how do you reply if the park police ask why you're hooking wires to the public hollyhocks? To talk to the flowers?

To begin experiments inside at home, remember that plants, like people, react sharply to a genuine threat to their well-being. If you wish, actually burn a leaf of the plant. This should give a definite reaction. Next, threaten out loud to burn the plant. Do you get anything? Then, *mentally* threaten to harm the plant. Compare the differences in reactions, if any. You may find that at first the verbal threat brings the bigger reaction, but in time the mental threat becomes the stronger stimulus. It is important to be able to control your thoughts and emotions so you can send clear communication. Vogel recommends meditation beforehand and prohibits alcohol and smoking during experiments.

When you think, *I'm going to burn that leaf with this match*, you must really mean it, you must intend at the moment to carry out your threat. If not, you'll get no reaction. Apparently, plants aren't anybody's fool. This finding—that to get a response from a plant you have to power your projection with genuine emotion—may give a clue to an ingredient of successful telepathy and prayer.

If you're going to use your plant over an extended period, it might be best to have someone else be the plant bully. Eventually, you may pick up some sort of plant reaction whenever the heavy is in the vicinity. If you have a house cat that likes to nip a leaf now and then, you'll probably get a reaction when the cat pads by.

Speaking of threats, if you do find you can get such reactions, what would happen if you presented a plant with its natural insect enemy? Would it have to be bitten once to be shy? Could it distinguish between a friendly bug and a predator?

Reasons for No Reaction

Naturally, check your equipment. Even though it is working properly, there are times when you may get nothing but a steady base recording. It's possible your greenery has blacked out in horror. Backster tells a story in this vein that bears at least one more repetition. While a visiting Canadian plant physiologist leaned over his shoulder, all the embarrassed Backster could get was a straight base line recording. Not a plant would respond. Finally, he questioned the scientist. Yes, she said, she *always* killed all of her plants at the end of her tests. Backster's philodendrons eventually came around—after the scientist had been safely put in a cab heading to the airport.

News that a vegetable can "faint" presented itself to one of us over Sunday brunch in the late fifties. Tomatoes say ouch when you stick them, commented *This Week*, the now-defunct Sunday supplement. Researchers in England, it seemed, were studying odd electrical reactions of vegetables. They claimed that tomatoes even stopped growing and became comatose when they "knew" they were about to be picked, pickled, or eaten. That nature provides a cutout, a blinking off for all life forms in extremis will prove as comforting as it is interesting to some. It may also ruin the repartee of one man who suffered moral lectures from his vegetarian friends. Having read of Backster's work, he decided that as a righteous carnivore, he could now cut any vegetarian dead with a quick "Suffering succotash!"

Some plants just don't respond to some people for unknown

reasons. It may be someone who is negative toward the plant. If there is no response, keep trying it on different days with different plants. On the other hand, it seems that a plant will sometimes suddenly tune in selectively to one person other than its owner in a group. Can you get this effect and can you make any sense of it?

An unhealthy, droopy plant doesn't work well and some plants just seem to turn off on occasion. One small one we'd transplanted from outside never budged from its base line during a session except once when it sent the needle to the top. A friend suddenly exclaimed, "Oh, I've got to be at the dentist's by 9:30 tomorrow"—a situation he didn't relish. He tried saying the same thing over a few times, but no response. The plant's original reaction perhaps reflected his single, genuine surge of emotion. Or it may have been a fluke.

Personal Response

Your plant's greatest reaction should be, generally, to you, owner and protector. Gathering evidence of this bond can be turned into a game.

Take any ten playing cards, excluding aces. Pick one as your target, keeping your choice to yourself. Have a friend turn the cards over one by one asking, "Is this yours?" You must pay a forfeit if he determines your card. Let him watch the plant monitor. Will your philodendron act as a party lie detector and give you away? Variations of this might make for some interesting experiments for poker players, especially if a player is holding a royal flush with a well-beloved plant hovering nearby.

If cards don't appeal, have someone in a group ask you semi-loaded questions involving your feelings about politics, sex, or particular people. Is your plant in harmony with you, do you get telltale reactions? You can also check what happens when you're listening to an exciting story, watching a thriller on TV, or listening to music that really churns your emotions. The needle on our plant monitor gave some very sharp kicks at appropriate moments while we watched Watergate hearings.

Monitoring Distance Experiments

Monitoring machines can make visible any link across distance you may have with your plant. Generally this should be done with a chart recorder. If using a device that only has a scale recorder, you'll have to employ an assistant who keeps very precise records of the time and strength of reactions. Tell him you will be sending thought to the plant at some unspecified moment during a particular fifteen-minute period. Ask him to keep his own thought calm, neutral, and as far from the plant as possible. Be sure to synchronize watches.

In another room or building, record the exact time, then shoot out a mental whammy to your plant. Threaten it. Or you might broadcast an intense thought of love and concern. If you get reactions, try to determine which of your thoughts or feelings carry best across space. How far away can you be and still prompt a reaction in your plant? Can you get a sympathetic response when you experience a surge of emotion not connected with thoughts of the plant? You might have a friend secretly devise ways to startle you—an ice cube down the neck, a spider on the arm—just make sure he really is a friend, you don't want to wind up as the subject in the next set of experiments.

Death Signal

Reaction to the death of any living thing is one of the most reliable of plant responses. The brine shrimp that Backster uses are fish food and may often be bought in aquarium supply stores. Any sort of bait will do, the only prerequisite is that *healthy* cells die. Vegetables and fruit may be used as long as they are truly fresh. Once you record the basic reaction to a death signal, you can use it to learn other things about plant perception.

We got some sharp reactions by taking a hint from Backster and using yogurt. As a gloxinia plant looked on, we mixed jelly into health-store yogurt and ate it. Acidophili in the yogurt were dying in the thousands or perhaps millions from the preservative in the jelly. The gloxinia picked up, the registering needle swept to the far end of the dial. Purposefully munching various types of food, such as blue cheese, in front of the plant seemed to unsettle the gloxinia. Our plant also seemed to "know" it when a fresh lemon met its demise and a green pepper was cut up. Toward the end of the chopping, the gloxinia seemed to get bored and settled back to normal.

Again like animals, plants seem to stake out a territory. Some dogs are concerned only about their house and yard, others worry about the street and the whole block. It may be possible to determine how much space your plant has claimed as its own by noting when it stops reacting to a death signal. Do you have to be two rooms away, three rooms, outside? What about the kitchen?

Hierarchies

Plant perception of death signals has uncovered a tantalizing curiosity. Your plant will eventually become conditioned to the death of primitive life forms and give no reaction. New plants must be used. However, in years of testing, supposedly, they do not become accustomed to the death of human cells and always react. Why should a plant care more for one sort of life than another? One might understand a burst of plant activity if its owner died, but we're dealing with death on the level of a scratch on the arm dabbed with iodine. It's flattering to think we're so special that the vegetation always remarks on human "death." But what is going on? What different information is broadcast from the demise of cells in shrimp, mouse, horse, man? And of course the irresistible question, Why? What does this mean? Probably everyone can summon up some theories on his own—can they be backed by experiments?

Plant Detectives and Detectors

Will we see the day when a mimosa points a trembling leaf at the dastardly jewel thief who murdered the dowager in her bed? For a dramatic, significant experiment, one that might be used for a science project, call in six volunteers. To lay the scene, set up three similar plants fairly close together in a separate room, then close the door and leave them to their fate. Have your six friends draw lots, one of which is marked X for "plant murderer." The murderer is not to disclose his identity to anyone. One by one, each of the six enters the room and spends three or four minutes alone with the plants. The rest of you wait far enough away to avoid hearing any sounds of scuffle. When the X-marked person is in the room, he must kill one plant. Pull it up by the roots, rip it apart, damage it beyond repair.

Set up your equipment at the scene of the crime. Monitor one or both of the survivors. Have the six suspects file in, one at a time. Can the plant-witness, by its reaction, point out the murderer? As plants do seem to have perceptions, it probably isn't sporting to throttle them for fun. However, done as a serious experiment, this test provides solid evidence for perception and short-term memory in plants. The validity of the experiment increases if you are able to repeatedly find the culprit using different people and plants. If you don't want to kill a plant, you might try having the culprit burn and otherwise badly damage a leaf of a plant. Monitor to determine if the plant can identify its assailant among the suspects.

The Wall Street Journal (February 2, 1972) reports that a precedent has already been set for the use of plants in an actual police case in New Jersey. A girl had been murdered in a factory office and the polygraphed plant witness helped in narrowing down the list of suspects.

Music and Plants

The effects of music on plants, mentioned in Chapter 2, are also interesting to monitor with the Emotion Meter. As an amusing thing to try, how do plants react to songs specifically about them or as emblems of a country or area? It would be intriguing, for instance, to monitor a maple leaf when "The Maple Leaf Forever" is played or sung for it, or rose leaves for "The Yellow Rose of Texas." "Edelweiss," "O Christmas Tree," and other songs could be tried out on the appropriate greenery.

Plant Thought Reading

At first Dr. Marcel Vogel hooked up the Psych-Analyzer to a small strip-chart recorder (well within the realm of any serious at-home lab) so that he'd have a printed record of his plant-conversation experiments. Later he got more sophisticated equipment. In a typical Vogel test, he asked a physicist to concentrate on a technical problem and took a pen tracing from his plant. Then he asked the scientist to think about his wife. A very different line pattern appeared. Vogel is pursuing the idea that plants can give us tracings or emblems of our different kinds of thought, different forms of consciousness perhaps. He postulates that mental states are reflected in the force fields of the body, which are in turn detected by the plant. With a team of doctors he is attempting to identify the specific patterns associated with particular mental diseases. If valid, this has obvious promise as a diagnostic tool, and could be an aid in the accelerating study of consciousness.

Are plants simply reacting to us the way iron filings dance this way and that with a magnet? Or do they have an inner life of their own? "Plants have a sensitive nervous system and a varied emotional life," asserted Sir Jagadis Chandra Bose, the turn-of-the-century great of Indian science. Using the crescograph—for which, among other inventions, he was knighted—Bose was able to tremendously magnify and observe plant reactions. A snail on this device, he said, would appear to race by like an express train. Bose stated plainly that plants have a nervous system. He found so many reactions in plants similar to those in animals that he proposed plants might one day be used in medical experiments to save animals from vivisection. According to Bose, plants know love and hate, joy and fear. Plants get hopped up on caffeine, flowers sway drunkenly on alcohol, and grandfather trees are able to survive the shock of major operations (transplantings) if uprooted under chloroform.

Plants don't have nerves as we know them, yet recent research on electrical activity backs Bose up. There seems to be an overall bioelectric principle that is expressed as nerves in animals and as something analogous in plants. Plants also appear to have acupuncture points as do humans and animals. We inhabit the same space as plants, but perhaps one reason we've been slow in communicating is that we don't always inhabit the same time. Greatly speeded movies of plants show them to behave, react, and recoil very much like animals. Our senses are not geared to their time and we don't generally perceive their world. As someone has remarked, to living forms on a much higher frequency than ours, we would appear as vegetative and unresponsive as plants.

Plant Memories

At the Timeryazev Institute for Photosynthesis and Plant Physiology of the Soviet Academy of Sciences, researchers have been flashing various rhythmic patterns of light at potatoes, cucumbers, and a host of other vegetables and flowers to test vegetative memory. According to Engineer E. Gruzinov, almost every plant tested was able to learn and remember the rhythm when the lights went out. Buttercups claimed the duration prize, recollecting for eighteen hours. Could plants be trained to count? Some people think so.

The idea is getting abroad that one can uncover plant memory with another Soviet technique—the one developed by Pavlov in his famous dog experiments. Target substances are brought close to the plant. (Backster has used seeds from different plants, one kind as target, the others as control.) Whenever the target is at hand, the plant receives a reward in the hope that it will learn to identify the target and eventually react without a reward. One snag is to decide what pleases a philodendron as much as a hunk of hamburger delights a dog. Backster's reward is light, others speak of a great burst of love—though you might run out of bursts in the repetitions needed for such experiments. Can anyone come up with data on what foliage considers a real treat? If plants can be conditioned, if they have a memory and can learn to identify different substances, a whole new field of potential use opens up. Reporting successful plant conditioning, using punishment rather than reward, Moscow physicist Dr. Victor Adamenko remarks, "On several occasions the philodendron gave a reaction when the [target] mineral was nearby, although now there was no electric shock; perhaps every cell possesses a form of primary perception." Going on to consider plants as live detectors and sensors generally, he says, "In time there may appear living triodes, receivers, generators, and other creations of biotronics." Adamenko echoes other investigators here and abroad when he suggests that with such biodetectors we may be able to pick up forms of energy not detectable with our nonliving instruments. And now it seems that some of the things that biosensors detect might just be termed out of this world.

From Plant to Planet?

On the evening of October 29, 1971, electronics expert L. George Lawrence and his associates took a break from outdoor work they were doing in California with remote biological sensing devices. Their equipment, according to Lawrence, was designed to pick up biological signals outside the known electro-magnetic spectrum. By chance as they rested, their detector was tilted skyward, aimed as they later determined at the constellation Ursa Major. Suddenly the detector's audio monitor drew their attention. Something was happening. Out of the blue they recorded about half an hour of signals. Signals?

Lawrence believes the pulses recorded that night are of intelligent character and that they came from far out in space. A copy of this odd recording now reposes in the scientific archives of the Smithsonian Institution. (Other signals have been intercepted by the detectors and an attempt at computerized decoding is planned. For more data see *Human Dimensions*, summer, 1971.)

Lawrence for some years worked in the missile arm of the defense industry and now directs the Ecola Institute in San Bernardino, California. He is the author of a great many scientific papers and text books on electronics, geophysics and the like. One would think he ought to know the difference between noise and an intelligent signal. He does know something about biodetectors. Lawrence became involved in plant reactions while working for the government. Then when Backster announced his discovery, Lawrence, interested, duplicated Backster's experiments and confirmed them. He went on from there designing plant systems. Today he possesses a three-ton instrument, the Stellartron, whose main feature is "a biological-signal transducer complex." His institute plans to start the Stellartron scanning the galaxy day and night, seeking signals from outer space.

Today of course a great many scientists believe that there may well be other civilizations in the universe. For more than a decade top Soviet astronomers and astrophysicists have not only held conferences to discuss how to contact extraterresterial civilizations, but they also discuss what to say if one should get through to us.

Perhaps the reason we have never gotten any definitive signals from extraterresterials, Lawrence speculates, is that we've been trying on the wrong frequencies, so to speak. Highly evolved civilizations may have moved past an electromagnetic form of communication to a biologically based form. Though it's a far jump from what we had in mind when considering plant communication, we now have to ask: Could biodetectors at last help us connect with other forms of intelligence in the universe? Researchers are about to man the Stellartron seeking messages from the universe. Whether or not this rather stunning venture bears fruit, it gives a glimpse of the new perspectives, the new worlds aborning with contemporary research into plant perception, other forms of energy, and a variety of things under the psi umbrella.

Lawrence's idea of a biologically based system being the communication medium of the universe shimmers with implications. It expands from Backster's root discovery of primary perception, of some basic, pervasive communicating link, of, it seems, some other form of energy. More and more scientists have come to think that the line between living and nonliving is not so firm as once believed. For instance, the theoretical physicist Dr. C.A. Muses, another supporter of Backster's work, remarks, "Absolute nonlivingness appears increasingly to be an illusion, the answering reality to which is that there is no end of biology in some form, however far we look below us or however far beyond."

It will be ironic, but true to form, if in our thrust to understand the world, we have overlooked what is closest to us—biology. Could the organizing principles and dynamics of biology in its broadest sense be working in particle and planet? Could this give us a new angle on the ancient dictum that man is a microcosm of the macrocosm, that the universe is reflected within him?

One thinks of the resolution of the film *2001*: the human fetus emerging, encompassing the far sparkling universe. Might it be biology, if not man, at the center? As applications begin, perhaps we are beginning to get a hint of where the opening made by Cleve Backster may lead scientists and artists, too, in the decades to come.

Plants That Turn on Machines

Plant engineers are beginning to sprout. Putting plants to work in systems can blossom into a fascinating, useful exploration for the creative researcher. It can be fun, too, as shown by the imaginative designs of Paul Sauvin, a New Jersey technologist and psi consultant for a research and development engineering firm. Sauvin took hold of the idea that you can cause your plant to react at a distance. An electrical signal can of course be amplified and transduced to trigger other reactions. How about a plant that trips a radio signal, which in turn activates the ignition of a car? Two and a half miles away, Sauvin let fly a burst of emotion toward his laboratory plant. Outside the lab, the car motor turned on. Sauvin also uses plants to mentally signal ''all aboard'' on a model railroad. Starting and stopping toy trains by thought may not be what the world most needs, but Sauvin gets the point across vividly that mental control of equipment at a distance is, with the help of plants, definitely possible. If you are of an electronic bent, perhaps you can get the kitchen geranium to turn on the electric coffeepot when you roll out of bed, or maybe you can wire your philodendron to switch on the house lights when you're not in. No one has figured a way to have the African violets let the dog out, too—but someone might work on it. Not much imagination is required to project more serious uses for telepathic plant systems.

Governments as well as individuals and corporations seem to be aware of the possible potential of plant perception. Apart from the various Soviet institutes mentioned, academician Dr. B. Dombrovsky reports that interaction between human psychological states and plants has been studied and confirmed in the biological laboratories of the State University of Kazakhstan. Plant research is proceeding in government labs in South America and recently, Mankind Research, Inc., of Washington, D.C., won a US government contract to explore plant response to external stimuli.

Kirlian Photography

Soviet researchers suggest that the Kirlian techniques can also show the interaction of humans and plants by changes in the plant's luminosity. If you're interested in photography and have built a Kirlian-type apparatus, some of the experiments mentioned in this chapter might be checked with Kirlian photos rather than with resistance or potential meters. It would seem to be eminently worthwhile for someone to attempt to correlate the two new techniques of plant exploration.

The Backster Effect

In a scientific sense, you are not duplicating—proving or disproving—the work of Backster or any other researcher unless you follow their controlled procedures exactly. Some of Backster's methodology may be found in "Evidence of a Primary Perception in Plant Life," *International Journal of Parapsychology*, winter, 1968. And an added cautionary: Unlike the science we are used to, these new areas involve mind and, to some extent—often to an unwanted extent—the interaction of the observer with the test. If you have any sort of friendly feeling for plants, you will most probably get good results. However there are states of mind that seemingly negate reaction no matter how good the equipment or methods used.

The Soviet physicist Dr. Victor Adamenko remarks, "Experiments appear to show that plants receive some kind of emanation at a distance of a hundred miles and that known methods of screening from electromagnetic waves, such as Faraday screens and metallic containers, do not prevent the plant from receiving the signal." Can your influence on a plant penetrate any barrier? Close-range tests may sometimes involve energies, while distance tests imply thought (which for all anyone knows may be an energy, but of a different order). In either growth experiments or monitored tests, set up a screen between you and the plant during treatment or put a container over it. (Do the same with the control.) Try glass, window screening, slate, wood, metal, plastic, etc. Distance experiments should be done with monitoring devices to check for effects.

Remember, psi tests have that added extra—expectation. Expectation can often be made flesh more directly in psi experiments than in the rest of life. What happens to people with different ideas about the effect of a barrier on their ability to get through to a plant? Do results confirm expectations?

The Scientific Question

If there is plant communication how does it happen? Many researchers are looking to psi fields and X-energies for explanations while others look to quantum mechanics, crystal resonance phenomena, even tachyons—theorized particles that speed faster than light. So many varied phenomena are appearing as researchers become more intimate with the plant kingdom that we suspect more than one thing is being revealed and that more than one explanation will be needed. For a suggestion of our own on the physical level, the Soviet discovery, a major one, that photons can carry information from one organism to another might literally bring a little light to the enigmas of plant communication. (See page 182-85.)

The unity of all being. It's a refrain as familiar and perennial as the rain and sun and it's beginning to appear in a new light. Human beings, it seems, are not cut off, apart from nature. We are connected. As for the meaning of the link, while you demonstrate for yourself some of the living pathways of connection, no doubt you'll come to your own conclusions. Perhaps you'd like to talk it over with your plants. . . .

Section Two

4

Auras, Coronas, Energy Surrounds—
Ways to Track the Invisible

"When there is the same interest or study given to things or phases of mental and spiritual phenomena as has been and is given to the materialized or material phenomena, then it will become just as practical, as measurable, as meterable, as any other phase of human experience." In 1939 that was the unequivocal declaration of Edgar Cayce, the "sleeping prophet." (Ref. 2012-1 Cayce files.) Cayce assured questioners that one day psychic phenomena could be shown directly with scientific instrumentation, measurements, and methodology.

How far have we advanced in developing techniques that will enable us to monitor, understand, and use the energy forces in and around the body, which psychics have claimed to perceive? Can newly developed and refined scientific instrumentation begin to make these energies visible to everyone? Can we discover the laws by which the energies operate so that we can use them to great benefit in fields from medicine to education to criminology to agriculture? Perhaps you will be the person who can help answer some of those questions.

New scientific developments, techniques, and instruments should be checked to see if any can help in the exploration of psi. Drs. Ullman and Krippner took a methodology and instrumentation from the field of electrophysiology to study telepathy. The famous Dream Lab experiments at Maimonides Hospital in Brooklyn showed that physiological monitoring of REM's (Rapid Eye Movements) could reveal a great deal about telepathy in dreams. Can new instruments help reveal more about such inexplicables as "auras," the "etheric body," energies circulating through invisible channels called acupuncture meridians, energy effects in psychic healings?

For centuries psychics and mystics have been describing a colorful aura (or "energy surround") around the human body. Early artists often showed this surround of energy in their paintings as a halo.

Ancient scientists in India and the Orient held that there were invisible energies circulating in and around the human body, and in China this knowledge was consolidated into the theory and practice of acupuncture, a healing method that claims to overcome illness by altering the flow of energy currents to the diseased area of the body. In addition, Western doctors visiting China have reported acupuncture is also used for anesthesia and pain control.

The concept of an energy body and of an aura, which has come down to us from the ancient sciences of the Far East and India, has formed a part of the doctrine of many groups that have made a study of these Oriental and Indian writings, i.e., theosophists and Rosicrucians. Swami Sivananda describes the Hindu and yogic theory of Prana—the universal energy considered more basic than atomic energy: "Whatever moves, works or has life is but an expression or manifestation of Prana. . . . Prana is the link between the astral (or auric) and the physical body. When the slender threadlike Prana (the silver cord) is cut off the astral body separates from the physical body. Death takes place."

The prana aura surrounding the physical body is said to be the means by which one person may impart healing energy to another by magnetic healing.

Until recently, however, we lacked the instrumentation and techniques to confirm the observations of the ancients (whose science had come from where?), and our main knowledge about these invisible bioenergies had to come from individuals with higher sense perception.

What do psychics see as the "aura"? Do they all see the same thing? And in what way do they perceive this energy surround?

American psychic Edgar Cayce saw a colorful surround about the body, from which he could diagnose illnesses and determine thoughts and emotions. Cayce described the flow of energy in the body as a figure eight with the lines crossing at the solar plexus. In addition he saw an energy body interpenetrating the physical body. This "energy body" (or "etheric body") vibrated at a higher frequency, he said. The energy body or etheric body is supposed to interpenetrate and extend slightly beyond the physical body, forming a part of the aura. Other psychics claim to see these same energy patterns.

Generally psychics assert there are many layers to the aura, the main ones being a dark quarter-inch layer close to the skin, an inner aura two to four inches out that is said to glimmer like heat from a pavement on a hot day, and a third, misty aura that extends much further out.

Dr. Shafica Karagulla, an outstanding medical doctor and a former colleague of Dr. Wilder Penfield of McGill University, has extensively researched clairvoyants' descriptions of patients' auras and coordinated their observations with medical diagnoses. Her years' long study of psychics' diagnostic abilities is detailed in her excellent book, *Breakthrough to Creativity* (DeVorss: L.A.). She reports that many psychics not only see energies emanating *from* the body but also energies pouring *into* the body from outside. There's a constant interchange of energies, she says, through the field around the body.

Dr. Karagulla, in her interviews with people who have higher sense perception, discovered that people often perceived phenomena such as the aura but had no idea that these perceptions could be classed as "psychic." Many artists and writers have sensed these auralike energy fields, whether aware of the psi aspect or not. For instance, British author Virginia Woolf in her masterful *To the Lighthouse*, describes a character, Mrs. Ramsey, as surrounded by a dome shape, and when Mrs. Ramsay reacts to those around her, she seemed ". . . at once to pour erect into the air a rain of energy, a column of spray, looking at the same time animated and alive as if all her energies were being fused into force, burning and illuminating. . . ."

The aura has generally been described as dome shaped, and Hindu descriptions of pranic energy identify it as "a fine spray of haze" all around the body.

Is the aura actually an optical phenomenon perceived with the eyes, or is it a different type of energy that psychics perceive in a different way? Ambrose and Olga Worrall, both outstanding psychics, maintain that "seeing" the aura is in no sense an optical function of the physical eye. Both Worralls maintain that one senses the aura with the "spiritual eye"—and quite spontaneously. Thus, it is possible for blind people to be aware of auras and for normally sighted people to "see" them when their eyes are closed. Olga insists that she "sees" the aura through the center of her forehead. Every living being—human, animal, or plant—radiates an aura, according to the Worralls; and this radiation is itself a life form. There's no aura around any dead thing. The Worralls feel, too, that the aura has something to do with magnetism and changes if a person is turned toward different points of the compass. For more details see their book, *Explore Your Psychic World* (Harper and Row, 1970), based on a series of seminars for the Laymen's Movement, Wainwright House, Rye, New York.

Jack Schwarz, one of a handful of thoroughly researched psychics in America, has worked with scientists since 1958 on physiological psi research to try to discover the scientific principles behind his dramatic paranormal abilities. At the Menninger Clinic in Kansas scientists explored his technique for conscious pain control and diagnosis of patients' auras even over closed-circuit television. He has personally trained many medical doctors to learn to see auras and to use this new ability in diagnosis. (See pages 57-58 for the how-to details.)

"What a psychic person sees as an arua," he says, "will vary, too, according to the psychic's own aura. After all, the psychic has to perceive through his own aura. If emotions or external conditions affect the psychic's energy field he will naturally see someone else's field with a different tinge." This may explain why some psychics say they can perceive the aura clearly on some days and poorly or not at all on others.

Says medical doctor William McGary, Director of the A.R.E. Clinic Ltd. in Phoenix, Arizona, "If we allow that all these individuals are not consistently hallucinating, then . . . we must learn to deal with the vibrational nature of the body if we are really to make progress in the therapy of the human body and in understanding its true nature." He asserts, "Our present understanding of the body is only partial and incomplete. . . ."

The study and understanding of the luminous emanation from people is pertinent not only to such fields as medicine and biology but to the area of religion as well. One does not have to go back to ancient times to find evidence of the intermingling of these energies in religious activities. Recently, the BBC of London had an extraordinary experience while filming a documentary on Mother Teresa, founder of the well-known Home for the Dying in Calcutta. Mother Teresa and the sisters of the Mission of Charity each day pick up the dying from the streets of Calcutta and bring them to the Home given to Mother Teresa to shelter the sick. Since 1952 they've picked up over 23,000 human wrecks from the streets of Calcutta, and of these abandoned and dying, saved over fifty percent. The cameraman for the film on Mother Teresa was Ken Macmillan, already renowned for his remarkable filming of the Kenneth Clark TV series *Civilization*.

Upon seeing the Home for the Dying, Ken told British author Malcolm Muggeridge, narrator of the film, that it was impossible to film it at all. The long cavernous room lined with dying bodies was almost dark and had only a few tiny windows high up in the walls. "Ken was adamant," Muggeridge recalls. They had no adequate lighting with them. Finally they decided to take some footage indoors to please Muggeridge and then film patients outdoors in brighter light.

When the film was processed, BBC technicians were surprised. The film footage shot indoors in the darkness was bathed in an exceptionally beautiful, soft golden and blue light.

"Ken insists that technically the result is impossible," reports Muggeridge. Ken Macmillan tried test runs with the same type of film under identical light conditions and got totally negative results. He could offer no explanation for the extraordinary gold and blue light in the Mother Teresa film.

Malcolm Muggeridge supposes it may be a religious phenomenon. "Mother Teresa's Home for the Dying is overflowing with love, as one senses immediately on entering it. This love is luminous," he says, "like the halos artists have seen and made visible round the heads of saints. I find it not at all surprising that the luminosity should register on a photographic film." (A frame from this sequence is included in Muggeridge's book. See References.)

Muggeridge showed the BBC documentary to a group of church officials and found that the reaction to the inexplicable light sequence was one of acute embarrassment.

If there really is a genuine luminosity pervading the Home for the Dying, what is this emanation? Could scientific instruments register and measure these energies? It's interesting that the luminosity was blue and gold, colors often associated with certain kinds of paranormal effects. Do Mother Teresa's prayers and concern for her patients manifest as an energy transfer or antenna to draw in forces similar to the energy sometimes seen by psychics between healers and patients?

The real question is what is this energy and what is the mechanism of its actions? The late Ambrose Worrall, being an electronics expert as well as a healer, maintained that it would soon be possible to develop instrumentation to monitor the forces of the psychic or energy body and the emanations given off by it. "We must consider all possible systems and force fields . . ." he advised. Like Cayce, he too believed that all these psi phenomena were meterable and measurable.

In recent years there have been a host of new technical developments in instrumentation and methodology in science which might help uncover some fraction of the whole range of energy phenomena in and around the human body.

Because so much of the energy interaction the psychic perceives is invisible to most people, its very existence has been denied; yet as Buckminster Fuller points out, ninety nine percent of what is happening in human activity and interaction within nature takes place in realms of reality utterly invisible, inaudible, unsmellable, untouchable by presently developed human senses and must be relayed to us by instruments. The invisible phenomena that psychics perceive may also soon be capable of being relayed to us through instrumentation. The following chart shows just a handful of recent scientific discoveries that pertain to investigation of the fields within and around the body. It may well be that some of them can be useful in elucidating further a specific fraction of a psi phenomenon as psychics see it or could be considered an analogy to the way psi happenings occur. The scientist working in his lab with sophisticated instruments may never have heard of psi phenomena, while the psychic who perceives these fields of force may never have the opportunity to visit a scientific lab to see whether the scientists' instruments show similar things.

The whole new thrust in the field of psi research and discovery has been in the development of instrumentation that can help us monitor and understand the functioning of psi energies. Soviet scientists, in particular, have led the way in this new instrumented exploration of the psi dimensions.

Some of these new instruments and the aspects of psi phenomena they make visible are discussed in the sections to follow. Where possible, simplified methods of constructing similar apparatus are included. The technical section gives references where you can find the complex material.

Aura Training Technique

Many people have learned to see emanations and fields around bodies of living things and believe that practice develops the ability to perceive this energy surround. They say the ability is akin to learning to look in the right way, and with the proper focus. One

FIGURE 2.

Energy Field Detectors

Scientific Term	Instrument That Registers the Energy Field	What It's Like	What Some Psychics Say They Perceive
Electro-dynamic fields	Burr volt-meter	Records energy fields of living things . . . patterns of energy controlling growth of embryo or seed, or healing wound. Shows energy changes in body during hypnosis. Shows effects of cosmic changes on body.	See energy fields of living things. See change of field when person hypnotized.
Convection currents of warm-air layer around body	Schlieren system	Three-inch-thick colored envelope of warm air moves from feet upward over body. At groin and armpits reverses direction. At shoulders spurts upward to dissipate in feathery plume five inches above head. Concentrations of bacteria and/or inflammation cause color changes, alter flow pattern. Used in diagnosis.	Two-to-four-inch colored field of energy—moves from ground up over the body. At shoulders, right and left fields join—travel upwards over head. If person ill, flow pattern blocked, colors changed. Used for diagnosis.
Ultrafaint luminescence	1. Supersensitive photomultipliers	Flashing signals of light in coded pattern coming from body. Advance diagnosis of disease before physical symptoms show up.	See various colored flares in field around body. See disrupted pattern of energy before illness manifests physically.
	2. Kirlian photography	May be an amplifier of above. Shows flare patterns revealing state of health and emotions. When part of physical body is cut away, photo shows "phantom" image of missing part. Different thoughts change the colors.	General pattern and color of energies reveal health and emotions. Can see phantom limb. Can determine thoughts from aura colors.
Force-field detection	Sergeyev detector	Detects pulsating field from living things some yards away from the body. Can determine anxiety, stress. After clinical death, records pulsing force fields of energy several feet away from body.	Psychics perceive wide, extended energy field around body. At death, see swirls of misty energy leaving body.

FIGURE 2.

Energy Field Detectors

Scientific Term	Instrument That Registers the Energy Field	What It's Like	What Some Psychics Say They Perceive
Acupuncture point locator	Tobiscope biometer	Detects acupuncture points on skin as points that conduct electricity more easily. Detects areas where energy flow is blocked.	See currents of energy flowing through body and perceive areas where flow of energy clogged.
Electromagnetic fields	Gulyaev auragrams	Show changes of energies around muscles. Diagnoses internal organs from electroauragrams.	Perceive changes of energies in internal organs.
Electromagnetic force field	Complex bioelectronics equipment	Shows fields around body as positively or negatively charged in different areas. Field polarities change with hypnosis, anesthesia, sleep, influence of external fields. Can be shown on modified TV screen.	See energy fields as polarized into positive and negative. Perceive change of polarities with hypnosis, anesthesia, sleep.

aura-training technique is as follows:

Sit down in front of a mirror. The background should be white or light colored. Relax and focus your gaze at a point approximately six inches above your head and two feet behind you in the mirror. Use peripheral vision to observe the outline of the body, especially head and shoulders. Gradually peripheral vision should reveal a thin line of light around the body. This may take several minutes. Move your head and see if this pattern of light moves with it. This helps differentiate whether the field is associated with you or not. Once you have seen this, try to figure out exactly how you did it so you can repeat the process. Another method is to use a black background and then illuminate yourself with a blue light. (Blue light bulbs can be used.) From there on it's a matter of practice, practice, practice. At first, they say, you may see a colorless or misty thin band of light around the body. Later with practice more layers may become invisible, extending outward. Colors may become clearer. Once you can see this emanation, you can begin experimenting with it. Try to gain conscious control over the pattern and shift it from side to side of the hand or head. In the same way as biofeedback, psi practitioners assert that through the aura you can gain psychic-physical control over body processes. If you succeed at aura training, then you'll be in a position to ask along with many others, "Exactly what is this energy field that I'm seeing?"

Aura Training Device

Dr. Walter Kilner of St. Thomas' Hospital, London, was one of the first to explore the aura systematically in the early 1900's. Using glass screens stained with dicyanin dye, he believed he could perceive a colorful area of radiation about six to eight inches around the human body which was affected by disease, mood, hypnosis, etc. Kilner describes his complex aura diagnostic system in *The Human Aura*, reissued in 1965 by University Books, 120 Enterprise Avenue, Secaucus, New Jersey 07094.

Contemporary research on the Kilner system has been continued by the Metaphysical Research Group, Archers' Court, Hastings, England. They have developed a device based on Kilner's work in the form of the aura goggles with filters dyed with pinacyanole. The group claims its students have had a high degree of success in seeing auras with this training device. Many scientists however consider the Kilner method highly controversial. If you would like to see for yourself, aura goggles and filters are available from Clark Publishing Co., PO Box 671, Evanston, Illinois 60204.

Sophisticated Aura Training Equipment

Jack Schwarz, a highly trained metaphysician, is a prime example of a new breed of psychic. As a teacher of metaphysics, far from viewing the new technology as a threat, he sees it as a fine means of opening up the paranormal, making it more accessible to all, and carrying highly beneficial knowledge into the mainstream of understanding.

Schwarz, who has worked for many years with such scientists investigating psi as Drs. Elmer and Alyce Green at the Menninger Foundation in Kansas, has developed a training program (charts and eye exercises) to enable people to extend their present senses and develop aura-vision. His program has been successfully used in training doctors to perceive energy fields around the body and to diagnose with them.

Schwarz has also developed a new device, an aura-vision trainer, which is called an Integral Stimulating Intensity Stroboscope (ISIS). The device is basically an adaptation of an optometrist's instrument and in conducting research with it in conjunction with an opthalmologist, it was discovered that it prepares the eyes for better vision by stimulating the rods and cones. "The original purpose of the ISIS was solely for auric vision training," says Schwarz. "However, while researching with ISIS other uses were discovered." The *Newsletter of the Association for Humanistic Psychology* reported in January, 1973, that when the ISIS was tested in a pilot glaucoma seminar, it was found to relieve excess pressure on the eyes. For best results as an aura-vision trainer, Schwarz suggests that the instrument be used in conjunction with the special training charts and eye exercises. For information on the ISIS Aura-Vision Trainer (Model 1204) write Aletheia Psycho-Physical Foundation, 515 NE 8th, Grants Pass, Oregon 97526.

5

Kirlian Photography

Human beings are "a spectacular panorama of colors, whole galaxies of lights. . . ." Throughout the 1960's extraordinary descriptions by prominent Soviet scientists appeared in the Soviet press of what humans looked like as seen by a newly developed form of photography. We're a world of "luminescent labyrinths," "fantastic galaxies," "alluring ghostly lights," and "multicolored flares," they said.

By the 1970's Americans, too, had constructed similar apparatus and were exploring a new picture of human beings: "a fascinating new world," "brilliantly colored bubbles and blotches," "the fabric of organic and inorganic life," flares pulsing out energy "like water from a fireman's hose."

Researchers East and West were viewing a brilliant emanation from the human body, which became visible when the body was placed in a field of high-frequency electrical currents. A Russian husband-and-wife team had developed a new way to make photographs, movies, and to visually observe brilliantly colored light plays surrounding and moving through the human body, animals, plants, and all living things. They call it the "Kirlian Effect" (pronounced keer-lee-an) after its inventors, Semyon and Valentina Kirlian. They had labored on their own for decades to develop and perfect this new form of photography with high-frequency fields.

Since the mid-sixties, teams of Soviet scientists from Moscow to Siberia have plunged into the study of these beautiful colored lights in living things and have come up with some intriguing new conceptions about the nature of life itself.

Among the initial findings: Disease shows up in a disturbed pattern of flares long before it manifests in the physical body in any diagnosable form. If portions of the physical body are cut away, the energy matrix or "phantom" of the missing part is still clearly visible in the photograph, although there is no tangible, physical substance there. Patterns vary according to mood and health and even thoughts. Hypnosis and drugs also alter the flare pattern and colors.

The patterns of the flares are substantially altered by weather; day and night; cosmic disturbances, such as solar flares. The brightest flares on the body show at the points on the skin known to be acupuncture points.

Soviet scientists began to work on applications of the Kirlians' high-frequency photography technique in agriculture, ecology, nutrition, dentistry, medicine, geology, criminology, archeology, and so forth.

The story of the discovery and development of Kirlian photography is given in three chapters in our book *Psychic Discoveries Behind the Iron Curtain*. After examining much data on Kirlian photography, we became convinced, as had a number of psi researchers in the Soviet Union, that the technique might also be applied in psi research to help make visible and studiable some of the psi occurrences whose mechanisms had previously resisted analysis. Can human thought or energy have an effect on plants to make them grow faster? The photography might make these effects visible as they occurred. Does a psychic healer emit some sort of emanation responsible for healing wounds?' Could Kirlian photography show what was happening? During the mysterious phenomenon of PK (moving objects by mind power), did the body emit a different energy pattern somehow involved with causing motion at a distance, and what was that pattern? Again, maybe the Kirlian technique could show us new things about psi events. It might be one more form of instrumentation that could help the rest of us understand what psychics claimed to perceive.

Of course, the Kirlian photography process itself is *not* a psychic event or psychic photography. The Kirlian technique per se has nothing whatever to do with occultism any more than the electroencephalograph. Yet instrumentation like the EEG and Kirlian device, developed for use in regular scientific research, can also be applied to studying psi to help us learn more about the electrophysiological processes taking place in the body when psi occurs.

The most basic Kirlian technique uses a Tesla Coil connected to a metal plate. Film and object to be photographed are placed on the plate in the dark. Switching on the current of high-frequency electricity causes the film to record an image of the object including a field around it. Nonliving things such as a coin, give a constant unvarying picture, but living things have continuously changing patterns. For what those patterns may mean, see Chapter 6.

The Kirlian technique, like the Schlieren technique or like REM (Rapid Eye Movement) monitoring, may reveal things about ESP.

Making photographs with electricity is not new. The originality of the Kirlian method does not lie in the development of the high-frequency spark generator itself, which has been around since the turn of the century, when Nikola Tesla first invented the Tesla Coil. (Tesla, the great genius of electricity who harnessed Niagara Falls, was probably the first to make photographs with high-frequency electricity.) Rather, the Kirlian technique is original in the wide range of patented apparatus that make it possible for the spark generator to be used in a whole spectrum of different photographic applications for fields from dentistry to botany and for instruments from microscopes to holography equipment. The Kirlians' patents on these adaptations have occupied a lot of space in the annals of Soviet photography and cinematography over the past twenty years. A very partial patent search reveals the breadth of their ingenuity in developing ways to apply the spark generator to photography. (See patents section.) It's curious that until 1973 some twenty years' worth of these developments in Soviet photography seem to have been overlooked by Western photography experts.

The tradition of photography with electricity goes back more than seventy years. At the fifth photographic exhibition in Russia in 1898 Yakov Narkevich Yokdo displayed photos created by an electrical discharge. In the early 1900's a Czech, B. Navratil, published on electrography and so did an American, F.E. Nipher. (Transactions of the Academy of Sciences of St. Louis, 1900.) In 1939 two Czech researchers, S. Prat and J. Schlemmer, published electrographic photos of leaves, showing sparkling corona patterns. They found the emanation would go through screens impermeable to infrared, visible, and ultraviolet radiation. They wondered: Could there be some additional unknown radiation involved? Again in 1949 a professor at Moscow University, Georgi Spivak, also succeeded in producing electrographic images.

The Kirlians, who have worked with the method since the 1940's, have developed a fairly sophisticated technology of electrography.

Our publication of material about Kirlian photography in 1970 and subsequent exchanges of data among scientists have helped respark interest in photography with high-frequency electricity in

America. To date, a large number of American researchers have succeeded in constructing electrographic equipment and making photographs. They have not only duplicated some Soviet work but also moved into new and different areas of research. In 1972 scientists from Stanford, UCLA, Newark College of Engineering, the University of New Mexico, Roger Williams College, among others, gathered at the First Western Hemisphere Conference on Kirlian Photography and Acupuncture in New York. Several hundred people attended. A second conference on Kirlian photography was held in 1973. After attending the conference, professionals from many fields have published enthusiastic articles. Editors of *Popular Photography Magazine* call Kirlian photography a "fascinating . . . developing technology-art-science," and in a profusely illustrated article (February, 1973) conclude, "What it may all mean and where it may go is for the future, but the imaginative possibilities are terrific." Dr. Dudley Chapman, a medical journal editor-in-chief, was so impressed with "this exciting new phenomenon" that he devoted the entire October, 1972 issue of *The Osteopathic Physician* to the topic of Kirlian photography.

The interested amateur experimenter who would like to get in on the frontier of this photography will find in Chapter 7 a way to make a very simple electrographic apparatus. This of course is not the same as the Kirlian equipment used in Russia. To the best of our knowledge, Westerners have not yet presented at any public conference, duplication of the most sophisticated of the Kirlian-type apparatus used in research at many universities from Moscow to Alma-Ata, although we've heard that a major military lab has begun work on such equipment.

New technology in the area of Kirlian photography could help us not only in psi research but in other disciplines.

Research on Kirlian photography is an area of psi that interests the United States government, and recently they have given several research grants to Mankind Research Unlimited Inc., of Washington, D.C., for work on the Kirlian effect. MRU, originally a subsidiary of a large engineering consulting firm, and now an independent company, considers the contracts ". . . 'firsts' for government-supported 'human engineering' research grants." Former Naval officer Carl Schleicher, who is president and research and development director of MRU, told us, "We have found that the government can and will support research in these areas [psi], if such research is properly communicated to them, provides a beneficial use of tax payers' funds and is conducted by responsible organizations.''

One of Carl's secrets of communicating with the government in order to obtain psi grants has been translations of occult and parapsychological terms into ''respectable'' technical jargon. Referring to a grant project involving the study of chakras (body energy centers, according to yoga), Carl told the *Washington Post Potomac Magazine* (July 22, 1973), ''. . . I can communicate this information to a government agency that doesn't know what the hell a chakra is . . . I just call them 'unique psychophysiological tools and techniques,' and they say, 'Fine, thanks very much.' '' By the same token, Kirlian photography, for purposes of government grants, was described as ''chemiluminescent and electro-photographic (Tesla effect) techniques,'' and ''certain . . . psychosomatic evaluatory areas.''

With Kirlian photography, as with everything else for which he has sought funding, Carl looks for pragmatic applications—techniques that can be applied to a problem, something to diagnose sickness, something that might even spot hijackers. MRU also markets Kirlian equipment, described later.

Many people seem surprised at the idea that anything springing from the occult could prove practical and useful; yet basically, if there had not been certain practical benefits from the occult sciences, they would not have survived to modern times. No doubt the future will see many more business enterprises along the lines of Mankind Research—companies that research and design equipment for useful applications of psi. (See pages 285-86.)

Says Professor Douglas Dean, former president of the Parapsychological Association, ''We have far to go to bridge the gap between certain areas of Soviet research and our own . . . particularly, Kirlian photography. But certainly we have much to gain by pursuing such research. The great unknown potential of Kirlian photography may open up areas yet undreamed of, which can be of great benefit to the whole of mankind.''

Exploring Psi with the Electrograph

When we first got back from Russia, late in 1968, with plans and scientific material on Kirlian photography, we could hardly wait to get started photographing so we too could see what it was the Soviets were all talking about. We translated Kirlian plans, scientific papers, patent material, and the more we learned of the multiplicity of applications of the Kirlian method, the more we were convinced the Kirlian technique could help in psi research. But we were in for a letdown. Electronics experts took one look at the material and stated flatly, ''No such machine can be built here. If it was, it wouldn't work—it would fry anything touching it. The project is impossible,'' they assured us, ''because Western electrical components are totally different from Soviet ones.'' They also claimed that Soviet scientific papers always leave out key details and Westerners have trouble following them.

One biophysicist who was enthusiastic about Kirlian photography hooked up the wrong equipment and electrocuted his plant.

Finally we decided the easiest solution to the problem of interpreting the Kirlian plans was to import equipment from a Soviet-bloc country. We succeeded finally in arranging for a high-frequency photography machine to be imported from Czechoslovakia. The Czech device is called an electrograph, and they say it gives results similar to those obtained with Kirlian equipment. They agreed to build a machine for us.

Eventually, by the beginning of 1972, a waist-high crate from Czechoslovakia arrived at Lynn's home in the US. After wrestling through the crate, she unearthed the electrograph—an apparatus about $10'' \times 15'' \times 6''$—housed in a wooden cabinet (see photo). To take a picture with the electrograph you put film and object on the exposure plate on top of the box and switch on the current for a second or so. Photography must be done in darkness. Flares are visible under the object or finger and a tingling sensation can be felt in the fingers. Could we get pictures similar to what the Russians had gotten?

One of our coauthors on another book, Professor Douglas Dean, is an electrophysiologist. At the Newark College of Engineering Psi Project he had pioneered physiological psi research. The minute the electrograph arrived he was eager to run some experiments. At a professional photography lab he and Lynn completed a series of photographs. They showed the corona effect just as the Kirlian pictures had. When two people placed their index fingers side by side, they showed streamer repulsion and thinning of the corona just as the Russian pictures had. In other words, the corona or radiation pattern folds back on itself and does not intermingle with another person's.

The Jersey Society of Parapsychology, of which Douglas Dean was then president, provided Dean with a small grant to carry out further Kirlian photography experiments, to see if the equipment could duplicate results the Russians had gotten photographing psychic healers. In *PDBIC* we mentioned one of the famous Russian healers, Colonel Alexei Krivorotov who works with his son, a medical doctor. Colonel Krivorotov does magnetic healing by placing his hands an inch or so away from the patient. Patients maintain they feel intense heat "like a hot water bottle" but no physiological indicator shows any change in the patient's or Krivorotov's skin. The colonel has been especially successful with back problems, infections, diseases of the nervous system. The Kirlians photographed Krivorotov's hands at rest and when preparing to heal. The Kirlian photos showed Krivorotov's hands had regular, average-sized flares before treating a patient, but when asked to prepare to heal, the flares greatly enlarged. Perhaps the Kirlian technique made visible an energy or information exchange between healer and patient that helps the patient reprogram himself for health. (See photo section, photos 2 and 3.)

Could the electrograph help tell us more about what happens during the healing process? Dean organized a series of electrograph photography sessions with Mrs. Ethel DeLoach, founder of the Jersey Society of Parapsychology. Mrs. DeLoach has become known for her healing abilities and has been permitted by some doctors to treat their patients in New Jersey and New York hospitals. Mrs. DeLoach had her index finger photographed while resting. It showed average flares. Next she was asked to think about healing. The flare patterns in these pictures showed a large shower of flares pouring from her finger. Each time the sequence was repeated, the same increase in flares showed up. Results matched those of the Kirlians. In color photos these flares are predominantly bluish. (See photo section, photos 4 and 5.)

Dean also did a photography series in color while Mrs. DeLoach was actually healing a patient. The *before* photo showed the usual small blue corona. Then the finger of one hand was photographed while with the other hand she attempted to heal a wen on the patient's left arm. The wen, a sort of cyst filled with dead cells, was about $1/4''$ high. During the laying-on-of-hands, Dean photographed a striking change in Mrs. DeLoach's finger. Not only had the flares increased substantially, but in addition a brilliant orange sunlike emanation appeared in the corona from the area just below the fingerpad. "It seems reasonable to think she was healing because the wen on the patient's arm disappeared the following day," says Dean.

These initial results were an encouraging indicator that the electrograph and Kirlian technique did seem to be able to make visible certain psi effects that had previously been difficult to detect and record objectively. For patients it could become a means of monitoring effectiveness of treatment. For healers, it could make objective whether or not treatment is having any beneficial effect on a person. At UCLA, Dr. Thelma Moss and Kendall Johnson also did a series of photographs of healers. They obtained a distinct difference in *before* and *after* photos of healers and patients: The healer showed a large corona just before healing and a small one after healing.

Subsequently Dean did many more series of experiments with our Czech electrograph, including setting up a closed-circuit video display. The pictures continued to back up initial photographic results. The initial comparative pictures of Mrs. DeLoach, although only preliminary, have been widely reprinted in European and American publications, including a medical journal.

Mr. Paul Sauvin of New Jersey (who was the patient in the above healing test) was one of the first people to whom we showed the Kirlian plans. Paul Sauvin has a good background in electronics and an eclectic mind and was one of the first to offer encouragement about the possibility of creating an American adaptation of the Kirlian equipment.

After weeks of testing out various alternative power supplies, during which he often spent evenings with his kitchen table all lit up with high-frequency currents due to a too-powerful generator, Mr. Sauvin finally suggested the type of commercial Tesla coil used by beauticians as being effective and safe. We followed up on his idea, obtained a High-Frequency Outfit and worked out several types of exposure plates to adapt it for photography. We found it gave excellent results. (See Chapter 7.)

We had hoped of course that publication of the Soviet approach to psi research in *PDBIC* would help stimulate some similar work to check out possibilities for this approach in the West. What the new Soviet work definitely stimulated was tourism to the Soviet-bloc countries. Hundreds and possibly thousands of journeys have been made by Westerners to the Soviet Union and East Europe to further an exchange of ideas in the field of psi.

Many more people brought back Kirlian plans and many varieties of equipment have been built, some based on a simple model-T ignition coil, others more complex, such as the unit at Stanford University.

In the winter of 1970 Dr. Thelma Moss, a medical psychologist and assistant professor at the Neuropsychiatric Institute, UCLA, made an important journey to the USSR, which eventually led her to set up the first full-scale Kirlian research program in America. The real credit for getting Kirlian photography off the ground in America must go to Dr. Moss and her coworkers.

After consulting researchers in Prague, Sofia, Moscow, and Leningrad, Dr. Moss then traveled several thousand miles east to the republic of Kazakhstan and the city of Alma-Ata near the Chinese border. The Kirov State University of Kazakhstan biology department has done much of the major research into scientific applications of Kirlian photography.

Dr. Moss made the trip at the invitation of Dr. Viktor Inyushin, a young biophyscist whom we'd met in 1968 in Moscow. She was invited to lecture at the university, visit the university lab, and learn more about his six years of research into Kirlian photography. She was greeted warmly by the Kazakh scientists, which was some comfort since the heat had gone off in her hotel and the temperature was two degrees below zero.

But the next morning Dr. Inyushin regretfully informed her that permission for her to visit his lab had been refused by authorities in Moscow. It was a great disappointment for Dr. Moss. Permission to visit Dr. Kogan's psi lab in Moscow had also been refused. Why? Many other Western scientists have also been refused at the lab door. Why? One may ask, too, why Westerners are not permitted to visit Soviet space installations and launching sites.

While the Americans run guided tours of Cape Canaveral, no one is even definitely sure where one of the major Soviet space cosmodromes is located—at Baikonur or Tyuratam, in Kazakhstan.

John Wilford, aerospace expert for the New York *Times*, asserts that the Soviets generally organize high-priority projects on a dual basis, one organization open and science oriented, the other secret and technology oriented. Members of the open organization are permitted to meet Westerners and attend international meetings. Members of the secret organization (often referred to as a "state commission") remain anonymous. These people exercise the real power in any project. For example, the men who actually run the Soviet space program have never been identified. Projects are shrouded in secrecy. Has the Soviet psi program been organized in the same way, with an open group handling visitors and a secret group operating behind the scenes? One Slavic psi specialist told us, "You will never even know who the key researchers are in the psi field in the USSR."

Whatever the reason, bureaucratic buck-passing or the Soviet policy of secrecy, Dr. Moss never got to see the university lab, but she did benefit from examination of published scientific material.

Once back at UCLA, she set out to replicate the Kirlian work at her own lab. She showed several American electronics experts the schematics of the Kirlian apparatus. The plans are "insufficient," "unfeasible," "absurd," the experts told her.

How she finally came by a Kirlian device will probably remain the highlight of her career as a professor, she says. During a UCLA extension-course lecture, she described her Russian trip, current research in psi and showed Kirlian pictures from Moscow and Alma-Ata. At the end of the lecture, a Mr. Kendall Johnson presented himself and said he'd like to make some Kirlian pictures.

"I would, too," she replied. She described the discouraging views of the experts and gave Ken the supposedly "undecipherable" schematics and the translated scientific papers. At the next-to-last class for the course he presented himself again, this time with what looked like an astonishingly good "Kirlian photograph." "Where did you get it?" Dr. Moss asked incredulously.

"In my father-in-law's garage," he replied.

With Ken's electronic ingenuity and several more weeks of perseverance in the garage they had a working apparatus. Their equipment is quite different from the Kirlians' as it pulses at a low frequency of 3,000 cycles per second rather than 200,000. Moss and Johnson have joined forces on research into what they now call radiation-field photography.

Says Professor Dean, "Johnson, perhaps because he had not been trained in electronics, finally succeeded in altering the Russian design so as to achieve the first modern Kirlian-type photos in the United States. This accomplishment served to verify that the Kirlian effect is a real one and inspired many other labs to start similar work. . . ."

Over the past three years, Moss and Johnson have taken substantially more than 50,000 radiation-field photographs, studied more than 500 persons and more than 1,000 leaves.

Dr. William Tiller, Chairman of Materials Sciences at Stanford University, traveled to the USSR with a group of scientists, doctors, and laymen from the Association for Research and Enlightenment, Virginia Beach. This group had a stimulating trip covering Moscow and Leningrad; and Dr. Tiller learned a great deal about Kirlian photography, which he has published in detail along with technical plans in the *A.R.E. Journal* (March, 1972, 75¢). At Stanford Dr. Tiller has assembled equipment designed to approximate the Soviet technique. He gives details in *Galaxies of Life*. He has already done some preliminary research studying metals with Kirlian photography.

At this point a great many people have developed equipment and have begun their own explorations.

Some Basic Kirlian Explorations

Here are just a few observations made so far by different researchers in the West:

- Altered states of consciousness can be made visible in Kirlian photos.
- Electrophysiological studies showed corona emanation does not relate to skin temperature, galvanic skin response, vaso-constrictions or dilations, or to perspiration.
- When a person is in a normal, healthy state, finger shows predominant blue and white corona. When emotionally aroused, anxious, or nervous, finger pad often emanates a red blotch.
- English researchers D.R. Milner and E.F. Smart, experimenting with DC high-voltage photography, found there's an energy transfer-interaction between a freshly picked leaf and a dying leaf picked twenty-four hours earlier.
- Studies of different states of consciousness through drugs (alcohol and marijuana): Intoxication with either produces a general increase in brightness and size of corona. One subject who worked his way up to his seventeenth drink went from a small close-knit emanation to a "rosy glow" eventually to being "all lit up."
- Moss and Johnson studied three people who claim healing powers—their photos showed the reverse of the Russian and Dean findings. A change was still evident but in this case the healers at rest had a very wide corona, but while healing a much smaller one. The patients had a small corona before healing and a larger one after healing.
- Hypnosis showed a similar pattern as above, though results are inconsistent.
- A psychic in his normal waking consciousness showed a very small emanation; in trance, a brilliant blue-white corona.
- In general each person has his own unique patterning.
- Plant leaves, when gashed or damaged, show red areas and bubbles.
- Thought energy directed toward an injured leaf by a psychic restored its original brilliance in the Kirlian photos.
- PK psychics' fingertips show a sharp, concentrated corona

during PK compared to normal state.

- During magnetic storms caused by sun spots, corona changed to large red flares.
- Music seemed to change corona, making emanation more concentrated and showing more globules.
- Colored light on skin seems to affect corona as seen in *before* and *after* pictures.
- Pictures vary according to time of day as a result of cyclical changes in the earth's electrical field. Field is maximum at 7 P.M.; minimum at 4 A.M. Greenwich Mean Time. (Convert to your own time zone.)
- A California researcher is working on developing a preliminary medical diagnostic procedure.

Here are just a few of the recent findings by Kirlian researchers in the Soviet Union:

- Specific thoughts a person has vary the electrobioluminescence —i.e., thinking of a fountain pen versus thinking of an interesting book.
- Pricking your finger near a plant makes the leaves glow fifty percent brighter.
- If a person trained in biofeedback or autosuggestion suggests to himself that his hand is getting warmer, there are specific structural changes in the luminescence observed only during the autosuggestion of warmth.
- If the trained person touches another person not trained in autosuggestion and the untrained person is photographed, he too shows the same structure of luminescence as the trained person.
- Plants were ideal detectors of this energy change. Holding one's hand near a plant and suggesting that the hand is warm caused the plant leaves to increase in luminescence. Suggesting that the hand is cold caused a decrease in luminescence of the leaves.
- Dew forms on the leaves of plants in exactly the same locations as the maximum flare patterns shown in the Kirlian pictures of the leaves.
- Kirlian photography was found useful in studying ways of preserving fruit and vegetables.
- Studying acupuncture with Kirlian photography: Stimulation of certain points on an acupuncture energy channel could cause brighter luminescence at other flare points on the channel.
- For nutrition: Studies of sprouts are interesting—luminescence

intensity of spring wheat root sprouts is considerably higher compared with other types of sprouts.

- Kirlian method can be used in ecology for early diagnosis of poisons in fish—photos of scales from poisoned fish showed clear difference compared to control fish. Could be very helpful advance warnings for poisoned lakes and rivers.
- In use of Kirlian equipment for early diagnosis, sharp flashes of energy occur in stress situations—useful in evaluating gravity of a patient's condition.
- A complex analysis of the whole luminescence spectrum has been done for use in analyzing the Kirlian photos and for diagnosis.
- Each different part of the body is generally a distinctive color: heart regions, blue; forearm, greenish-blue; thigh, olive.
- Detailed analysis of Kirlian pictures of various types of cancer tissue as an aid in diagnosis: Compared to normal tissue, cancer tissue from the stomach showed a microdiffused discharge pattern with fine white or gray granular shadows. Researchers analyze the nature of the discharge channels, their geometry, and energetics to elucidate tumor diagnosis.
- Kirlian diagnosis can be done with a person as a whole or with their cells.
- It can be used for registration of emotional condition; medical diagnosis (especially cancer); monitoring effects of drug treatments on a person; monitoring effects of radiation treatments on a person.
- Hope to use the method with X-rays and ultrasound holography to make a person transparent to a certain depth.

(For more details on these Soviet findings see *Bioenergetics Questions, Material of the Scientific Methodological Seminar in Alma-Ata*, 1969. Available from Southern California Society for Psychical Research, 170 South Beverly Drive, Beverly Hills, California 90212.)

6

Kirlian Photos: Can They Show Us What Psychics See?

An aurora borealis of brilliantly colored lights pouring from the human body! That's how some Soviet scientists have described Kirlian photos. Are these the luminous energies of living things that psychics claim to see? Do the photos show us any element of the aura or etheric forces? Or do the Kirlian photos simply show us nothing more than the electricity with which they are produced? This was the controversy that began to rage when Kirlian photography with high-frequency electricity was first heard of and replicated in the West.

If you succeed in making Kirlian photos, you too will be asked, "What are these pictures about? Do they show the aura, psi energy, or just electricity?" Within the last year there's been more new scientific evidence all pointing to the same conclusion—that you're really seeing the activities of a genuine natural-energy emanation from living bodies in your Kirlian pictures.

In the Soviet Union scientists have differing opinions. Some think that stimulating the skin with the high-frequency charge used in Kirlian photography simply causes the body to radiate electrified particles, which show up in the photos as different patterns in the corona. They call this "cold electron emission," and physicist Victor Adamenko says it might have its roots in the same level of substance as the aura. Some Western scientists say this theory cannot account for all the light given off. Other scientists insist that Kirlian photography is amplifying a *different* energy within the body, which they call "bioplasmic" energy.

At the Kirov State University of Kazakhstan a group of scientists in the biology department led by the famous academician B.A. Dombrovsky, assert that the energy visible in the pictures is a form of plasma, the fourth state of matter. They claim that this bio-plasmic energy forms the energy matrix of all living substances. They envisage the bioplasma body as a kind of energy counterpart of the physical body. The bioplasma body is not the mere radiation of the physical body, but rather the physical body is the mirror of the energy body. Thus, disease strikes first in the energy body before it reaches the physical body. The Kirlian photos have so far proved to be a means of early detection of illnesses, which show as disturbed energy patterns in the pictures.

It is possible, then, to prevent illness, too, by rebalancing these disturbed energies seen in the Kirlian photos, and this might be what acupuncture treatment does.

This energy body apparently reflects the emotions of a person, states of mind, reactions to sound and color and the whole environment, and also picks up psi information. It is also theorized that the bioplasmic body broadcasts energy as well as receives it.

Talking to the Kazakh scientists, Dr. Moss learned that they consider bioplasmic energy similar to the energy of *prana* as defined by Yoga.

Within the last few years several exciting discoveries that may hold the key to Kirlian pictures have been made by scientists working in different areas of biophysics. Back in the thirties it was a Russian scientist, Alexander Gurvich, who announced that living things could generate light. After years of careful experimentation he was able to show that some sort of radiation coming from some living things had an effect on other living things. He called this mitogenetic radiation. Gurvich believed this energy to be more powerful than the ultraviolet light reaching us from the sun. To other scientists it seemed incredible that living beings could generate such energy. They couldn't see the "light" and Gurvich's work was bypassed.

Living Luminescence

However, by the 1960's biologists around the world knew it wasn't just glowworms that glimmered. People glowed, too. In the Soviet Union a principal investigator of extremely faint rays of light from plants and animals was the well-known Dr. Boris Tarusov of Moscow University. To see this luminescence researchers used highly sensitive amplifiers of light called photoelectronic multi-pliers. These are similar to the snooper-scopes used to see in total darkness in military activities. Photo multipliers are also used in star tracking in astronomy. With photo multipliers biologists saw infinitely small rays of light coming from leaves and even individual cells. But there was still a mystery—the why of the glow.

At first it was assumed that active chemical compounds in the living bodies of humans, animals, and plants were responsible for the glow. Some researchers assumed that the faint light changed according to the metabolism of the plant: chilled plants—low glow; warm plants—high glow. Others thought the glow had to do with the earth's electrical field. The puzzle shone on.

At the State University of Kazakhstan, where scientists researching Kirlian photography had developed the theory of bioplasmic energy, the idea grew that the processes observed in the Kirlian photos might be related to this natural ultrafaint luminescence researched by Tarusov. *"We submit that ultrafaint luminescence in biological systems represents plasmic processes,"* says Dr. Viktor Inyushin of Alma-Ata. *It's possible to strengthen this ultrafaint luminescence in living things by the use of Kirlian photography,* Inyushin asserts. [Italics ours.] (See *Bioenergetics Questions,* Paper 3.) In the opinion of the Kazakh experts, the Kirlian process changed the natural luminescence of the body from weak to bright so that it was easier to see what was going on in it. By 1972 a team led by Dr. Boris Nikolaevish Tarusov, Chairman of Biophysics at Moscow University, made an important new breakthrough. Long and patient observations of ultrafaint luminescence with the latest type of supersensitive photo multipliers paid off. They found that plants didn't always glimmer with a *steady* light and that the glow variations were tied to much more than metabolism.

Sometimes these almost invisible rays would suddenly burst with power, almost as if the plant were sending out a light-flash signal. The Soviet scientists found that plants could "talk" with their signals. A specific light pattern meant too much water or salinity around roots. Other signals corresponded to lack of fertilizer or excess. Most importantly, luminescence flashes seen with the photo multipliers showed—just as Kirlian photography does—that diseases can be diagnosed from the light patterns given off long before any physical symptom of the illness can be detected. A specific pattern of increased luminescence in plants turned out to be a sign of a coming bacteria and fungus attack. Studying the flashing luminescence in cotton plants, they found a specific signal, a warning pattern that the deadly wilt disease was threatening long before the plants showed any physical sign of ill health. The Kirlians had found the same thing with their electrical photographic technique.

One unexpected benefit of the luminescent plant flashes: the plants themselves indicated which of them would do best—grasses or shrubs—in a new area where gardeners had not previous experience. There began to be more and more evidence. Many of the patterns that show up in Kirlian photography also show up in natural radiations from living creatures even when they aren't illuminated with high-frequency electrical fields.

Another new finding has come up to strengthen the idea that Kirlian photography is indeed showing natural energies active in and around the body. Out in Siberia an enterprising scientist, Dr. Vlail Kaznachaev, decided to have another look at Gurvich's contention that organisms radiate some kind of energy. Rather than trying to make living radiation visible with such things as photo multipliers and Kirlian photography, Kaznachaev and his coworkers decided to search for any effect such radiations might have on other living things.

Results were stunning. Among other things they found diseased cells emit rays that carry information, rays that can penetrate through quartz glass to healthy neighboring cells and make them sick, too. (See Energies Section, pp. 182-85.)

Interestingly, Kirlian researchers have found that different diseases show specific light patterns in their photos. They have speculated that these flashes of light may well be transmitting information. There are similarities here, as Kirlian people point out, to Kaznachaev's finding. The discovery that there is radiation from living cells that carries information is a major one, something few scientists believed possible. Kirlian investigators are now attempting to correlate this confirmed light radiation from living things with the light patterns so beautifully shown in their pictures. The idea is, of course, that the radiation could carry not just information related to illness but could, like computer cards, carry programs for all sort of phenomena—in particular, perhaps, for psychic healing.

At Alma-Ata, Dr. Inyushin and his colleagues have also been developing new ways to register these X bioenergies and correlate them with the energies appearing in the Kirlian pictures. Inyushin explains that he obtains a recording of the subject's energies without changing him from his normal condition for the experiment, i.e., without turning on high-frequency electricity. Again based on Gurvich's theories, the Kazakh scientists found a way to register extraordinary emanations from people's eyes. They used a special film emulsion sensitive to the ultraviolet spectrum along with selective filters, and they suppressed all heat radiation. They got some very strange pictures on the film. *"We discovered an emanation from the eyes of animals and humans,"* reported Dr. Inyushin at an international conference on bioenergetics in Moscow in 1972. The energies coming from human and animal eyes vary with emotions and environmental conditions, says Inyushin.

To record these extraordinary emanations, they used a film emulsion of very finely divided particles placed in a cryostatic (low-temperature) element together with photocells. Even through opaque screens and thin metallic sheets, *"We obtained from human eyes, under conditions of autosuggestion, after an exposure of only one-thousandth of a second, very clear images on the emulsion."* [Italics ours.]. (*Journal of Paraphysics*, Vol. 6, No. 5.)

Could it be that Kirlian photography amplifies these as yet uncharted radiations from the human body? Just as brain waves must be amplified many times over before they can be made recordable, it may be that the high-frequency electrical field amplifies some of the energies involved in such phenomena as ultrafaint luminescence, radiation to neighboring cells, emanations from the eyes on film.

Across the USSR scientists are again examining the theories of Alexander Gurvich on natural radiations and glowing light from humans. Their findings are beginning to prove Gurvich right. Humans seem to radiate energies and the Kirlian technique may make them visible to us all.

Benson Herbert of the Paraphysics Lab in England stresses the extraordinary importance of coordinating all this new research into the natural radiations and luminescence of the human body with the research on Kirlian photography. If bioplasmic energies, radiations, luminescence, can be registered from the body in its natural state without putting a person into a high-frequency electric field as Kirlian photography does, and if in both cases similar energy patterns are found, it may settle once and for all "the controversy which is still raging—at both ends of Europe." Some believe the patterns appearing in Kirlian photos are exclusively due to the electric field applied to the body and that there are no energies of the body being revealed.

Referring to the current work at Alma-Ata, Herbert says, "Success in this experiment would in fact give encouragement to those Western parapsychologists who like to believe that some connection may exist between the Kirlian patterns and what is referred to in occult literature as the 'aura.' . . . It would at least leave open the question as to whether the 'aura' and the corona may have certain common features in their nature or causation. . . ."

For psi researchers, the work of Dr. Boris Tarusov on ultrafaint luminescence; Dr. Vlail Kaznacheev, Dr. Alexander Gurvich,

George Lakhovsky, and the researchers at Alma-Ata on radiation from living things, are all very important. New research techniques, especially those using supersensitive photo multipliers, may also be valuable in tracking general psi happenings as well.

The View from Here

Some US psychics who have seen the Kirlian pictures and are familiar with metaphysical theories see a resemblance between what the photographs show and the Yogic theories of *prana* energy. Other psychics think that what is made visible is the effect of the aura on the high-frequency discharge.

Generally the consensus among psychics here is that the Kirlian pictures may show us etheric energy.

Professor Dean describes what it looks like in motion based on Kirlian movies shown at a 1972 Moscow psi conference. "The flares shown in the stills periodically shoot out energy every few seconds, like water from a fireman's hose, and change color from one burst to the next in the motion picture. In addition globules are shot out from a leaf or finger," he reports. The flares were said to come from acupuncture points on the skin. "These effects are very difficult to understand," says Dean. He points out that the standard calculations for known energies done by physicist Dr. Tiller cannot account for all the energy displayed. Dean, Moss, and Johnson see a striking correlation between radiation-field photographs and descriptions of an energy body given in metaphysical literature, such as A.E. Powell's *The Etheric Double* (1925): "Every solid, liquid, and gaseous particle of the physical body is surrounded with an etheric envelope. . . . In size it projects about one-fourth of an inch beyond the skin. . . . In appearance, the etheric double is a pale violet-grey, or blue-grey, faintly luminous and coarse or fine in texture, according as the dense physical body is coarse or fine." Blue and violet colors consistently appear in Kirlian photographs of living things in their normal state.

Powell discusses the phantom pain many amputees experience. "This is due to the fact that the etheric portion of the limb is not removed with the dense physical portion." The Russian photos of leaves with portions cut off show "phantoms" of the missing portion.

"It is by means of the etheric double that *prana* [energy] runs along the nerves of the body. . . . Furthermore, just as the particles of the dense physical body are constantly changing and being replaced by fresh particles derived from food, water, and air, so the particles of the etheric body are being constantly changed and replaced by fresh etheric particles, these being taken into the body . . . in the form known as the Vitality Globule.'' Could these be the globules and bubbles that seem to shoot out of leaves and fingers in the Kirlian movies? Powell describes the invisible energy of the body as ''rose-colored'' and sustaining the nervous system. He claims that it is this type of energy that may be transferred from healer to patient.

Kirlian photographs of healing situations of both people and leaves have often shown a rose-colored emanation glowing distinctly and pinkly. Researchers Moss and Johnson conclude, ''Kirlian photography might be able to provide physical evidence for some type of energy system that exists within and extends beyond the physical body.''

Douglas Dean asserts, ''For nonpsychics the intriguing possibility looms that everyone may now be able to see on film what psychics claim to see naturally. . . . The possibility of seeing what was hidden before is generating excitement in this new method of photography and is making dozens of laboratories turn to it.''

No matter what it turns out to be that generates the patterns in Kirlian photos, American researchers Moss and Johnson and Dean are convinced that Kirlian photography can reveal a great deal about ourselves.

(For more details, see luminescence references.)

Experiments with Human Luminescence

Even without costly photo-electronic multipliers (snooperscopes for seeing in the dark) or expensive lab equipment for studying cell cultures, you can experiment with human luminescence and the Kirlian pictures.

To try a basic experiment you'll need some highly light-sensitive black-and-white or color film. You can use either sheet film or roll film. Polaroid color film that comes wrapped in individual sheets can also be used if you have access to a Polaroid camera to develop it.

If you are using regular film, take a sheet of film, or cut a section from a roll of film and wrap it carefully in lightproof material so no fraction of light can penetrate. Tape this piece of film on your arm or any part of your body and wear it all day. Note how many hours you wear each piece of film and the location. Have the film developed, or if Polaroid, develop it in a Polaroid camera. Very often you will find a kind of blurry pattern of colors on the film. This is an experiment that the psychic healer and engineer Ambrose Worrall used to do to demonstrate there were definite emanations given off by the body that could affect film. Sometimes, if you think strongly about a particular image while wearing the film, the pattern on the film will vaguely reflect that image. Is it body heat that causes the pattern? Dr. Thelma Moss of UCLA tried heating and chilling film but the film remained blank. Only humans wearing the film for several hours gave unusual energy patterns. If you have the time, try placing a strip of film over your eyes and leaving it there for an hour or so. See if the emanations recorded from the eyes are different from those from the fingertips or the arms. Consult an acupuncture map and try locating film on an area where there appears to be a great many acupuncture points clustered together. Does this area give off more luminescence than other areas where the acupuncture points are sparse? If you know someone with Kirlian equipment or have built some yourself, try correlating the patterns of emanations on film with what appears in the Kirlian pictures.

Try making film pictures at different times of day. We all exist in the earth's electrical field and the earth's field changes twice a day. It's at its minimum everywhere on earth at 4 A.M. Greenwich time in London and at its maximum at 7 P.M. Greenwich time. Add or subtract hours to convert Greenwich time to your local time zone. See how your biofield changes at the hours the earth's electrical field is shifting gears. Some researchers have found that luminescence pictures can change depending on the change of the earth's electrical field.

For more details, see Section Six.

7

How to Make a Kirlian
Photography Device

The following instructions are designed to enable a person without any knowledge of electronics to put together a simple, inexpensive, high-frequency photography apparatus. (People with a technical background are referred to the Kirlian patents section and the references containing diagrams of the various schematics.)

The Kirlians themselves prepared a booklet, *In the World of the Miraculous Discharge*, giving a simplified account of how to assemble and build a small spark generator from scratch for photography purposes for the do-it-youself home hobbyist. The more complex schematics were published in regular scientific journals. (See Section Six.)

Kirlian photography is done without a camera and without light by the use of a high-frequency spark generator and an exposure plate. To make a picture, the film is placed directly on the plate and the object to be photographed is placed on top of the film. The high-frequency unit is turned on and the high-frequency electrical charge running through the object causes the film to be exposed.

The very simplest way to photograph is to use the high-frequency spark generator just as it is sold, with its glass electrode as the "exposure plate." The film is placed in a lightproof envelope against the skin and touched briefly with the glass electrode to make a picture. This can be done in daylight. With the glass electrode it is possible to view the discharge process as it occurs. The following method, however, gives far better photographic results.

The next simplest unit can be made with the spark generator, a wire, an exposure plate, and a box to house the whole thing. With this setup photography can be done in darkness or daylight.

Where to Obtain a Spark Generator

The type of spark generator we found to be the safest and easiest to adapt while at the same time producing good-quality pictures, is a commercially made Tesla Coil, designed for use in beauty and barber shops. This is a simple, plug-in coil, fully enclosed in a large, bottle-shaped bakelite handle with a tuning switch in the base. It is fully shockproof, and the unit is designed with an angular molding to prevent slipping and rolling off surfaces. These high-frequency units generally are sold with a choice of glass electrodes. When the glass electrode bulb is inserted in the Coil and the current is turned on, it glows with an ultraviolet light and makes a slight buzzing sound. In beauty and barber shops the operator rubs the glass electrode over the patron's skin to give facials, scalp treatments, and skin treatments. This high-frequency spark treatment gives the skin a pleasant tingling sensation, which beauticians apparently believe stimulates circulation and thus helps the complexion and scalp. The ultraviolet light released by the glass electrode bulb is believed to be effective in knocking out local infections. High-frequency outfits are also used for grooming circus animals—no doubt because the spark treatment is supposed to facilitate a luxuriant coat.

A beauty operator who gives such treatment has usually taken a special course before using such equipment, and we do not suggest that you try to use the equipment on your own for this purpose. We are merely giving the background data on the type of Tesla Coil you will be using in photographing.

We have checked out alternative power sources for use in high-frequency photography, such as the Model-T Ford ignition coil, but feel that for the amateur experimenter with Kirlian photography, the commercial Tesla Coil described above is more versatile and safe. (It's a high-voltage and extremely low amperage unit.) Over a two-year period we have tested this easily portable photo device and found it gives good results. Mankind Research has also thoroughly tested this type of power-supply unit for application in electrophotography and reports it "supplies the high frequencies required to give reasonably good photo resolution and definition."

Also it's interesting to note that this type of Tesla Coil is the one some experimenters adapted many years ago for use in the Lakhovsky Multiwave Oscillator used in radio-biological research. (See pages 285-86 for details.)

Both Dr. Tiller and Professor Dean caution experimenters that it may be possible that some types of spark generators give off X-rays or other as yet uncharted rays and that experimenters should take care not to overdo exposure to the radiations. Professor Dean points out, however, that the Kirlians themselves worked with this form of photography some thirty years or more and lived to a healthy old age. And the Kirlians apparently felt the technique safe enough to publish it in a do-it-yourself booklet for young people as well as a regular mass-circulation Russian photography magazine.

The type of Tesla Coil we suggest has of course been in use by beauticians for decades, and is considered beneficial; so, providing that you carefully follow all the safety regulations provided with the instrument you purchase, there should not be a problem. In particular the instructions state that the unit should not be operated continuously more than ten minutes at any one time or it will overheat. However, for photography, exposure time is usually little more than several seconds at most. During exposure time the device can sometimes cause static on a radio or TV set in the same room (but not those in other rooms) just as an electric razor often will do. However, exposure times are seldom over a second or so and the static is scarcely noticeable.

We urge that experiments be done in a well-ventilated room because ozone is given off during exposures and ozone is considered an air pollutant. Do not touch the appliance or attempt to connect it to an electrical outlet when your hands are wet, and do not use the unit in connection with water, any inflammable lotion, or medicament containing alcohol. Do not allow the body to come in contact with metal—and this includes metal furniture—while using or operating this device. When the apparatus is not in use, remove the plug from the electrical outlet.

High-frequency appliances may be obtained from your local beauty-supply company; or if they do not have any in stock, you can obtain one directly from one of the following:

> Illinois R. S. Company
> 865 North Sangamon Street,
> Chicago, Illinois 60622

(Ask for High-Frequency Unit No. 10 and the No. 1 General Electrode.)

> Nu-tone Products Corp.
> 49 East 21st Street,
> New York, N.Y. 10010.

(Ask for Master High-Frequency Unit No. 9. The General Electrode No. 1 can be purchased separately if desired.)

There are a number of more expensive models available also, but this basic unit works well in photography.

The price for the basic high-frequency unit including one glass electrode will be in the $30.00 to $40.00 range. (Additional types of glass electrodes cost about $5.00 to $6.00 each.) These high-frequency units plug into standard electrical outlets, 110/120 V. The tuning knob in the base of the unit permits adjustment of the electrostatic voltage field from approximately 22 kilovolts to 40 kilovolts. This type of Tesla Coil operates on frequencies from 120 Hertz to 900,000 Hertz per second. Wave-form is square wave.

Mankind Research Unlimited also sells this same type of high-frequency unit along with instructions for converting it for use in photography. (Their setup differs from ours.) Price for this light-duty unit (suitable for intermittent operation for 10-minute periods) is $39.95 plus $1.50 postage. Power supply equipment (heavy duty) for one hour duration and continuous operation is $69.50 plus $1.50 postage. MRU also sells a 76 page data package containing translations of Russian articles and details of their own Kirlian electrophotography procedures. $4.75. Mankind Research Unlimited, 1143 New Hampshire Ave., NW, Washington, D.C. 20037. A variety of Kirlian units, including professional lab instruments, are available from Edmund Scientific, Barrington, New Jersey 08007.

Setting up the Equipment for Photography

Though the instructions that follow are quite detailed, the basic setup is extremely easy to put together. Once you've obtained a high-frequency spark generator, you will notice there's a tuning knob in the base of the unit. This provides the spark (or voltage) adjustment. Turned to low, sparks are tiny and a buzzing sound is barely audible; turned higher (clockwise), sparks are larger and the buzzing sound gets louder. For comparison photos you will want to keep the spark adjustment constant. Tape or paint an indicator arrow on the knob so that you can make approximately the same dial setting. Generally the knob makes about 4 turns to maximum.

On-Off Switch

For photography, the high-frequency unit should be plugged into a cord with an on-off switch or better yet, a timer. If you turn the unit off by turning down the spark adjustment to zero, you'll have a variety of spark pulses in the picture. Also, sometimes, the pho-

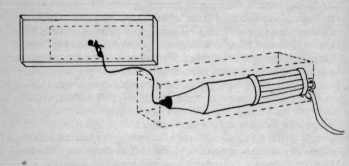

FIGURE 3.

Diagram shows how to assemble Kirlian components. See instructions.

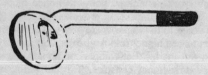

FIGURE 4.

General Electrode No. 1—the glass electrode that comes with the high-frequency unit.

tography is done in the dark and without an on-off switch, you will find yourself fumbling in the blackness to find the outlet to pull out the plug. One type of on-off switch available is a three-way connector cord. One end has a plug to go into the wall socket, the other end has a handy on-off switch and in the middle is a socket into which the high-frequency unit can be plugged. These three-way cords with on-off switch are often sold for use with Christmas decorations. In Canada, Noma sells such a cord called "Christmas Convenience Cord" ($2.00-$3.00). An on-off foot-pedal switch is available from Lafayette Electronics at nominal cost (111 Jericho Turnpike, Syosset, New York 11791.) Put a strip of luminous tape on the on-off switch to make it easy to find.

Summary of Parts for Kirlian Device

(See Photo 20)

- high-frequency unit with one glass electrode ($30-$40) available: beauty supply
- copper-clad boards, any size (few cents to $2.00) available: electronics store
- extension cord with on-off switch ($2.00-$3.00) available: electronics or hardware store
- six feet of copper wire encased in plastic (few cents) available: electronics or hardware store
- three or four small alligator clips (few cents) available: electronics or hardware store
- electrician's tape
     available: electronics or hardware store
- rubber plug or eraser
     available: stationery or hardware store
- wooden or cardboard box

Summary of Instructions (See Figures 3 and 4)

- Punch small hole in middle of box lid; punch two large holes at one end of box near bottom.
- Tape 2'' wire in middle of copper side of board.
- Tape copper-clad board copper side down on lid; push wire through hole.
- For 12'' wire to connect generator to board: Push one end through hole in rubber plug; attach other end to alligator clip; push rubber plug into socket of high-frequency unit so wire

touches metal socket; clip other end of wire with alligator clip to 2″ wire from board.

- Put high-frequency unit in box. Push cord through one hole and knob through the other and close box lid.
- Plug cord into extension cord with on-off switch.
- To photograph coin or leaf that is not grounded, use grounding wire—24″ wire with alligator clip on one end. Clamp clip to box. Tape other end of wire to exposure board so it touches object. Hold down leaves with a piece of glass.
- To operate: Turn spark-gap knob and test for strength of spark on exposure board. Spark should be set low. In darkness put film and object on exposure board. Turn on unit for one second to make the photograph.

Exposure Plate

For the basic exposure plate, we found a copper-clad un-perforated laminated board was ideal. These copper-clad boards are available at any electronics store. The boards generally have a very thin layer of copper laminate on one side and a bakelite finish on the other. Copper-clad boards are used in electronics for wiring together transistor circuitry. The boards come in a variety of sizes from 3″ × 2″ to 9″ × 12″ and sell for a few cents up to a couple of dollars for the big ones.

For use in high-frequency photography these copper-clad boards have a number of advantages. The copper side, which will serve as the electrode, will be completely sealed down so there's no danger of having a plant or finger come in contact with metal and getting nipped by electricity. The bakelite surface makes a smooth photography surface. The distance between the object photographed and the copper electrode will always be the same—i.e., the thickness of the bakelite. (In some photography setups the metal electrode is left bare and a nonconducting substance placed over it as a screen between plate and film—but the width of such a screen may vary, or a piece of metal might remain exposed.) Copper-clad boards are also available with an epoxy glass backing. Each type of backing (or screen) adds its own distinctive character to the photographs. To start with, you may want to buy a 4″ × 6″ copper-clad un-perforated board, large enough for 4″ × 5″ sheet film.

In addition to the exposure plate, you will need about six feet of plastic-encased copper wire; electrician's tape (black plastic-backed type); several very small alligator clips; a small rubber plug about 1/2'' × 3/8'' (can be made from eraser); a wooden or cardboard box about 13'' × 6'', about the size of a shoebox. The box the unit comes in is suitable.

Cut a two-inch length of copper wire and remove a bit of the plastic casing at both ends. With electrician's tape, firmly tape down one end of the wire in the middle of the copper side of the copper-clad plate. Punch a hole in the lid of the cardboard box in the exact middle. Place the copper-clad plate on top of the lid, copper side down, and run the wire down through the punched hole. Tape the plate down on the box lid all the way around with electrician's tape.

Cut a length of copper wire about two feet long. Remove the plastic casing at each end. Attach one end to an alligator clip. (Wind the end of the wire around the screw on the clip.) To attach the other end of the wire to the high-frequency unit, use a round rubber plug about 1/2'' × 3/8''. Put a hole down through the center of the rubber plug and run the end of the copper wire through it, allowing a half inch of wire to be exposed at the end of the plug. Push the plug tightly into place in the socket of the high-frequency unit so the wire contacts the metal of the socket. (This wire can be soldered in place in the socket if you wish, though that wouldn't permit switching to the glass electrode.)

Place the high-frequency unit inside the wooden or cardboard box. Note where the cord and knob touch the end of the box and cut holes for each of them so they're easily accessible. Clip the alligator clip on the copper wire to the two-inch piece of wire protruding through the lid. Close the box. Plug the cord into the socket on the cord with the on-off switch. Instead of a box, some people have housed units in an attaché case, although the metal trim and clasps on the case tend to draw sparks.

Grounding Wire

The unit you have constructed can be used to photograph a plant sitting in its pot or a person's finger. To photograph a leaf by itself or any object that's not grounded (i.e., on a surface through which electricity can be conducted to the ground) you need a grounding wire. Cut a length of copper wire two or three feet long, peel back the copper casing for an inch or so at each end. Attach one end to an alligator clip. Hook the clip to the edge of the box lid. With electrician's tape attach the other end of the wire to the exposure plate so it touches the leaf, coin, or object to be photographed. The wire carries electricity back to the box, which serves to ground the object being photographed.

Type of Film

Various kinds of film can be used. Dr. Moss states that almost every kind of film produces satisfactory pictures. Flat sheets of film are the easiest and most convenient, but roll film can also be used.

- 4″ × 5″ or 2 1/4″ × 3 1/4″ black and white Kodak Tri-x-pan professional thick base film #4164; also Kodak ortho 4154 thick.
- 4″ × 5″ Kodak Ektacolor short exposure S6101; or Kodak Ektachrome 6115.
- Kodachrome X, 35mm, ASA 64, 20 on a roll.
- Ektachrome X 35mm, ASA 64, 20 on a roll.
- Polaroid color pack of eight #108 or Land type #58.

Some experimenters have used Polycontrast paper with good results.

Patterns and colors vary according to the type and speed of film. Kodak Ektachrome tends to give bright blue and violet colors when photographing fingerpads.

Roll film is harder to use because the metal cassette must be taped down and kept completely out of contact with the exposure plate. If using a roll of 35 mm to make slides, an empty film cassette and winder key can be obtained at a camera store. The film can be advanced from one cassette to the other as you photograph. Several turns of the key will advance the film about one frame. A flat cardboard holder will help keep the film in place on the exposure plate. When getting the film developed, it should be marked "Do Not Mount." The film will be returned uncut and after you clip each picture from the roll, you can buy slide mounts to mount them.

Polaroid film must be developed with a Polaroid camera or a developing unit from a Polaroid camera.

Exposure times can vary and you will probably find your own optimum. Professor Dean has standardized exposure at three seconds for black and white and eight seconds for color. Dr. Moss has standardized at one second for both. Mankind Research suggests one-tenth of a second to five seconds and says an exposure time of a fraction of a second gives the sharpest detail. For Kodachrome II (ASA 25) they use one-half to two seconds.

Photographic Time Switch

For accurate timing of exposures you will want to incorporate a timer into your photography setup. A timer capable of timing fractions of seconds on up to sixty seconds can be obtained at most electronics or photography stores for a reasonable amount. Lafayette Electronics sells one for well under $10.00. The timer also serves as an on-off switch.

How to Photograph

- Have everything you need handy, objects to photograph, film and supplies. You'll have to locate items in the dark.
- Work in a well-ventilated room. Ozone is given off during photography. Make sure the floor is dry.
- First, do a test run to adjust tuning knob in the base of unit for the desired size of spark. It's advisable to start with it set at low.
- Set timer if you are using one.
- Turn out all lights. Room must be totally dark.
- Place film on exposure plate, emulsion side up.
- Put object to be photographed on top of film. If photographing fingertip, press down lightly, not heavily, on exposure plate.
- Turn on unit for one to three seconds, then switch off.
- Never use apparatus on head.
- If photographing a finger, blue flares will be visible under the finger in the dark and a tingling sensation felt in the finger pad.
- If using black and white film, you may want to have pans of developer, rinse, and fixer handy so you can see results immediately.
- If object to be photographed is dirty or sticky, put a sheet of thin transparent acetate between object and film.

If you're an amateur at developing, a photography hobby kit is available at most photo stores with all materials included. Film can generally be developed in the usual way by a photo processor.

Photographing in Daylight

Method 1.

To photograph in daylight it's preferable to use flat sheet film. Each piece of film must be wrapped in a black completely lightproof envelope made of material—such as paper—that doesn't conduct electricity. These envelopes are usually available at most photo stores. Get several. You must go into a darkened room to transfer a sheet of film into each envelope. Note which is emulsion side up. The film encased in the envelope is placed on the exposure plate in the usual way. The object to be photographed is placed on top of the film also in the usual way and photographed as above.

We found in experiments with wrapped film that the definition and clarity of pictures was not as good as with unwrapped film photographed in the dark, however it may be possible to find a type of lightproof wrapping for the film that does give equally good results.

Another daylight Kirlian setup uses a photographer's black changing bag. Exposure plate and film go inside, objects to be photographed are inserted through the bag sleeve. A bag can also be rigged up to use Kirlian equipment with a Polaroid camera.

Method 2.

Wrapped sheet film is used as in Method 1. But instead of using the exposure plate on the box, this time the glass General Electrode is used. Disconnect unit from wall socket. Remove the rubber plug from the socket of the Tesla Coil and remove the whole high-frequency unit from the box. Insert the General Electrode bulb in place, following the directions that came with the appliance. This method is helpful for photographing different areas of the body.

Place the wrapped sheet film over the area of the body you wish to photograph. It can be held in place with a rubber band. If photographing an object, it must be grounded. Then simply touch the film with the glass electrode for two to three seconds for black and white, four or five seconds for color. Film can thus be wrapped all around a round surface for a more complete photograph than could be gotten on a flat exposure plate.

Kirlian Movies

The very simplest technique for making a Kirlian movie involves setting up the reel of movie film so the film can be passed over the Kirlian exposure plate and can be wound onto a takeup reel on the other side of the plate. A movie of a fingertip can be made by placing it on top of the film on the exposure plate. If filming an object, such as a coin, it must be weighted down on the exposure plate so it doesn't slide along with the film. The spark tuning knob should be turned to minimum. After switching on the Kirlian equipment in darkness, the film must be wound evenly onto the takeup reel.

This movie technique is very crude, of course. Without a lens the flare patterns are not clearly focused. Patterns change so rapidly it's impossible to trace specific colored flares emitted and images sometimes look like a nontelecasting TV channel. Despite its inadequacies it might be possible to record gross overall changes in luminescence with this method. In a film we made to see the reactions with and without music, we found the flare patterns of the finger seem to pulse occasional flares of bright pink while music was being played, in contrast to the usual blue without music. We wonder if this is characteristic of changes caused by music or just a fluke.

Kirlian movies as an art form could make an interesting light show to go with music—especially if the film is of your fingertip reactions coordinated with a record or tape of the music.

(A more sophisticated movie technique involves using a visual display device usually made with a cathode ray tube to show the Kirlian discharge as on a TV screen. The focused image can be videotaped or filmed from the luminescent screen. See patents 118135 and 209968 in technical section and *A.R.E. Journal*, March, 1972.) (Photomultipliers may also be used for movies.)

Polaroid Kirlian Photos

Instant Polaroid Kirlian photos can be made in daylight by using a photographer's black changing bag. A Polaroid camera, using Polaroid 108 Color Pack, is required (least expensive—the Polaroid Big Shot). Load camera as usual removing the black cover sheet. Place Kirlian exposure plate and camera inside bag. Open camera inside bag and remove film pack. Place entire film pack on exposure plate, film side up. To photograph fingers, have subject slide hand in through the sleeve in the bag and place fingers lightly on the film surface—well away from the metal rim on the pack. Exposure time, 1/2 to 3 seconds. Keep voltage at minimum. Additional exposures can be made on the same film surface. Return film pack to camera inside bag. Remove camera from bag and develop photo in the usual way. Repeat procedure for each print in the Color Pack. Pictures can also be done without the bag in a dark room.

General

The simple basic Kirlian type apparatus described will enable you to embark on a fascinating new area of photography and, if you wish, to apply this form of photography to exploration of psi effects. Of course the Kirlians' main contribution wasn't basically the idea of using a spark generator to photograph with high-frequency electricity (which had been done before), but the invention of scores of different systems to adapt the high-frequency generator to a host of applications. They devised both still and motion-picture photography; optical systems; adapters for microscopes; equipment to utilize the technique for varied shapes of objects and for diagnosis in dentistry and medicine; devices to apply the technique in areas from metallurgy to criminology to archeology.

Some of these varied devices are detailed in the patents section of this book and in the *A.R.E. Journal*, March, 1972. If you are technically oriented or have a friend who is, you may be able to adapt some of these devices for use with the basic spark generator. Information is also available from: International Kirlian Association, 144 East 90th St., New York, N.Y. 10028.

4

Experiments, Projects, Art,
with a New Form of Photography

Tips for Improving Kirlian Photographs

● If the exposure plate should become scratched or marred in any way, replace it with a new plate. Any unevenness on the surface will conduct the high-frequency current unevenly. One researcher thought he'd found an amazing effect in Kirlian photos, then found it was just bumps on the plate.

● In making any comparison photos, always place the objects to be compared in exactly the same spot on the exposure plate. On this simple equipment there's no control over whether or not the current is dispersed evenly over the whole plate. If you were to compare a picture in one corner on a sheet of film with one in another corner and there's a difference, the effect could be due to less electrical current in one corner. To avoid wasting film and yet get the exposures in the very same spot, cut up the large sheets of film into small squares.

● In making comparison pictures from day to day, remember that the earth's electrical field is different day and night and things will have more brilliance in the photos depending on the hour. (Seven P.M. maximum, four A.M. minimum. Greenwich Mean Time—convert to your local time zone.)

● Overexposure results in a large white circle around finger or object, obliterating some of the streamers.

● For any serious research, of course, all variables—such as temperature, humidity, and so forth—have to be controlled. (For more suggestions, see "Methods and Techniques of Photography in High Frequency Current Fields," Frantov and Mikhalevsky, in *Bioenergetics Questions*.)

Kirlian Photography as an Art Form

When you first get your high-frequency photography equipment setup, you will probably want to start out by getting some idea of the kind of photographs possible with the device. You may want to take pictures of plant leaves, coins, jewelry, sprouts, insects, fingertips, etc., first of all just for their sheer beauty. Researchers describe the photographs as a ''spectacular panorama of colors,'' ''luminescent labyrinths,'' ''fire world.'' For the artist or hobbyist in photography, the device may provide a means of creating a new art form. Friends, too, may want a picture of their plants, pet, or fingertips. Finger pads seem to give the most interesting photographs because apparently the play of flares from the body is most volatile from the fingertips. A person with very sensitive hands, such as a musician, is said to have unusually beautiful torchlike flares coming from the fingers.

Some beautiful pictures of plant leaves done with radiation field photography by Kendall Johnson have been displayed at a photographic exhibition in Los Angeles.

Kirlian photos on transparencies can be displayed on light boxes as a collage for an intriguing effect. They also make an interesting design motif.

A simple plant leaf looks like a decorated Christmas tree. The black and white pictures, too, have a special translucent quality. An inorganic substance, a coin, for example, has an unchanging corona—but organic things, such as leaves, have continuously changing patterns. Pictures can be done in depth as well. Put several layers of sheet film below and above a leaf or a dime and penny back-to-back, to make a sandwich. Different images will appear on each piece of film.

You will want to try out different exposure times and varied techniques for unusual art effects.

Kirlian Posters

You'll have a genuine conversation piece if you turn some of your best Kirlian photos into posters. Kirlian posters of plant leaves or fingertips make intriguing wall decorations. Most local photo shops have a fairly inexpensive service available for making posters up from photographs in black and white or in two colors. Full-color blowups for posters are more expensive. If a photo poster service is not available in your neighborhood, you can find one in the ads in any major photography magazine and have posters made by mail order.

Exploring Psi with Kirlian Photography

One of the most exciting aspects of researching psi effects with high-frequency photography is that it seems to render visible in photographs some of the energetic effects taking place when human thought affects living detectors such as plants. In Section One on plants, you will see how some of these so-called psi effects can be monitored with instruments, but with this modified version of Kirlian photography, you can actually see in photos the effects step by step as they take place. One of the most fascinating things to photograph with high-frequency photography is a plant leaf.

In doing any pictures you wish to compare, always use the same type of film and always place the object in exactly the same spot on the exposure plate.

Keep complete and detailed notes of what you photograph, date and time of day. Time of day will affect pictures because of earth's electrical field—maximum 7 P.M., minimum 4 A.M. Greenwich Mean Time—convert to local time in your area. Keep records, too, of exposure time so you can have it precise for any comparisons. If photographing several objects or several fingertips at one time, keep records so you can identify who's who afterwards.

Important: If you want to try any serious exploration, the same picture must be done over and over, five or six times each at least, to be sure you're not just getting a chance effect and that it's definitely something that happens repeatedly.

Setting Up Plants to Detect Human Thought and Energy

If you photograph the leaves of a plant while they're still on the plant, have the plant sitting on a surface with no metal on it. Put the Kirlian device near it and raise or lower it to reach the plant leaf. As long as the plant is grounded—sitting on a surface that will conduct the electricity back to the floor (and thus to the ground), you won't need the additional grounding wire. If you photograph a leaf by itself, one end of the grounding wire must be taped to the bottom of the leaf with electrician's tape. A piece of glass should be placed on top of the leaf to hold it flat against the film.

Life and Death of Plants

Several photographs of plant leaves several hours apart show the fascinating phenomenon of the disappearance of the luminescence from the leaf. Start with freshly plucked leaves. Photograph them again eight hours later. Then photograph them eight hours after that, and again eight hours after that. Gradually you will find the luminescence departs from the leaves like the lights of a city going out until finally there's just total darkness. Even dampening the leaf does not seem to restore the brightness. (See pictures series in *Galaxies of Life*.)

Often it seems flares and globules are given off as the luminescence dies out. This is an interesting thing to try to photograph with the depth method, sandwiching the leaf between several layers of film to see which direction these globules take as they go out of the leaf.

Soviets have photographed lilac buds in their normal state, then gradually sliced off the bud little by little. The top of the stem glowed like a roman candle. (See pictures in *PDBIC*.)

Injured Leaf

Start with two leaves from the same tree or plant in their normal condition. Photograph both of them. Then gash or cut a hole in one of the leaves. Again photograph both of them. The Kirlian picture of the gashed leaf should show red patches or streaks and bubblelike flares given off, though neither the red nor the bubbles are visible on the leaf to the naked eye. Try heating leaves in the oven or cooling them in the refrigerator. Note any changes in the photographs.

Kirlian photos also show a distinct pattern if a plant is sick. Get leaves from diseased plants to photograph and see if you can spot the patterns that show illness in a plant.

Photographing Effects of Your Thoughts on Leaves

Photograph three leaves of the same size and type in their intact state. Next, gash two of the leaves and photograph them again. Choose one of the gashed leaves and take some time now to try mentally to heal the plant leaf and send it energy. In your mind's eye, see the leaf rebuilding itself and recovering from the injury. Hold the leaf in your hands and try to impart energy to it. Then photograph the three leaves again. If your thought is powerful enough, you may see a change in the radiance of the flares coming from the leaf you thought about, compared to the other gashed leaf. Of course this experiment should be repeated many times to assure yourself the effect is genuine.

Dr. Thelma Moss of UCLA conducted a whole series of leaf experiments with a healer, Mrs. Olga Worrall, of the New Life Clinic in Baltimore, Maryland. In each experiment Mrs. Worrall held one of the leaves in her hands and gave it a "healing" treatment. When each "treated" leaf was again photographed in the high-frequency field, it shone more brilliantly than in the first picture and photographic evidence of the gash was gone although the gash still appeared in the physical leaf.

Mrs. Worrall says, "Kirlian photography is registering an energy of some type that apparently affects the plants. Perhaps it is the same energy which is used with the laying-on-of-hands with people. . . .

"I can feel the energy in my hands, flowing out to the person I am healing, and it was the same with the leaves," Mrs. Worrall reports. (See photos, *Human Dimensions*, Vol. 2, #1, spring, 1973.)

You can try another type of energy-transfer experiment, too. Dr. Inyushin reports that if you prick your finger near a plant leaf, the leaf will glow fifty percent brighter when photographed immediately with the Kirlian method. You can also try photographing the plant's response to the death of tiny brine shrimp plunged into boiling water.

Kirlian photography may be able to show us more about human energy transfer to other things aside from plants such as living crystals, salt, gems and stones, and so forth.

Sprout Photos

Another type of experiment with plants and thoughts can be done with sprouts. Beans available from any store can be sprouted. Set up two pans, one for control and one for the thought test. Photograph several sprouts from each pan. Beam positive thoughts at the sprouts in one of the pans to make them grow even faster. Photograph some from each pan each day to see what effect your thought is having. (See plant section for more details.)

Music and Chanting—an Energy Effect?

Photograph several leaves in their normal state. Place them near a record player or stereo and play a record for them, or play some music on a musical instrument. Rephotograph the leaves. We have found that music seems to change the pattern of luminescence in living things, making it more concentrated and sometimes making bright globules show up. Effects seemed to be different with different kinds of music. In particular we had extremely interesting results playing a record of glass harp music. This is music produced by running the fingers round the rims of crystal glasses. Glass harp music was considered to have hypnotic powers in previous eras. Photographs done after the glass harp music had been played showed very striking changes in the luminescence of leaves and fingertips. (See photo section.)

At the University of New Mexico, Larry Amos and Jim Hickman, who have done some excellent work, also found with their electrophotographs that after music had been played the luminescence of finger pads seemed to show up more intensely.

A group led by Al Manning in Los Angeles tried chanting to see what effects it would have on the luminescence. They used the time-honored mantra *Om Mane Padme Hum*. The *after* pictures showed a much wider band of luminescence around the fingertips (*Cosmos*, December, 1972).

In the plant section you will find more details about the impact of music on plant growth. Perhaps a sprout experiment could be set up with one pan of sprouts getting music and one not getting music to see in photographs how the music stimulates growth. Different kinds of music—classical or rock music—seem to have differing effects on plants. This is a most intriguing area in which to explore the energetic effects of music on life. Could Kirlian photography monitor the effects of music therapy?

Ancient chants could also be explored for their relative impact. Do some work better than others? Are certain sound patterns related to different functions? These are all areas worth exploring.

Psi Detective

The point of this experiment is to try to see, through Kirlian photography, if you can determine which of several living leaves another person may have been thinking about. Take three similar leaves and number them. Photograph them in their normal state. Show someone else the three leaves and tell them to pick one of the three leaves for some special attention while you go out of the room. They must try to give this leaf energy in some way—think about how great it is, prick their finger near it, try to send it energy. They can do this for ten or fifteen minutes. You return to the room and Kirlian photograph the three leaves. It may be possible from the photographs for you to select which leaf was thought about.

Your Food and Kirlian Photos

All these experiments with plants have many implications for the food we eat. You might try some of these before and after pictures of the ingredients of a salad. How about the energy transfer to the food of a person preparing a meal? If a person is extremely angry or depressed while putting a meal together, would the energy mix in with the dinner? Try photographing a lettuce leaf in its normal state and again after being handled by someone who is angry. How about someone who loves to cook? Do their thoughts mingle with the food and constitute a secret ingredient of their gourmet specialities? There may be many areas of exploration of the interaction of human energies with living things around us that may yield interesting insights. Would a difference show up between organically grown foods and those grown with pesticides? (See plant section for general experiments to be tried with Kirlian photography.)

"Phantom" Effect

Soviet researchers have found that if a small fraction of the physical body of a living creature is missing, the image of the whole body will still show up in the Kirlian photographs. One test is to sandpaper away a fingerprint. The Kirlians say the regular fingerprint picture will still show up. This relates also to the work of Dr. Harold Burr of Yale (*Blueprint for Immortality, The Electric Patterns of Life*), who showed through registering electrical fields the energy matrix of living things.

You may also try to get the "lost leaf" effect. A live plant should be used for the test. Photograph the leaf of the plant in its regular state, then shave off a tiny millimeter strip from the edge. Photograph it again. See if the image of the missing part is still there. Then shave a tiny bit more. Some say around ten percent of the leaf can be cut away and still have the whole image of the leaf appear in the photo. (See photo 6.)

In connection with this "phantom effect" the work of Russian émigré George Lakhovsky may be pertinent. In tests on plants with tumors, the application of a high-frequency field to the plants, such as that used in Kirlian photography, appeared to strengthen the energy matrix of diseased plants so that the tumors dried up and fell off, new tissue regenerated, and the plants became healthy again. (See *Waves That Heal*, translated by Mark Clement, available from Health Research, Mokelumne Hill, California 95245.)

Richard Miller of the University of Washington, Seattle, reported at the 1973 Prague psi conference that he had duplicated the ghost phenomenon with a leaf. He feels the lost-leaf effect is reminiscent of the xerox process. (Of course the xerox theory wouldn't explain why a person's fingerprint would still be visible after being sandpapered off.)

At this same conference, G. Clauzure of the Institut Métapsychique International of Paris reported the intriguing results obtained by a French researcher in the early 1900's with a photography process similar to Kirlian. Alphonse Bouvier, a magnetic healer, made numerous experiments in which he gave lengthy magnetic healing treatments to amputees, with particular attention to the area of the amputee's missing limb. Then he made a high-frequency photograph of the amputee, particularly the area of the missing limb. "In this way," the French report, "he obtained an image of the limb which no longer existed materially. . . ." Bouvier felt that this was proof of the existence of an energy body and that it tended to prove that the surgeon's scalpel had left intact the "bioplasmic" body in its original form.

This might be an interesting experiment to try. Perhaps a healer is able to heighten the energy of the bioplasmic body to the point where the pattern of a missing limb can be made visible with the high-frequency process.

Photographing Small Creatures

At the University of New Mexico, researchers Hickman, Amos, and Krumsiek have photographed a variety of small creatures—salamanders, cockroaches, race runners, etc. For photographing small lizards they told us they'd found it helpful to refrigerate the creature for a few minutes to slow it down so it wouldn't zip off the exposure plate before its picture was taken. (See their results in *Galaxies of Life*.)

Photographing Hidden Objects

Semyon and Valentina Kirlian say that high-frequency photography can reveal items concealed in paraffin. They suggest a basic experiment from which you can extropolate. Take a small cardboard box. Put several items, such as a piece of china, a bit of metal, a coin, etc., inside it. Then melt paraffin and pour it into the box so that the whole box is encased in paraffin and the objects are totally buried in it. When the paraffin hardens, take an electrographic photo of it. You may want to use a second exposure plate on top, attached to the grounding wire to make a sandwich. The Kirlians report that unlike X-ray, which gives a shady image, the electrograph pictures should show the silhouettes of the buried objects in varying degrees of brilliance, according to the electrical conductivity of each object.

Effects of Suggestion

If you have learned autosuggestion or any biofeedback techniques, such as being able to control the temperature of your hands to make one warm and one cold, try photographs to see if there are distinct changes. You may also note changes of mood and interrelations with other people—with two fingers side by side. (See photo section.)

Effects of Color

Bathe the hand in colored light for ten minutes or so, and then photograph a fingertip. Compare with normal state. Try each of the colors in the spectrum to see if there are variations in response to each color. Check out your results with color therapy theories regarding the effect of each color on the body. Kirlian photography might be a way to monitor color therapy.

Influence of the Cosmos

Kirlian photos have shown changes in living things during magnetic storms caused by solar flares. Get data from a local observatory on magnetic storms and try to get pictures on key days. Dr. Anatoli Podshibyakin of Kiev discovered that body energies immediately shift at the time a solar flare occurs. Japanese researchers found sunspots affect the blood. This would be another key area for exploration. (See chapters on astrobiology in *Natural Birth Control*, Bantam, 1973, for more data on recent research on possibly photographable cosmic influence on living things.)

Photographing PK

People able to do PK (move objects by mind power) have also been photographed with Kirlian photography. At the moment they were ready to move an object, the picture of their fingertips showed sharp jagged flares and a more concentrated corona than normal. Pictures of PK psychic Alla Vinogradova's finger were published in the *Journal of Paraphysics*, Vol. 6, No. 5, 1972. We have photographed a PK psychic in Buffalo and gotten similar results. Uri Geller, a PK psychic being studied at Stanford Research Institute, had a Kirlian photo taken of his hands and he claims he was able to make the image of a number appear in the photograph.

Setting up a Telepathy Experiment with Photography

Physiological research on telepathy at Newark College of Engineering showed that at the moment someone in another room looked at a card giving the name of a person known to you, a medical instrument called a plethysmograph would register a change in blood volume in your finger. (See *Executive ESP* for details.) Would these same physiological effects show up in a Kirlian picture too? This might be an interesting project. Make up three cards each with the name of a person you know (especially those you do *not* like) mixed in with three blank cards. Have a sender shuffle them and go into another room. Cut six small squares of film. At set times, when the sender is looking at each card, take a picture of your fingertip. There may be a difference in the pictures when the sender was thinking about people you know.

Magnetic Effects

Leaves in a magnetic field show quite a distinct change in luminescence, according to the Soviet photos. (See photo section.)

Ambrose and Olga Worrall maintain that they see a difference in the force field of the body as a person faces toward different points of a compass. Try photographing a leaf first pointing north, then south, then east, then west, to see if alignment makes any difference. Use a compass for accuracy.

Kirlian Photography and Acupuncture

Soviet researchers have succeeded in photographing the

acupuncture points on the human body using the Kirlian technique. (See Kirlian photo of the acupuncture points on the human chest in *PDBIC*.) These 700 or so points appear as areas of greater brilliance on the skin in the still pictures and in Kirlian motion pictures appear to emit bright flares.

It is known that acupuncture points have a higher electrical conductivity than the skin around them. Soviets developed a small pen-shaped device called a Tobiscope to locate acupoints with precision. Dr. Victor Adamenko of Moscow invented a variation in *Bioenergetics Questions*. German, Italian, Japanese, English and other companies also market acupuncture point locators of varying designs.

The Korean acupuncture researcher Kim Bong Han has shown that if radioactive phosphorus is injected into an acupuncture point on a specific acupuncture meridian or channel, the radioactive substance flows along the meridian and can be monitored at other acupoints on this same meridian. When the radioactive substance is injected in a nonpoint area, it cannot be detected at the acupoints. Professor Kim Bong Han also went on to demonstrate a physiological basis for the acupuncture points and meridians. When we visited the USSR in 1968, Soviet scientists stressed the importance of Kim Bong Han's research and pressed upon us a Russian edition of his book. Later we were able to find an edition in English: *On the Kyungrak System*, Journal of the Academy of Medical Sciences of the Democratic People's Republic of Korea, 1963, No. 5. Medical Science Press, Pyongyang, Korea. We shared it with some of the A.R.E. scientists who went to Russia and Dr. Tiller has prepared a summary for *Galaxies of Life*.

Recently another breakthrough has been made in charting the energy circulation system postulated by the acupuncture points and meridians. Dr. Victor Inyushin of Alma-Ata reported a new way of using the Kirlian method to show a connection between the acupuncture points on the skin and the different organs of the body. In his first experiment with fifteen subjects, he used the Kirlian optical system plus photoelectric equipment so he could give a numerical value to the amount of luminescence coming from specific points on the skin.

He first monitored the intensity of luminescence of one nonpoint area and seven acupoints on various parts of the skin that Chinese theory says are connected to the teeth and interior of the mouth. Then the subjects' mouths were irradiated by gas laser and the luminescence on the skin measured again. Luminescence of the acupoints on the skin on the meridian connected to the mouth increased one to two times after irradiation of the mouth. The control point remained the same. The light from the mouth was conducted to distant points on the skin! Inyushin has repeated this experiment many times with similar results. He declares, ". . . objective control of the electrical state of the human body can be accomplished by using the acupuncture points and conductance channels and is entirely realistic." He considers further research in this direction a necessity. (See *Bioenergetics Questions.*)

Photographing Acupuncture Points .

You may wish to attempt to photograph acupuncture points on the skin with Kirlian equipment. You will need an acupuncture chart showing the location of the acupuncture points on the skin and the twelve different meridians. According to acupuncture theory the hands and feet are the areas where the flow of energies through the body changes polarity and these points may be the easiest to photograph.

You might try an experiment in photographing changes in the luminosity from acupuncture points. For instance, select an acupuncture meridian that runs from the feet to the hands and photograph a *before* picture of the hands. Then for several minutes, direct a sunlamp to the area of the feet where the majority of the points on that meridian are located. Rephotograph the acupuncture points from that meridian on the hands to see if there is any difference.

Acupuncture massage can also be used to stimulate specific points and to relieve pain. It is possible that changes might show up in Kirlian photos. Some helpful texts include *The First Book of Do-In*, which deals with acu*pressure* healing and is available for $1.50 from Happiness Press, 1607 North Sierra Bonita Ave., Hollywood, California 90046. Also, *First Aid at Your Fingertips* by D. and J. Lawson-Wood deals with massage of acupuncture points as a first-aid treatment in emergencies. It is available for 75 pence from Health Science Press, c/o Thorsons Publishing Group, Denington Estate, Wellingborough, Northants NN8 2RQ, England.

The Washington, D.C., firm Mankind Research Unlimited has produced some interesting Kirlian pictures related to acupuncture. A before-and-after sequence by MRU was published in the Washington *Post's Potomac Magazine*, July 22, 1973, showing the fingertip of a man suffering the pain of arthritis. The *before* picture, instead of the usual blue corona, shows a large plume of brilliant red emanating from the top of the fingertip. Researchers believe the red plume might be an indicator of pain. After treatment by acupuncture, the man said the pain had disappeared. The red area is gone too in the *after* Kirlian picture, which shows a regular blue corona.

Dr. Thelma Moss at UCLA has also begun to explore acupuncture with Kirlian photography.

Acupuncture and Psi

What does acupuncture have to do with psi? A very great deal, if the theories of some psi scientists are right. They feel that the theories of acupuncture which postulate a kind of energy circulating in the body can be helpful in explaining many energy effects observed in psi phenomena such as psychic healing or PK.

Researchers in Japan and the USSR have used acupuncture-monitoring devices to study the energy exchange involved in psychic healing. They monitored both healer and patient before the healing treatment by laying on of hands. Before the treatment, the healer's energy pattern showed normal while the patient's showed an imbalance. After the treatment, the acupuncture points on the healer showed a slight imbalance while the patient's pattern was more balanced. It seemed as if the healer had given up a certain amount of energy while the patient had gained energy. (*Paraphysics Journal*, Vol. 4, No. 4.)

Soviets Adamenko and Raikov have used the Tobiscope to study various states of consciousness—the ordinary waking state versus various forms of hypnosis. By getting readings from several acupoints it is possible to objectively measure changes in the body's bioplasma energy, they say. Adamenko and Raikov found with this technique that the flow of bioplasma energy between acupoints responded directly to the hypnotist's commands. In other experiments researchers found that the bioplasma reacted sharply when a telepathic message was sent to a subject.

The patterns of energy monitored at acupoints also seem to resonate with the universe. At the Institute of Clinical Physiology in Kiev, Dr. Anatoli Podshibyakin made a startling discovery. By charting acupoints he found that a person's bioplasma seems to tune in to changes on the surface of the sun. Solar flares occur: The electrical potential of the skin's acupuncture points changes. Graphs of sunspot activity and the changes in the electrical rhythms of the skin appear to correspond closely. As solar explosions occur, the energies of the human body react, though cosmic particles rejected by the sun would not reach the earth for another two days. East European researchers believe that the energies circulating through the body that are postulated by acupuncture would naturally play a role in the creation of human life as well. It has been demonstrated that the sun and moon can affect these vital energies—therefore, the influence of the sun and moon may play a role in human fertility and infertility and in determination of sex. (See ''The Sun and Us'' and ''The Lunar Beat'' in *Astrological Birth Control.*)

Could it be that the demonstrated connection between the bio-plasmic energies of the body and energies in the universe might help account for such findings as:

- telepathy in dreams is heightened at full moon (Maimonides Dream Lab)
- ESP tests give better results at full moon (Institute of Suggestology, Bulgaria)
- PK occurs more easily during magnetic storms caused by solar flares (Sergeyev, Leningrad)

The links between acupuncture and psi could be a most important area of investigation. Acupuncture diagnostic devices and/or Kirlian photography could be used in monitoring psi processes such as psychic healing, color sensing with the skin, telepathy, PK, dowsing, etc., in order to gradually increase reliability of these psi functions, making them repeatable and dependable.

Acupuncture Research

Many Westerners who have heard about acupuncture only recently seem unaware of the decade or more of scientific research done in other countries to explore the dynamics of acupuncture from the viewpoint of Western medicine. In 1956 the Soviet Union sent a group of doctors trained in Western medicine to Peking to study acupuncture at the Institute of Experimental Acupuncture directed by Madame Chu Lien. The practice of acupuncture is medically accepted in the USSR as it is in many European countries. Those interested in recent Soviet findings might contact: Laboratory of Reflexotherapy, Moscow; Laboratory of Chen-chiou Therapy of the Institute of Neurophysiology, Leningrad; Acupuncture Lab of the Bechterev Psychoneurological Institute and Polyclinic No. 5, Leningrad; Department of Therapeutics, Gorki Hospital, Gorki; Department of Diseases of the Nervous System at the Kazan Institute of Advanced Medicine; Department of Therapeutics at the Armavir Hospital.

An excellent Soviet text on acupuncture reporting contemporary research on the mechanisms of acupuncture treatment as monitored with modern scientific equipment was prepared by Dr. Vadim Vogralik, Professor at the Gorki Medical Institute named after C.M. Kirov, in Gorki, USSR. *Principles of the Chinese Healing Method—Acupuncture*, 1961, available from Gorki Book Publishing, Kremlin, second building, Gorki, USSR (1 rouble 33 kopecks). Western books on acupuncture by Dr. Felix Mann and Dr. J.R. Worsley are especially helpful.

For a German acupuncture point detector see: C. Overhof, *The Physical-Physiological Fundamentals of Electroneural Diagnostics*. Bühl-Baden. Verlag Konkordia A.G., 1960, 119 pages and R. Croon *Electro-Neural Diagnostics and Therapy*. Bühl-Baden, Verlag Konkordia A.G., 1959, 128 pages.

Electrodynamic Fields and Kirlian Photography

Dr. Harold Saxton Burr of Yale University, an internationally recognized neuroanatomist, made an extraordinarily important discovery some forty years ago—namely that all living things from men to mice, from trees to seeds, are molded and controlled by "electrodynamic fields," which can be measured and mapped with standard modern voltmeters. He considered these fields of life or L-fields to be the basic blueprints of all life. Monitoring L-fields with voltmeters, he discovered such illnesses as cancer could be diagnosed long before the usual symptoms develop; that the healing of wounds both internal and external could be continuously monitored at a distance; that internal processes such as ovulation, could be precisely and accurately monitored according to changes occurring in the electrodynamic fields of a woman's finger.

Like the Kirlian researchers and like Alexander Gurvich even earlier, Burr came to the conclusion that the energy matrix shapes the living form in matter. Burr monitored the voltages of the electrical fields around frogs' eggs. The area giving the highest voltage reading always became the frog's nervous system. He learned that there was a distinctive pattern of energies that would later form the blob of protoplasm into each element of the physical body. Rearranging the protoplasm did not disrupt the final form. L-fields even radiate some distance away from the embryo, he discovered.

Like the Kirlians, Burr and his colleagues also studied the energy fields of plants. Like the Kirlians, Burr also found that energy fields of trees and plants vary not only with sunlight and darkness but also with the cycles of the moon and with magnetic storms and sunspots. L-fields also were indicators of the vitality of seeds. Using the voltmeter, Burr could segregate those seeds with superior growing power.

Burr's student Dr. Leonard Ravitz made the dramatic discovery that L-fields also reflect people's mental states. Like Kirlian photography, the Burr method revealed altered states of consciousness, varying degrees of hypnosis, changes of emotions and so forth. Ravitz found that even the recollection of an emotion such as grief showed a marked energy change of several millivolts as monitored by the voltmeter. Dr. Ravitz states unequivocally, "Emotions can be equated with energy." Like the Soviet acupuncture researchers, Ravitz also found that the action of the sun and moon (sunspots, phases of the moon) affects the body's electrodynamic fields.

After researching hypnosis for years with the voltmeter, Ravitz asserts that hypnotic depth can be defined electrometrically, and he feels that hypnosis should be looked on as an energy-field effect.

Burr believed that just as our bodies and brains are maintained by permanent electromagnetic fields which mold the ever-changing material of the cells, so in turn these fields are influenced by the greater fields of the universe so that man is an integral part of the universe and shares in its purpose and destiny. With the development of new electronic instruments and techniques, said Burr ". . . an entirely new approach to the nature of man and his place in the universe became possible."

The spectacular array of discoveries Burr and his colleagues have made over the past thirty years and their vast implications can scarcely be touched on here. The extensive Burr findings form an impressive body of work against which to measure the data now being made visible by Kirlian photography. Do the two systems interrelate? Do Kirlian photos show visually some of the same things measurable with the voltmeter such as advance diagnosis of illness, energy fields of wound healing, effects of sunspot activity? Do the L-field polarities of the human body and their changes match the energy patterns of the body that psychics perceive? Could the voltmeter be used to monitor the effects of psychic healing, telepathy, PK and poltergeists, dowsing, and could it tell us about puzzling psi experiences such as "out-of-body" travel, or the mechanism of mediumistic trance?

The instrument used in Burr's epoch-making experiments is the Hewlett-Packard DC Vacuum Tube Voltmeter Model 412A, available from the Hewlett-Packard Co., Palo Alto, California.

A popular account of Burr's lifetime research is given in his own book, *The Fields of Life*, Ballantine Books, PO Box 505, Westminster, Maryland 21157 ($1.50). The book includes a complete list of all of Dr. Burr's papers. An important book about Burr's work and its implications for psi, psychiatry, and philosophy is Edward Russell's *Design for Destiny*, now available in paperback from Ballantine Books ($1.25).

General

The above are just some basic indications of things to photograph with Kirlian equipment.

Anyone seriously interested in doing Kirlian photography should check out the resource material from both East and West. (See Section Six.) Publication on Kirlian photography has burgeoned within the last couple of years and many books and periodicals are crammed with new research and technical methods, new theories, new findings.

Some of the key publications to get might include: *The Osteopathic Physician*, October, 1972; *Galaxies of Life, Questions of Bioenergetics*; *Popular Photography*, February, 1972; *Psychic*, July, 1972; *A.R.E. Journal*, March, 1972; *Journal of Paraphysics*; *Proceedings of the Academy of Parapsychology and Medicine*. (See Section Six for details.)

9

The Schlieren System—
An Aura Detector?

Surveys of individuals who claim to see auras describe the aura as a pulsating, moving field, composed of one of many colors, around the human body. The colors are said to vary according to the health, emotions, or thoughts of the subject. According to a *Fate Magazine* survey conducted by Louis J. Vacca, respondents see first a narrow dark band, one quarter inch wide next to the skin. Beyond this, projecting from two to four inches, they see a second aura, the inner aura, which they said was very clear. Past this region of the energy envelope they perceived a third aura, misty and without sharp outlines, extending out six to eight inches.

The two-to-four-inch inner aura is only faintly colored—silvery, greenish, or golden, they told the pollster. Some respondents reported that *"the inner aura is similar to heat waves shimmering up from the pavement on a hot day."*

This description given by aura-seeing individuals is strikingly similar to observations being made by contemporary scientists studying heat convection currents surrounding the human body. Normal body heat creates currents that form a pulsing envelope of warm air from one to three inches thick. This layer is warmer than the general environment; and, though invisible to most of us, it shows up as a halo on photographic plates, using a nineteenth-century German technique, called Schlieren photography, developed to detect flaws in glass. When the convection currents are made visible by the Schlieren system, the envelope of warm air around the body appears as a "shimmering, rainbow-colored aura," according to David Heiserman of *Science Digest*.

A team of doctors at the City University of London, led by Dr. Harold E. Lewis, discovered that this "heat" aura is laden with bacteria, particles of inorganic matter, and microscopic bits of skin. This halo contains up to 400 percent more micro-organisms than the immediate environment and may explain formerly unaccountable inhaled doses of airborne bacteria, says Dr. Lewis. Experimenters have also theorized that some diseases hang on because the envelope of warm air tends to trap bacteria and act as a breeding ground for them.

Does this heat envelope around the body correspond to the field psychics perceive? Or could its action pattern be similar?

Schlieren photography, which is also used to study airflow in supersonic wind tunnels, is now revealing some fascinating things about the pulsating warm airflow around the human body. Just as a prism breaks up light into a band of colors, convection currents in air can also break up light into color patterns. Each layer of air in the human air envelope has its own color, depending on its density and temperature. The Schlieren optical system makes these color patterns visible on a screen.

An American psychiatrist with psychic ability, Dr. John Pierrakos, director of the Institute for Bioenergetic Analysis in New York, has studied the energy fields of the body for some fifteen years, simultaneously with his medical practice. He believes these energy fields, which he is able to perceive psychically, are tied up with the body's metabolism, heat, emotions, rate of breathing, and with humidity, atmospheric conditions, and other factors.

Dr. Pierrakos psychically perceives a kind of "corpuscularlike movement" of small particles in this four-inch inner aura. As part of a complex, detailed description of this pulsating, shifting field around a human subject, he observes, ". . . the field moves from the ground up on the inner side of the legs and thighs, up the trunk and outer side of the hands, forearms and arms. The two mainstreams meet and travel upwards towards the neck and over the head. At the same time there is a movement at the inside of the lower and upper extremities towards the ground."

Researchers at the City University of London used the Schlieren optical system to research and photograph the convection currents around the human body, and here's what they see happening: "Starting at the soles of the feet, the air layer moves slowly upward over the body. At the groin and under the armpits it reverses direction briefly. At the shoulders it spurts upward to dissipate in a feathery plume about five inches above the head." Both psychic and scientist now claim you have a halo! Classic descriptions of the auras of the hands indicate there are bands of energy between the fingers and rays of energy projecting from each finger. Schlíeren photographs show a similar pattern, perhaps again revealing some aspect of the aura or providing an analogy to it. (See Figure 5.)

FIGURE 5.

Sketch of warm-air currents emanating from the human hand, as seen with the Schlieren technique; bears resemblance to some psychics' descriptions of the aura of the hand.

Could these warm-air convection currents play a role in what some people are seeing as the inner aura? Could this flowing heat envelope be functioning in a similar way to the actual aura, following the flow patterns of auric energy fields? Certainly the surround of colored energy around the body made visible by the Schlieren system may be *only a part* of what psychics see, yet there are a number of similarities. Perhaps coordinating what psychics see with what the Schlieren system reveals might provide more clues about aura diagnosis—there may be certain patterns in the heat aura that match anomalies in the psychic aura.

Aside from the basic flow pattern of the auric energy up from feet to head and down again, Dr. Pierrakos also observes that there is an alternate upward and downward movement of the aura in each half of the body: ". . . The field pulsates from the midsection of the body towards the head and feet simultaneously both in the front and back and the sides of the body," he says.

The overall movement of the aura energy he sees can roughly be represented by a figure eight crossing over the solar plexus. He finds that each individual has an energy of a different tone, rhythm, color, and vibration. These luminous forces around the body "thunder" and "quake" with strong emotions, he says. Especially anger and rage seem to make them cascade like an avalanche. In diagnosing from energy fields, he looks for blockages, deflections of energy, change of flow pattern, dull color, slowing of vibratory movements.

That a medical doctor should be able to perceive these auric energy fields and diagnose from them is not all that unusual, according to Dr. Shafica Karagulla in her intriguing book, *Breakthrough to Creativity*. Many of her colleagues were willing to confide in Dr. Karagulla, a medical doctor herself, and revealed their unusual "secret" ability to perceive beyond the range of the normal.

Many doctors, like the outstanding diagnostician she met from the Mayo Clinic, could instantly perceive the energy fields of patients and check for pathology the moment the person walked in, though to protect their medical standing they said nothing and put the patient through routine lab tests. She encountered a large number of doctors and psychics across America, who, like Dr. Pierrakos, see a living, moving web of energy frequencies involved with the body. Some also saw vortices of energy at certain points along the spine connected with the endocrine system. Says Dr. Karagulla, "You begin to get a picture of man not only as a dense physical form, but man made up of several types of energies, and that the solid form is the byproduct—the final condensation—rather than the primary factor."

It may be that scientific instruments such as the Schlieren system might show the *effects* of the auric energy on the heat envelope around the body. Just as psychics claim to be able to diagnose from examining the aura energy patterns, doctors researching with the Schlieren system have found they can also diagnose from the body energy patterns.

They found striking changes of color in the heat surround that coincide with an increased bacteria count due to infection and unusual changes in the flow pattern that coincide with areas of inflammation. Observing the flow pattern of the heat aura they discovered that the bacteria-laden warm air flowed toward the nose where it was inhaled—possibly accounting, they thought, for certain bacterial and viral infections such as the asthma attacks children get after eczema. Illnesses, such as arthritis, for instance, in which joints become inflamed, cause a rise in heat in certain areas and changes in the flow of convection currents. Doctors have already succeeded in mapping body temperatures with a heat-detecting instrument called a thermograph to provide an early diagnosis system for rheumatoid arthritis at its earliest stage, when crippling is most preventable.

Dr. Glen W. McDonald of the US Department of Health, Education and Welfare says that every human body emits infrared radiation. "If the eyes were structured to see this emission," he added, "each of us would have an incandescent glow." The thermograph can "see" this glow. And because areas of inflammation emit more heat than other regions, the glow from such joints is different from normal glow.

Though science has so far begun to make visible just a part of the vast sea of energies psychics perceive around us, nevertheless even this expansion of perceptions has paid dividends—could combining data from thermograph maps and Schlieren pictures help give us an analogy of what and how psychics diagnose from the aura?

Would a psychic's description of his perception of a subject's inner aura coincide with the shimmering currents made visible by the Schlieren technique? A person suffering with an inflammatory disease such as arthritis might first be looked at by psychics, to study the effects of the inflammation on the energy flow of the inner aura, and then studied with the Schlieren technique.

In addition, could the Schlieren technique help make visible changes occurring during various kinds of psi phenomena? Human relations constitutes another fascinating area that could be investigated to see whether the psychics see the same thing the optical system amplifies. Dr. Pierrakos says, "If you could see this luminous and colorful phenomenon around the body and between people, you certainly would have the feeling that people swim in a sea of fluid with brilliant colors which constantly change and vibrate." It would be interesting, too, to coordinate Schlieren-aura findings with other research on the aura and Kirlian photos.

A professional Schlieren System is available from Edmund Scientific for around $100.00 (No. 71,014), but the amateur experimenter can construct a simple Schlieren system for just a few dollars.

How to Construct a Schlieren System

The basic Schlieren system is made up of a light source, a viewing screen, several magnifying lenses, and screens with pinholes. (See Figure 6.) Light strikes the object being observed (a hand or candle flame, for instance) and the heat currents cause the light to break up into bands of color, which are magnified by the optics onto the viewing screen.

You'll need three ordinary magnifying glasses, the large round type with a handle, available in most stationery stores. In addition you'll need some aluminum foil, clothespins, pieces of cardboard and several small-necked bottles.

As a light source you can use a slide projector, a powerful photography light, possibly a sunlamp, or a high-intensity goose-neck lamp. The light should be very strong for this experiment.

If you have a projector and screen, the screen will be ideal for viewing the Schlieren picture. If not, a piece of white cardboard will do.

Cut two squares of aluminum foil 2″ × 2″. Punch a tiny round pinhole into the exact center of each one. A stand is required for each foil square. A clothespin taped to a box or small bottle makes a good holder.

FIGURE 6.

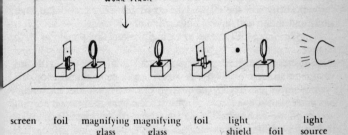

| screen | foil | magnifying glass | magnifying glass | foil | light shield | foil | light source |

How to assemble a simple Schlieren system to make visible in color the warm-air aura of the fingers, hand, or a lit candle.

A holder stand is needed for each magnifying glass. Several small-necked bottles about the height of the handle will do. The handle goes inside the bottle and the lens rests on the neck. A box will also work. Or you can improvise a holder from anything handy. The magnifying-glass handles must stand perfectly straight.

For a stray light shield, a square of cardboard around 8 1/2″ × 8 1/2″ can be used. Cut a one-inch round hole in the exact center. Tape the bottom edge of the board to a bottle or box as a stand.

The components of the Schlieren viewing screen can be set up on a table or cardtable or, if you wish, on a four-foot plank of wood.

Set up your viewing screen or tack a white cardboard viewing screen on the wall. It should be almost level with the table. Place the table about six inches away. Set up the slide projector or lamp independently three or four feet away from the other end of the table. Center the light beam in the middle of the viewing screen. (See diagram.) Put one of the magnifying glasses on the table closest to the light. The stray light shield is set up three or four inches in front of magnifying glass #1. Move it around until the light is focused clearly through the glass and the hole. Next line up a foil square an inch or two in front of that so again the light focuses sharply through it. Put magnifying glass #2 in front of the pinhole and focus it so an image of the pinhole reflects on the viewing screen. Magnifying glass #3 goes six inches in front of #2. The space between these two magnifying glasses is the area in which you insert objects to be observed. Put the second foil square in front of magnifying glass #3 so the light is focused on the screen.

To view an object on the screen, place it between magnifying glasses 2 and 3. A small lighted candle is interesting to observe. Keep adjusting the components until you get the best possible image. Colors from the heat of the flame will begin to dance on the screen. Blow on the flame and check for any component that's misaligned and causing any distortion in the image. To view clearly, you will probably need to extinguish most of the lights in the room.

Any hot object placed between lens #2 and lens #3 will show dramatic rainbow effects. The experimenter can gain practice, too, with objects previously warmed up in the oven. After experience with very hot objects, try to observe the heat convection currents given off by the hand. This may require more delicate alignments to make the colors perceptible.

Once you have the apparatus working well, try looking for the intermingling of patterns when two hands are brought together. See what happens when several people's hands are seen together. Try a dog's paw, if your dog is cooperative.

When you finally are able to observe the field around the hand, see if you can gain conscious control over the amount of heat given off. Recent biofeedback training has shown people can change the temperature of their hands at will. Try shifting heat and energy from one side of the hand to the other.

Check other sections for further ideas for experiments.

You can draw sketches of the Schlieren auras seen on the screen, or if you use a rearview projection screen, you can photograph the image from the other side of the screen.

Section Three

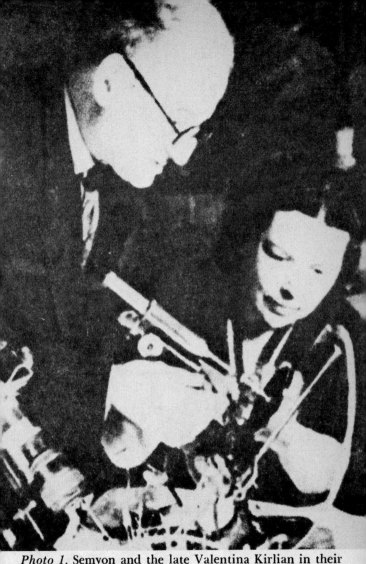

Photo 1. Semyon and the late Valentina Kirlian in their home lab photographing and observing plants, using their high-frequency method and patented optical devices. Developed over twenty years ago for plant research, the Kirlian method now finds application in psi research.

Photos 2 and 3. Kirlian photos of the fingertip (magnified) of Russian healer Colonel Alexei Krivorotov. Top: at rest in his normal state. Bottom: when asked to "heal" someone by laying on of hands, his fingertip shows increased luminescence.

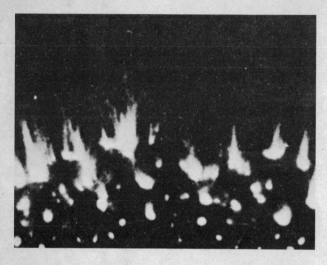

Photos 4 and 5. Kirlian photos produced in the US with equipment imported by the authors from Czechoslovakia. Photos of the fingertip of American healer Ethel De Loach researched by Professor Douglas Dean show: (photo 4) healer at rest; (photo 5) healer, when asked to think of healing by "laying on of hands" displays more luminescence. During moment of healing, a brilliant orange flare develops at the base of the first finger joint.

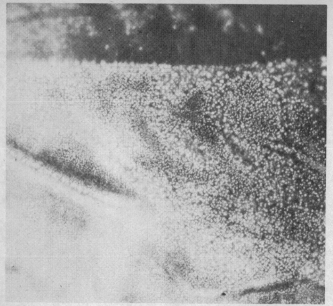

Photo 6. Phantom phenomenon: several millimeters of this leaf have been cut away (top of photo).

After removal of part of the leaf, a Kirlian photo still shows the *entire* leaf as before, though fainter in the area where the portion of the leaf is actually missing. If a person's fingerprint is sandpapered off and the finger photographed, the original swirls of the fingerprint still show in the Kirlian photo.

Photos 7, 8, 9. Photos by the Kirlians of the death of a leaf: (top) freshly picked leaf; (center) same leaf ten hours later; (below) same leaf twenty hours later. Sparkles fade as leaf dies. American researchers have photographed this same life-death sequence and find no sparkling emanation comes from any dead thing—plant or animal.

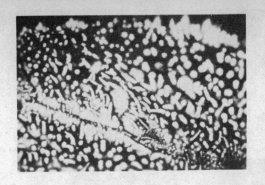

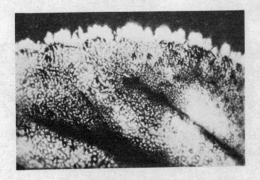

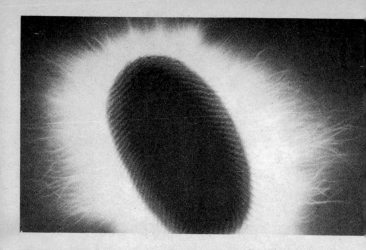

Photos 10 and 11. Music appears to have an affect on luminescence. (Above) tip of middle finger before music; (below) same fingerpad—*after* Bach's Brandenburg Concerto Number Three was played—shows sharply decreased corona with highly defined flares and several luminous bubbles emanating from the area of the finger joint. Different kinds of music elicit various kinds of patterns.

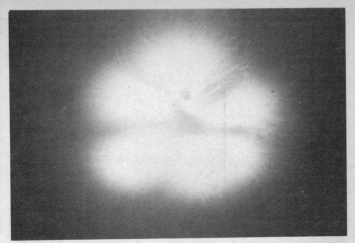

Photo 12. Soybean sprout after twelve hours' germination, photographed by the authors. Dr. Harold Burr's electrometric research, using the microvoltmeter to study electrical emanations of seeds and embryos, showed they had the most powerful fields of all living things.

Photo 13. Kirlian photo shows flare patterns of paw of a five-year-old Scotty dog.

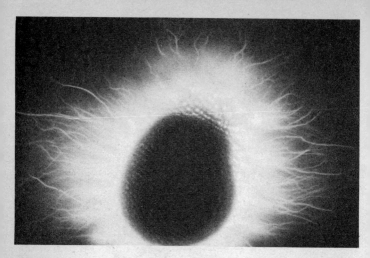

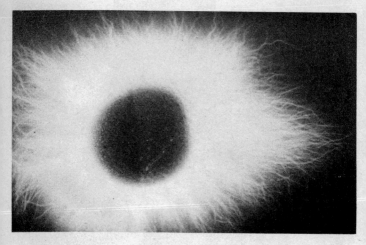

Photos 14 and 15. Photo 14 shows Mrs. Sechrist, of the Edgar Cayce Association for Research and Enlightenment, during prayer, in Photo 15 she had switched to meditation, both patterns differ from the normal and from each other.

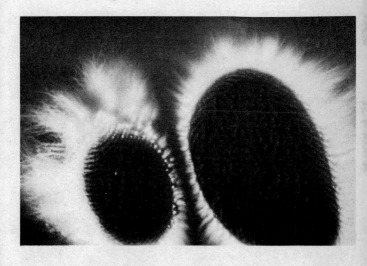

Photo 16. As fingertips of two different people near, rather than intermingling, flares usually draw back.

Photo 17. Top: Kirlian photo from Alma-Ata of a geranium leaf in its normal condition. Bottom: Same leaf when in a magnetic field, shows sharp decrease in size of corona and dozens of white bubbles over its surface.

Photo 18. The Electrograph—a high-frequency photography device—imported from Czechoslovakia by the authors. The instrument operates on a frequency upwards of 100,000 to 3 million hertz and generates 40,000-volt pulsed square waves. Discharge frequency can be adjusted from one to fifty cycles per second. Insulated copper plate on top is the electrode-exposure plate.

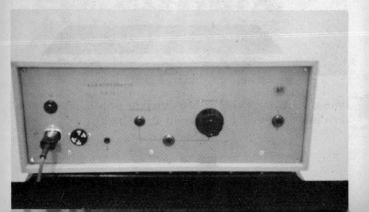

Photo 19. Kirlian photos make intriguing posters.

Photo 20. A simple high-frequency photography unit: Tesla Coil; copper wire with alligator clip on one end and rubber plug on the other; copper-clad board.

Photo 21. A teleflasher concocted from a slide sorter. Sample winker plug and flasher button shown in left foreground.

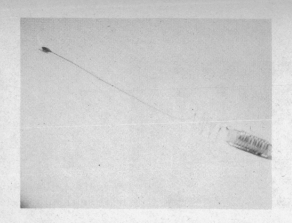

Photo 22. An impromptu dowsing rod, easily made from wire, plastic, and a fishing sinker.

Photo 23. The Czechoslovakian original red and white plastic pyramid for razor-blade sharpening. It stands slightly less than three inches tall. (Base of triangle: 11.4 centimeters, side: 10.8 centimeters.)

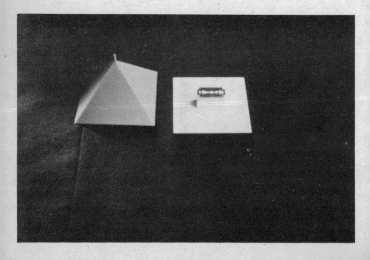

ČESKOSLOVENSKÁ REPUBLIKA

ÚŘAD PRO PATENTY A VYNÁLEZY V PRAZE

STÁTNÍ ÚŘAD PRO VYNÁLEZY A NORMALISACI V PRAZE

PATENTNÍ LISTINA

ČÍSLO 9 1 3 0 4

ÚŘAD PRO PATENTY A VYNÁLEZY V PRAZE

STÁTNÍ ÚŘAD PRO VYNÁLEZY A NORMALISACI V PRAZE UDĚLIL PODLE § 18 ZÁK. Č. 34 1957 Sb.
PATENT NA VYNÁLEZ S NÁZVEM:

Způsob udržování holicích nožíků a břitev ostrými

V ROZSAHU PŘIPOJENÉHO PATENTNÍHO SPISU.

PŮVODCE VYNÁLEZU: Karel Drbal, Praha

PATENT BYL ZAPSÁN DO PATENTNÍHO REJSTŘÍKU POD SHORA UVEDENÝM ČÍSLEM.

VYNÁLEZ BYL ODEVZDÁN STÁTU.
PRÁVO K VYUŽITÍ VYNÁLEZU PŘÍSLUŠÍ STÁTU.

V PRAZE DNE 15.srpna 1959

PŘEDSEDA

PŘIHLÁŠKA VYNÁLEZU P 2399-49

Photo 24. The Czech patent that started it all—awarded
to Karel Drbal for his razor-blade sharpening pyramid.

Photo 25. Czech researchers discuss biogenerators. From left to right: Karel Drbal, patentee of the pyramid; Robert Pavlita, designer of psychotronic generators; his daughter, Jana Pavlitova-Zapadlova; Dr. Zdenek Rejdak, World President, International Association for Psychotronic Research.

Photo 26. A selection of the more than seventy psychotronic generators created by Robert Pavlita.

Photo 27. Generator attracts nonmagnetic and magnetic substances under water.

Photo 28. Aluminum umbrella-wheel inside copper collar is turned by "energy" from cylindrical generator at left. We watched Pavlita demonstrate this system. The wheel revolved with no apparent evidence of trickery.

10

Teleprompting with the Teleflasher

**Game Theory and Telepathy—Learn
While You Play to Develop ESP**

If a picture is worth a thousand words, sensing a picture telepathically is probably worth many more. The theme of this handbook is experience-experiment, and you can probably learn more, or at least something different, about what makes telepathy click by experiencing it than by reading volumes of case histories and theories. The most sophisticated "instrument" you can have to explore the whys and wiles of telepathy is your own mind. Some grounding in telepathy is a good entrance point to other extrasensory phenomena. And building up some ability might have other bonuses. Many people at the top in everything from business to the arts say that psi is an element in their success; and scientific studies of psi and success are beginning to confirm their claims. Serious, out-in-the-open consideration of psi—with an eye to practical application—is beginning to grow in the business community. (See *Executive ESP*, Prentice-Hall, 1974.)

Are you telepathic—or can you be? Numerous researchers and most psychics agree that everybody has potential psi ability. Generally the world's famous psi practitioners insist that they trained themselves to be psychic. Psychic ability, it seems, can be developed just as you would learn to play golf or tennis, learn to sing or speak a language. The basics for success in learning any of these include: training, practice, enjoyment, and continued use to keep developed ability from getting rusty. These requirements probably apply to learning telepathy, too, which is the catch, sometimes. How do you practice telepathic arias? Or how do you keep up your telepathic form? You can't go out to a course or a court as with golf or tennis and pick up a game. But if you have a little creativity there is something you can do to entice others to join in and to circumvent the boredom barrier to telepathy training. You can try the "Learn while you play" format.

Today, game theory and game stimulation are widely used to help people develop and sharpen skills. Traffic controllers, executive trainees and military officers, to name just a few, have taken up game-playing training programs. Specially designed games might also be helpful with ESP training it seemed to us. If you've already developed some basic psi ability, game playing is a good way to keep in practice.

Games can be designed from a variety of angles. We began mulling the semi-truism that most of us think of ESP as extrasensory *perception*. But what about the other side of the coin, extrasensory *projection?*

In the usual telepathic demonstrations, the psychic star does the receiving and an anonymous member of the audience does the sending. Yet famous mentalists, such as Dunninger, point out that if the sender does not form an image or thought clearly, the psychic has trouble picking it up. Until recently, the sender seemed to be the forgotten half of the telepathic connection, not only in public demonstrations but even in lab research into ESP, where it seemed that anyone handy could serve as the sender.

In spontaneous crisis telepathy, certainly the sender seems the key. It's the person caught in the emergency who blasts out a mental SOS. If the sender's signal is strong enough in any situation, it may impress itself on another. Psi projection is probably also a live element in that elusive but very real something—charisma or star quality in politics and entertainment.

Soviet researchers have long centered attention on the projection part of ESP. They consider that the sender as well as the receiver is a psychic. The Russians have been tinkering with a multitude of methods from visualization training to the use of electromagnetic fields to stimulate their telepathic senders. All of this got us thinking about various aids to psi development and practice that might enhance visualization and concentration.

The importance of game theory, the telepathic sender and mechanical training aids—these three ideas came together for five of us a few years ago and resulted in a flash—to be exact, a flashing light box or screen on which you put symbols, pictures, colors, names, aces, kings, and queens to be transmitted telepathically.

The idea of a simple device that might help get telepathy pulsing came from Soviet engineer Vladimir Fidelman, a psi investigator at the Bio-Information Section of Moscow's Popov Institute. In the late sixties, rather than trust a telepathic sender's own ability to clearly shape and pulse his thought, Fidelman went electric. He put a number—8, for instance—on a light and flashed it over and over at a telepathic sender. "Chant," he commanded. "Chant eight, eight, eight, rhythmically with the light." He told the sender to immerse himself in 8 until he could visualize nothing but 8 in vivid clarity on an imagined screen in his mind. Using this technique, Fidelman reported that his senders successfully transmitted 100 out of 134 numbers to a receiver over a mile away.

As Fidelman no doubt knew, both of the Soviet Union's best-known mentalists, Wolf Messing and Mikhail Kuni, like the American, Dunninger, agree it's tricky for them to pick up an impression if the sender's thought is vague, fuzzy, and formless. Messing and Kuni claim that the deaf and dumb make the best telepathic senders—because, as compensation, they have learned to visualize superbly.

Fidelman's flashing lights seemed, at the least, to be an aid to concentrated visualization. They also echoed some other ideas. Neurologist and inventor Dr. Andre Puharich, a psi researcher who often seems to be ahead of the field, some years before had turned high-speed strobe lights on the closed eyes of the Dutch psychic Peter Hurkos. Hurkos was able to adjust the strobe to the speed that "pleased him." Bathed in the bright, rhythmically pulsing light, Hurkos experienced "verifiable heightened telepathy and/or clairvoyance," according to Puharich.

A flashing light is rhythmic. Yogi Ramacharaka, in the *Hindu-Yoga Science of Breath*, writes that "rhythm will augment the sending of thought by several hundred percent." Send after rhythmic breathing, he advises. As a side note, it's interesting that certain yogis have long used special "strobe candles" that produce a fast flicker, supposedly to improve meditation and often as an unwanted fringe benefit, psychic powers. As yogis and so many others have pointed out, the psychic and spiritual realms are not the same.

It's foolish to try enhancing psi with high-speed strobes on your own, outside of a medical lab; the "wrong" frequency can give you a lot of problems—epileptic fits for one. But what about a plain, flashing rhythmic light such as those used in window displays. To attack fuzzy sending, with the help of three friends, the teleflasher came into being . . . a kind of teleprompter. Anyone can make one easily. To keep practicing with the flasher, we turned to games. The combination clicked for a number of us.

Our cohorts on the game project knew a lot about psi. One of them had been associated with a professional parapsychology association where part of the job involved investigating psychics. Two were test subjects for some of the early research on physiological telepathy in the US more than a decade ago and had taken part in numerous workshops and psi development programs. They had also been subjects in an extensive study on parent-child telepathy. These friends helped us put together some prototype teleflasher models and devise new games. They found that the rhythm, the focusing of concentration and improved visualization sparked by the teleflasher did seem to heighten their telepathy more than many other techniques they had tried.

Over the years, starting back in college in our respective countries, we too had off and on looked into psi development. With the flasher, telepathy seemed to work better for us than before and we found it hard to resist practicing, i.e., playing.

To make sure we weren't a bunch of ringers, our friends played flasher games with various people—even a parapsychologist. Everyone seemed to get a kick out of playing. Some found the flasher very relaxing and conducive to psi generally. One highly cerebral doctor who'd thought ESP was for the birds was stunned when he got a run of eight out of eight right and decided telepathy might be worth looking into.

And this was where we were going to say, "On with the games." But then suddenly, after this chapter was written, we learned of a remarkable, creative piece of telepathic research. It looks as if medical researchers with the Toronto Society for Psychical Research have made an important discovery, a leap in information eminently worthy of being included for its own sake. But as you will see, we also have a secondary reason for writing about this work that was introduced in *New Horizons* by geneticist Dr. A.R.G. Owen, who declared, "We believe it to be one of the most important papers ever to be published in the field of parapsychology."

This probe of telepathy is a perfect example of turning established equipment and techniques to new potential by applying them to psi. In Toronto a team of doctors led by an M.D. highly qualified in medical research began with a regular physiology test. They beeped a single note of sound in short, regular, rhythmic, blasts at a person in the lab. Each time the tone sounded, a synchronizing light flashed indicating that signals from an EEG measuring the subject's brain activity were being fed through an instrument known for short as CAT (a computer of average transients). This produced a chart recording showing a wave pattern in the person's brain evoked by the sound. The doctors weren't surprised. It's been long and well known that this wave pattern, called the average evoked response, occurs in the brain following a sound.

Next, the doctors did something that may well surprise a lot of people. They switched off the sound generator and they substituted a telepathic sender for the tone. Each time the light flashed indicating the CAT was analyzing brain waves, the sender attempted to transmit a telepathic image—a cup of coffee, a cup of coffee—to the subject. One second elapsed between each signal.

The physicians found that *rhythmically* pulsed telepathic thoughts aimed at the subject "evoked responses in the EEG which are similar in form, and comparable in magnitude to those evoked by physical stimuli such as sounds." In other words, they found something going on in the receiver's brain, a wave pattern very similar to the one the tone had caused. Apparently—and this is of prime importance for research—the sending of a telepathic image can be correlated with a clearly observable event in the receiver's brain.

Here is new and first-rate evidence that psi communication can and does occur, that something does get through. And, perhaps most noteworthy of all, the subject never realized when thought was being beamed at him nor that anything was happening inside his head. These test results are ripe with implications, too many to go into here, but one question seems worth asking: Something does get through to the receiver's brain—could a trained telepathist bring it to consciousness?

Dr. Owen, director of the Toronto Society, declares of this Canadian first that it "opens up so many exciting prospects for objectively based researches of many kinds that it may legitimately be recognized as signifying the advent of a new era in psychical research with potential repercussions on the behavioral and other sciences." (*New Horizons*, summer, 1973.) A respected, established scientist, author of numerous works on genetics and an award-winning author on parapsychology, Owen doesn't make such glowing remarks lightly.

Obviously a fine medical experiment and the teleflasher games aren't in the same category. There isn't a direct link. But as you can imagine, we couldn't help noticing that a telepathic image sent at a steady rhythm got through to the receiver. Visualizing an image and sending it clearly, the doctor in charge noted, "requires considerable practice."

Which brings us back to our teleflasher games. For some of us they seemed a way to get someplace. When you've developed a good telepathic technique, you can take off without the flasher.

Once you get going, you may find the most interesting way to explore telepathy is by making up your own games—someone has to invent the Monopoly of the Aquarian Age.

Some of the games we've included are for more serious psi development, while others, such as psychic roulette, bingo and flash poker, are for play—with a slightly ulterior motive. Games are a way to pull in people who wouldn't want to be caught at a psi development class, who "don't think there's anything to it," or say "it could never happen to me." You're only playing a game, there's nothing to argue about. Though there can be something for your friend to wonder about if he starts hitting telepathically. You can also play games with a bone-cold skeptic. Let him play on the laws of probability, while you try for an extrasensory assist.

Another bonus to using games as an exploratory technique is that you avoid the often freezing connotation of a test or a trial. ESP card tests have their place, but they lack a lot as a teaching technique. Unless you possess an unusual character, a paralytic boredom sets in. Besides, you wouldn't give someone an exam on the piano before he'd ever taken a lesson. It would hardly enhance his ability or desire to learn, not to mention his confidence. The time to test your telepathy would seem to be after you've developed it.

No one can guarantee that you'll become telepathic. In part, it's up to you. How much do you want to work at it? And levels of psi talent no doubt vary as with any other ability. Very few of us become opera stars, but most people can at least learn to hum a little. Of course no one can say that you won't metamorphose into a telepathic star. And chances aren't bad for people bursting forth above the telepathic hum level.

How to Make Your Own Game Set

Materials you'll need for a game kit for psi development or any psi games are easy to make from inexpensive items around the house. For basic sending material, make up some tele-sets. These are sets of five: letters, numbers, symbols, colors. We tried out a great many different combinations. The sample tele-sets included seem to work best with a minimum amount of confusion and similarity between shapes. For numbers try, 4,5,6,7,8. For letters use, B,A,Z,O,W. Symbols are Fish, Clover, Rain, Tree, and Crescent Moon. (See Figure 7.) And the colors used are red, yellow, blue, green, and purple.

Tele-Sets

FIGURE 7.

Above is the Tele-Symbol Set. Draw each figure on a sheet of paper.
For the Tele-Number Set use: 4, 5, 6, 7, 8.
For the Tele-Letter Set use: B, A, Z, O, W.
For the Tele-Color Set use: Red, Yellow, Green, Blue, Purple.

Using a felt marker, draw each image on a separate sheet of paper. Or you may instead cut the images out of black construction paper. These dark symbols placed on the teleflasher screen will be highlighted by the light pulsing around them. If you prefer, you can draw the silhouette of an image on a piece of white paper and blacken the rest of the sheet. In this case, a light symbol will flash at you against a dark background.

There are various ways to put color on your flasher. Use thin colored paper or tissue paper or try pieces of colored cloth. If you have pieces of colored plastic, colored celluloid, or glass around,

use those. You can also use opaque and colored construction paper.
Cut into circles or squares and put them in the center of the flasher so
the light pulses around them. Or you could paint colors on paper to
use in the same way. If you're using transparent colors, you can
make green by combining yellow and blue; purple by combining
red and blue.

You'll be using one tele-set—numbers, letters, colors, or
symbols—at a time and will have to figure out a way to choose the
target. To pick a letter for instance, you can roll a die after assigning
each letter a number. Keep a list by your flasher showing which face
on the die signifies which target in each of the tele-sets. Another
method, perhaps easier in the long run, is to convert a spinner from
an old game. Tele-set figures are put on the spinner in concentric
circles. (See Figure 8.)

FIGURE 8.

Design of spinner used in teleflashing. Draw to pattern, cut out, put over
face of old game spinner or construct your own with spinning pointer.

Tele-sets, die, or spinner are basic game equipment whether or
not you're using a flasher.

How to Make a Teleflasher

A teleflasher is basically a light box with a flashing light inside. Teleflashers can be made in three different formats:

1. If you happen to have a slide sorter, it can easily be converted to a teleflasher by simply adding a winker or flasher plug. These plugs are available at most hardware stores. The slide sorter plugs into the winker plug, which in turn goes into the wall socket. Winker plugs are used in many store display windows and they flash at a comfortable speed.

A slightly more rapid flash can be obtained by using a small flasher button (about 1'' in diameter and 1/8'' thick), which fits in the light socket. Flasher buttons are available at many hardware stores. *Before inserting the flasher button, be sure the slide sorter is unplugged.* Remove the lightbulb, insert the flasher button in the light socket and screw the lightbulb back in place.

Ideally the flash rate should be around the speed of your pulse—about seventy-two pulses a minute. The flasher buttons are around this speed. Many people prefer the slower pulse, however, and find it more relaxing and conducive of telepathy. The winker plugs flash at this slightly slower speed. You might try both to see which is more effective for you.

If you are converting a slide sorter for use as a teleflasher, remove the lightbulb that comes with it and substitute a fifteen-watt bulb, which you'll probably find is much easier on the eyes.

Several inexpensive types of slide sorters have recently come on the market, some of them made of specially treated, heat-resistant cardboard with an opaque plastic screen, others in handy foldover metal boxes. Any of these models can be easily adapted as a teleflasher. (See photo #21.)

2. A teleflasher can also be made from a plastic food-saver box or food-crisper box or any sort of plastic or polyethylene box. The box should have a smooth, opaque top to use as a screen. It can be round, square, or rectangular. Cut a circular hole large enough for a light socket to fit into in one side of the box. Punch air holes all over the sides and bottom of the box. Insert the light socket and install a fifteen-watt lightbulb. As above, a winker or flasher plug can be attached to the plug on the light-socket cord, or a flasher button can be inserted inside the light socket.

3. A portable teleflasher can be made by using a battery-operated flasher lantern or a flashlight with a flasher switch or an auto safety-flasher unit. These are available at most automotive stores.

The red cover over the flasher unit should be removed. The flasher unit can be placed inside an opaque plastic box large enough to house it. Holes should be punched through the underside of the plastic box to permit heat to escape.

Setup

If you haven't made much of an attempt to experiment with telepathy, before plunging into specific games you might want to try some warm-ups with the materials used in most of the games that follow.

You'll probably find it easier to start with just one or two other people with whom you have good rapport. Put the teleflasher on a table or desk, anyplace where the sender will be comfortable and the receiver cannot see the screen. If you wish, dim the lights in the room. If the sender wears glasses make sure reflections in the lenses aren't visible to receivers.

How to Send Thought Telepathically

Sending couldn't be easier. Put the image on the teleflasher and send in rhythm with the flashing light. For high-power sending, here are some techniques culled from the pros most of whom believe telepathy is a skill you can learn.

Relax physically and mentally. Feel sure of success.

Concentrate and saturate yourself with the target image. (The flashing light helps keep your thought focused as it pulses a bright, vivid image.)

Chant the name of the target silently to yourself. (Again the flasher helps keep you in rhythm.)

Send pulsing images to a definite destination, the mind of your receiver. Release each image, send them out on the mental waves one after another. Keep going up to two minutes or until the receiver gets the telepathic message.

How to Receive Thought Telepathically

Relax. If possible, lie down in a comfortable position. Close your eyes. And don't try too hard.

Visualize a blank screen in your mind. Look for the image to appear like the channel number of a TV station. Some receivers prefer to visualize sparkles of energy or a pool of water or a long corridor in which an image will take shape. Find out what works best for you. Command your unconscious mind, ''Give me the answer now.'' A sort of uncaring alertness works best.

Wait for an image to form. Don't guess. Sometimes the right image will immediately pop into mind. Other times it may take up to two minutes for the right pictures to take clear shape.

Differentiate, try to notice cues that indicate the difference between the right and wrong image. Often incorrect pictures flicker and dissolve.

If you want to embark on serious schooling in telepathy, see pages 139-40.

Playing with Basic Tele-Sets

Choose a tele-set that appeals to you. Make sure your receiver knows the images included. Suppose you're playing with numbers, spin for a target and send. When your receiver calls out a number, tell him if he's right or wrong immediately. This will help him learn cues to spot a genuine image. If he is wrong, simply say no and keep right on sending until the image gets through. This kind of feedback is a key element in training.

Sometimes two numbers come into the receiver's mind and he can't decide which is correct. He should say, ''It's a five or an eight'' (or whatever). If neither is correct, the sender says no and keeps pulsing thought. If one number is right, the sender concentrates on the key points that differentiate the number.

When your receiver gets the number, choose another. If the same one comes up, flash it again. Keep track of which of the receiver's calls (first, second, third, fourth, or fifth) was correct. Some receivers are almost always right on their second calls. If that happens, wait longer for the image to stabilize before calling.

The receiver should never try to outguess the die or spinner. There is no logical way to figure out what number will come up next. If you as the receiver find yourself thinking, ''it's probably not a four because that came up last time,'' forget it. Trying for an edge with rational stratagems only hampers telepathy. There is no way to determine the correct image—except psychically.

Some senders find that it helps to outline the shape of the number or other image with their finger (out of sight of the receiver, of course) to give a kinetic boost to their sending.

According to the laws of probability, the receiver will get one out of five numbers right on the first call by chance. Anything more may mean telepathy has clicked on. But don't specially send sets of five. Forget about testing yourself against the laws of chance at the beginning. The main thing is to get the feel, the mood of it. (When you feel adept and want to test your ability, see page 138.)

After a while switch roles, with the sender becoming the receiver. But if you felt communication was improving, you might want to stick with the same setup. Trust your intuition. Two of the Soviet Union's most famous telepathists, Karl Nikolaiev and Yuri Kamensky, report that their telepathic hookup seems to be a one-way system—successful only when information goes from Yuri to Karl. A few of the people who've tried the teleflasher report the same one-way flow.

Don't send the same tele-set for too long, switch from numbers to letters to symbols. That way the receiver won't get a batch of five all blurred together in his mind, and the sender won't get bored looking at the same thing.

Try the tele-set letters, B,A,Z,O,W. Again keep records of correct calls. After a little experience, begin to try any number or letter of the alphabet. You'll probably notice that some images become confused—"M" coming through as "W" and "3" as "8." See if you can find your own cues to differentiate.

The Fish, Clover, Rain, Tree, and Crescent Moon seem to come through well as they differ enough in shape and meaning. When the target comes up Rain, try to get some of the motion, the driving, slanting feeling into your sending. Once you and your receiver get the hang of it, start flashing your own symbols. Use well-known ones, particularly those that mean something to you.

Impressing a color on someone else's mind has a different feeling to it than sending a symbol and some people find it easier. As the color pulses, imagine it all around you, engulfing you—then send it out to your receiver. Chant mentally the name in unison with the flash. See nothing but color, color, color.

Tele-Clock

Perhaps because we are all trained to visualize a clockface clearly from childhood, many people find it one of the easiest things to send and pick up telepathically. If your progress seems slow with other images, try the clock. It may work better for you. To make a flasher image: Draw a round clockface on a white sheet of paper with a felt marker. Number one to twelve. Cut out two strips of black paper, one short for the hour hand, one long for the minute hand. If you want, pin them in the center of the clockface. The only other thing you need is a random method of choosing the numbers one to twelve. Again, you could convert an old spinner. You can number cards one to twelve, shuffle, and choose; or you can number slips of paper, chips, or even bottle caps to shake in a bag. (Dice won't work because the number one must have an equal chance of showing.)

Once you've chosen a target hour, say three o'clock, put the clockface on the teleflasher and position the hands. To send, concentrate strongly on the angle of the hands, tracing the angle repeatedly with your eyes. Chant "three o'clock" (or whatever) mentally in time with the flash of the light. Receivers sometimes get a first impression that the time is on either the right or left side; they should call out "left side" or "right side" and then go on to tell the exact hour.

On a chance basis, you would only get one out of twelve calls right with the tele-clock. But the clock seems to set telepathy clicking in a lot of people, and they can tell the psychic time fairly often. Once you are experienced with the tele-clock, use the minute hand as well as the hour hand and communicate exact times to your receiver: 12:15, 2:30, 9:45. When you come to making up your own games or experiments, a clock face can be easily used as a compass.

And Furthermore . . .

Some days you and your partner's psi may be working better than others. Fatigue, illness, and emotional upset usually diminish ESP. And there are other factors as yet uncharted—among them, weather—that seem to affect telepathic power. Soviet and Bulgarian scientists and also Dr. Puharich and Dr. Krippner in the US have found that telepathy is more potent in their labs during the time of full and new moon. Try your telepathic powers when the moon is full or during a lightning storm. Does it make a difference?

One of the great psychics of our century, Eileen Garrett, believed that extrasensory perception worked better when more of our regular senses were stimulated. Some people like to have perfume around them or incense burning. Try it.

According to the science of yoga, rhythm is the key to heightening telepathic powers. The power to send a telepathic thought can be augmented, yogis say, if a person first does rhythmic breathing. The best rhythm to use for ESP breathing exercises, according to yoga, is the rhythm of the heartbeat. By harmonizing breathing with the pulse of the body, it is said the whole body catches the vibration and harmonizes with the will. By unifying the vibrations of the body, a person can more easily impress his thoughts on others and attract thoughts of others keyed in the same vibration. You and your receiver might both try their ideas.

To do the preliminary breathing exercises for ESP, become aware of your pulse rate—it should be fairly close to the pulse of the flasher. Inhale for six pulses. Retain the breath for three pulses. Exhale six pulses. Count three pulses between breaths. Repeat several times until you are consciously aware of the rhythms of your body. Then harmonize the image you want to send with the same rhythmic pulse pattern.

Telepathic Pictures

Try using your teleflasher as a mental slide projector, communicating pictures and scenes through ESP. Choose any interesting pictures—of scenery, city landmarks, famous paintings, famous ads. Advertisements are particularly good because associations with the product are so ingrained and constantly reinforced. You can also use picture postcards, your own slides, or pictures cut out of magazines or calendars. Select pictures with strong shapes or silhouettes.

Communicating pictures from out of the blue is of course, more difficult than transmitting a one-out-of-five image. The receiver is not likely to pick up the image whole, but will rather move in on it gradually. While the sender concentrates on the picture, the receiver calls out impressions as they come to him. You could be sending a picture of a long curving seacoast. The receiver might say, "I see a sweeping curve." Tell him he's right and ask if he can tell you more. Take your time. Do not hurry him between impressions. Guide the receiver into the target the way a control tower guides in a pilot flying blind. Ask him to concentrate on the right side of the picture, or the top, or wherever a particularly prominent feature may occur. If one color predominates, ask your receiver to tune in to it.

Swan with Snorkel

Receivers often get pictures, or parts of pictures, symbolically rather than literally. For instance, a receiver who was trying to pick up a picture in which a dollar sign was prominently featured said, "I see a swan; it's very rounded like an S. The swan seems to have something like a straight snorkel rising above its head.'' This receiver was getting an impression of the correct shape, but she had no thought at all that she was trying for a dollar sign. When a receiver gets a shape right symbolically, or a feeling (such as ''cold'' or ''desolate'' for a winter scene), tell him he is correct symbolically. Ask for more impressions to zero in on the specific picture. But don't get into a guessing game. Communicating pictures telepathically can give you fascinating insights into the workings of the mind, how we interpret symbols, and how one association leads to another. The more you experiment, the more you may find yourself learning about the normal avenues of thoughts and communication, as well as about the paranormal avenue of telepathy.

People

Sending images of people introduces a new psychological element. Start with photos of five people that your partner and you both know well. Or use pictures of five famous people you feel strongly about one way or another. Try to immerse yourself in the person—not only what he looks like, but also his personality. Try to see him through your receiver's eyes. Repeat the name over and over silently to yourself.

Events

Scientific studies have been done with senders viewing dramatic events in tests using movie clips. Scientists found that events were easier to communicate than static pictures. You might want to use a home movie, but if that's too complicated cartoon strips make ideal event-sending material. Use a multipanel cartoon strip from the newspapers that has well-known characters and a clear-cut storyline. The sender should spend a few seconds sending each panel of the cartoon story, then try to get across the overall theme and sequence of events.

Another interesting psi experiment involving sending events can be done with your TV set. Select a station-break time between programs when a whole group of different commercials come on. The receiver must go into another room out of earshot of the set. The sender selects one of the group of ads and tries to strongly impress the content and theme of the commercial on the receiver. Generally brief commercials make good event material because they are designed to get over a clear-cut dramatic message in a very brief time with very vivid visual and auditory effects. The receiver scores if he is able to describe any outstanding element of the ad material or the product.

Long-Distance Teleflash

Though it's still debated, distance does not seem to diminish telepathic power. If you and your partner live in different houses, try sending messages over the rooftops. If you live together, get as far apart as possible. If one of you is on a trip—even halfway around the world—it's a golden chance to see how far your mental connection can reach.

Synchronize watches. Decide on an exact time that transmission will begin—let's say eight P.M. Send the first image for two minutes. Rest two minutes. Then begin sending the next image. Agree beforehand how many images will be sent. Each of you should write down in order the images sent or received. When your psi session is over, get together (in person or on the telephone) and compare notes.

What to send. At first, practice linking your minds across space using the tele-sets that you've already communicated at close quarters. Then start experimenting with messages of your own. Codes are a natural for long-distance telepathy. So are time and place signals. See if you can make an appointment by ESP.

Emergency

The annals of psychic research are crammed with accounts of spontaneous telepathic messages that got through in a time of crisis—a ship going down, a woman smothering from a gas leak, a construction worker trapped in an unnoticed cave-in. Sometimes the receiver acts on the mental impression, bringing about a rescue. With your partner, decide on signals that you could use in time of real urgency when there is no other way to get a message through except telepathically.

Secret Messages and Codes

In both the Communist and Western worlds, researchers are

tinkering with coded telepathic systems. These scientists believe coded telepathy can soon be put to work in space travel, in emergency situations and, perhaps, in military operations.

You might try experimenting and developing some codes of your own to transmit messages. This could even be useful, if you live in separate houses, or if you've forgotten to buy bread for dinner. Using number and letter sets, decide on some such key as the following.

4 — Phone me after we're through with this session.

5 — Beware.

6 — I'm going to be late.

7 — Bring home milk.

8 — Meet me at the rendezvous tomorrow.

B — SOS.

A — Write me.

Z — Come home.

O — I love you.

W — I'm okay.

If you want to set up a rendezvous psychically, agree beforehand on a place and time. Make up any messages you want—things that are amusing or helpful to you—to go with tele-sets. Or use symbols of your own device.

At first, practice sending codes at agreed-upon times. Teleflash the code symbol for thirty seconds, rest thirty seconds, then teleflash the same signal again. Then check with your receiver (by phone or in person) to see if he got the correct message. Keep practicing regularly. When you achieve a measure of success, try sending coded messages without warning. For instance, send out a powerful number 8 ("Meet me at the rendezvous tomorrow")—present yourself at the rendezvous—and see if your receiver shows up, too.

Sending Book Codes

Advanced telepathists can try more complex codes that are almost impossible to break. Choose a book or magazine and make sure your partner has an exact copy of the same edition—a pocket language guide for tourists with lists of useful sentences is ideal. Number pages that seem particularly appropriate, 4, 5, 6, 7, 8. You may add five more numbers if you wish.

Assign the first five or ten sentences on each of these pages a tele-letter. To send a message, turn to the page with the sentence you want and mark down page number and sentence letter.

Telepathically you only have to get through two images, for instance, 5 Z to communicate a whole sentence or paragraph. Using a code book, you can send fifty to one hundred communiqués. Send the full messages at least three times.

Try Your Own Clairvoyance

You can use your teleflasher by yourself as well as with a partner. To start with, try a simple experiment. Select one tele-set—let's say the letters. Put the five letter cards in five envelopes and shuffle them so that you do not have any idea which letter is in which envelope. Number the envelopes one through five. Take one envelope to a table across the room from the teleflasher. If necessary put heavy paper or cardboard inside the envelopes to keep the letters from showing through.

Put the color blue on the teleflasher. Watch the color pulse, get into the rhythm. Wait and see if an image of the letter in the envelope begins to appear on your mental screen. When you feel you've gotten an image, jot it down. Retrieve the first envelope and note down the number on it opposite the letter you wrote. Repeat the procedure with all five envelopes, one by one. Do not open any until you are finished with the experiment. When you have finished the first five, check your list to see how many letters you got correct. Try the experiment with the number set and the symbol set. Eventually, if you seem to have developed a knack for clairvoyance, try projecting your mind outward—ready for anything—while sitting in front of the teleflasher. Try different colors; some seem to work better with different individuals. Can you get any impression of a distant scene that can later be verified?

Creating Your Own Games

Once you get into the swing telepathically, start experimenting and creating games. You'll have fun testing out your inspirations, even those that don't work in the long run. You'll also learn something about what your psi powers can do.

Figure out how to adapt your favorite games into telepathic ones. Often working the entire game into a psi format is too slow and cumbersome. Choose a critical point and let that be the place where a player may get an assist from telepathy if he's developed his ability. Think about tic-tac-toe, checkers, or even chess.

At least at first, try to keep the psi elements uncomplicated. Play with simple, easily transmitted symbols such as the tele-sets. If devising games that depend on odds such as those on page 142 ff., actually work out the probabilities so that you have a real game and a fair one.

Make up treasure hunts, story games, and team games. You might try a relay match with the members of each team having to pass on a different telepathic image to the next in line. First team through wins.

You don't have to confine yourself to transmitting images. Get into kinetic telepathy (see page 145-46) and go on from such standards as pin the tail on the donkey, blindman's bluff, and treasure finding.

Scientists have verified the telepathic transmission of taste. Start with basic sensations: sweet, sour, salt, bitter. Have the sender savor sugar, lemon, salt, or instant coffee granules. Do receivers come up with the proper psychic mouth watering? Can you make this into a game? If you are psi gourmets, try conveying anything, wine, whipped cream, or hasenpfeffer. If nothing else, you can always eat the game material at the end. Creating psi games for children can be good practice, not to mention enlightening. Many children take to psi naturally, particularly if no one has ever told them it's impossible. That a special telepathic rapport often exists between parents and children and between siblings is well documented. For what it is worth, and as a sign of the times, commercial psi development courses increasingly report that children who've gone through training with their parents are able to pick up telepathically the right answer to questions their schoolteacher has in mind. It might be a good idea to let the children help make up the games.

For younger children especially, keep the games short, simple, fast paced. Award points or prizes. Try to work in some action or humor. An example of a children's game is Psychic Animal Crackers. For sending material, cut out or draw a pig, cow, donkey, duck, and snake. Pick one at random, put it on the flasher and while sending, mentally chant the sound the animal makes: oink-oink, moo, hee-haw, quack, hsss. About ten seconds before you stop sending, let your receivers start making the sound of the animal they feel you have in mind. Keep sending. If a quacking child notices that most of the group is mooing, he can change his tune. But caution all beforehand that a first impression is often right, and perhaps one should stick to his quack. Call a halt and let loose the correct animal call.

Psi Games with Pets

If you're tired of playing fetch with your dog, you might make up a telepathy game. Documented instances of canine-human telepathy do exist, and most dog owners will assure you their pet can read their minds. Can you mentally call your dog to you, make him sit or lie down or bring you his favorite toy? Try this when you're sitting down with your eyes closed—or at least not in your usual stance when giving a command. You can also try directing the dog to one of two or three balls, bones, or dishes of food. If successful, keep going, maybe a canine telepathic star has been born. Remember, however, that a dog is a very keen observer and easily picks up minute sensory cues you may unconsciously be giving him. When researchers look into this sort of thing, they often screen the human end of the telepathy team, out of sight and hearing of the receiver.

Testing

Today scientists have many ways to test telepathic ability. Until recently the most popular method was the statistical card test. The point was to prove that psi existed. You don't have to prove telepathy is a fact. Scientists and psychics have labored through countless tests to prove it for you. But you may want to check how your own abilities are doing. You can take two routes. The first is statistical.

Tele-sets come in groups of five. The law of probability dictates that you should get one out of five right by chance. Choose the set you like best. Take twenty-five index cards, write down each image in the set on five different cards, shuffle them *well* and put the pack face down. Turn over the first card and place the image noted on it on the flasher. Send the entire deck in this manner. Expected chance score is five right. Parapsychologists find that most correct calls are made toward the beginning and end of the run, as if the test itself had a built-in dampening effect on telepathy. See if you can overcome this effect.

For a proper statistical test, you should run through the twenty-five cards at least four times and combine the scores. Chance, of course, is twenty out of a hundred. If you score considerably below chance you'll find out something about how your telepathic circuit works (and maybe something about your feelings toward tests).

Parapsychologists call this ''psi missing,'' which means you are using psi in a negative manner, using telepathy to *avoid* hits. This may sound odd because we often wrongly think of card tests in terms of our old school tests, where only high marks show proficiency. Card tests are a different sort of animal. The point is how close you come to the chance mark. If you score widely above the mark, something other than chance is at work. Similarly, if one is to believe statistical theory at all, if you score way below, "something other" is at work. (Currently, a number of investigators are departing from the old test scheme and allowing subjects to pass rather than forcing them to guess when they don't feel they have connected with the psi target.)

A less precise but more adaptable way of testing your ability is by trying it in various situations. Most famous telepathists have developed their power by *use*. See how many correct symbols you send *in a row*. Try to get over codes and images. Try to tune into other people's thoughts. Try sending unknown pictures and scenes. If information gets through, telepathy is probably at work. No one can calculate the odds against getting information by chance about any particular picture out of the millions there are in the world. The odds are astronomical.

Relaxation Training

If you are serious about developing telepathic ability and want to carry it a lot further than game playing, then it's important to look into the science of relaxation training. Psi practitioners generally stress the importance of relaxing the conscious mind for success at ESP, but it's not enough to just say to yourself, "Relax," if you don't know how. A methodology is essential. Recent scientific tests have shown relaxation to be highly conducive of ESP. Subjects scored between eighty-six percent to one hundred percent in a series of different telepathy tests after relaxation training. (See "Preliminary Explorations of Psi-Conducive States: Progressive Muscular Relaxation," W & L. Braud, *Journal of the American Society for Psychical Research*, January, 1973, cost, $3.00; 5 West 73 St. New York City 10023.) The article contains a transcript of one type of relaxation method.

The two year study on ESP training mentioned above was based on preliminary research conducted at Motivation Research Center in Austin, Texas.

Yoga Relaxation Technique

Most psychics would agree that to heighten psi *perception* a state of relaxed alertness or pseudo-passiveness helps. Generally our normal perception is directed toward the immediate world around us; and unless one can switch out of this attitude, more concentration simply focuses *normal* perceptions. Meanwhile the unconscious may pick up information that normal perceptions cannot pick up, provided the conscious mind does not interfere. The key to successful perceptions, many psychics say, is to train oneself consciously to hold conscious processes in leash while giving deeper unconscious processes the go signal.

To achieve relaxation of the conscious mind and alerting of the unconscious, many people find the basic relaxation exercises from Raja Yoga are very helpful. Yoga holds that mind and body are linked, and whatever happens to one affects the other. Physical tension is seldom found apart from mental tension. Mental tension always arises first and is the cause of physical tension. The Savasana exercise in Raja Yoga is designed to teach an individual to relax the physical body, thus relaxing the conscious mind.

General Relaxation

The first step is to relax the body as a totality. This letting go of body tensions involves letting the force of gravity do the work. The relaxation exercise can be done lying down face up on the floor or in a comfortable reclining chair or chaise lounge. Lie down with your feet about twenty inches apart and your hands palm up, about ten inches out from the body on either side. Make sure your shoulders are flat and your head is in a comfortable position. On each out breath feel your arms and legs becoming heavier and heavier. Picture yourself sinking into the floor. Let the natural pull of gravity take over.

Yogis believe there are sixteen key areas of the body that control relaxation: 1) feet, 2) shins, 3) kneecaps, 4) thighs, 5) abdomen, 6) solar plexus, 7) upper chest, 8) spine, 9) hands, 10) forearms, 11) upper arms, 12) throat, 13) back of head, 14) jaw, 15) eyes, 16) scalp.

Five out of the sixteen zones pertain to the head.

Each area should be specifically relaxed in turn starting with the feet.

First create a mental picture of the area. Then try to mentally sense the bone, muscle, tissue, and blood in the area. After increasing awareness of the area, mentally will a state of relaxation and heaviness in that zone. Continue through the sixteen areas. Take at least thirty seconds for each zone. When you have completed the sixteen zones, mentally examine your body from outside. If there is any zone that is still not fully relaxed, visualize it again and sense it becoming heavier and more relaxed.

Some expert psi percipients suggest that these relaxation exercises should be done at a specified time each day if a person is genuine and sincere about developing ability at psi perception. Psi researchers of the past point out that patience and persistence are essential.

For the percipient, the next step after relaxation is to hold an image in the mind of a blank TV screen or a blank movie screen. At the moment the sender is trying to pulse out an image, the percipient should give the unconscious mind a silent order with as little mental exertion as possible . . . "I want the picture presented to my consciousness. What is the image? Give it to me now. Give me the answer now." Visualize turning on the mental TV set and seeing the correct image.

The ability to relax is important in tapping any psi channel. Dr. John Mihalasky, for instance, stresses it when speaking to management executives, think-tank groups and engineers about ways to pull in precognitive information to assist in good decision making. A professor at Newark College of Engineering, Mihalasky along with Douglas Dean has correlated high scoring of company residents on precognition tests with the success of their firms. From their extensive research it would seem that psi as an applied science is hardly new. It's been used quietly but successfully by people at the top for a long time.

11

Group Telepathy Development Techniques

Whatever else telepathy may be, it is a link between one mind and another. Telepathy is a connection. And naturally many people find it most rewarding to try to develop and understand psychic talents with a group of friends. Include only those who are harmonious and comfortable with one another. Try to meet regularly and remember that the longer you practice together, the better you should become, If possible, have one or two people in the group who have demonstrated some psi talent. Keep the atmosphere friendly and informal. You're not setting up a contest or a chemistry experiment. You're embarking on an exploration. Any trip brings new experiences, sometimes new insights, and once in a while a discovery. In a group excursion into telepathy you may discover something about yourselves—something about all of us.

A teleflasher can be used with some of these informal group psi experiments and development techniques, although it is not an essential. To start your group off, familiarize them with the basics of telepathic sending and receiving. (Sēe pages 128-29.) Run through some of the tele-sets to help everyone get the feel of the process. Let each have a few turns at sending. Once settled into the basics, you're set for the experiments particularly designed for groups. (If you're without an interested group, these ideas may be tried with only one other person or in some cases turned into party games.)

Exploring Token Objects

In this experiment, inanimate objects act as a sort of link to the sender's mind. They afford a way of tuning in to his conscious memories. The sender puts some small personal belonging—a ring, watch, pin, pen—on the teleflasher or he may just hold it in his hands. Whatever, be sure it is not seen by the rest of the group. Begin sending. Concentrate on the object, let it fill your consciousness, immerse yourself in the shape and the associations of your object.

- Group members try to pick up both the object and some impressions associated with it. For instance, if a wedding ring is the focus of attention, receivers may see images of a church, a season of the year, a celebration or festival.

Each receiver can write down impressions as they occur to him and read them all out at the end of a session. Many development groups, however, find it helps if each person simply calls out impressions as they come.

Don't hurry the receivers. Let the group continue as long as they feel something interesting is happening. They need not necessarily come up with the correct name of the object—the cluster of associations is often more interesting and more meaningful than actually hitting on *ring* or *tie clasp*.

Sometimes rather startling associations pop into a receiver's mind—events or emotions connected with the object that the sender is not consciously thinking about—information filed away in his memory. When an heirloom is used, receivers may pick up information associated with previous owners. On rare occasions, correct impressions of people and places unknown to the sender may come through. If a particularly vivid and insistent image appears that means nothing to the sender, he might later check to see if it portrays any important happening in the life of the person who previously owned the object.

As a variation, put a flasher in the middle of the group with a blue color on it. Pass the token object around. In this case, of course, everyone knows what the object is; people are trying for associations, for events linked with the token. Let each person hold it as he stares into the pulsing light attempting to gain some impressions. This sort of reading of a token object by a psychic is called psychometry. The object itself seems to be a focus or recorder of information that can, under certain circumstances, be activated and played back by the human mind. It's as if thoughts seem to cluster about an object. As yet no one knows how much information can be stored and reactivated. Perhaps your group can bring forth some understanding of this unknown.

Telepathic Tracking

The sender concentrates on a person known to him but unknown to the group. The sender writes that person's name with a black felt marker on a piece of paper, and places it on the teleflasher. A photograph or object belonging to that person may also be used.

Receivers, since they do not know the person, will not be expected to get his name. But how close do they come to describing the personality, character, history of the unknown individual? As in the preceding experiment, very strong images may occasionally be received that do not mean anything to the sender. Try to check these out. See if they do apply.

Receivers should recount their impressions no matter how ridiculous or beside the point they may seem to the logical mind. One receiver persistently "saw" a woman walking down a path with a lion. It seemed too absurd to mention. Later he discovered that the woman had been married for thirty-five years to a man named Leo.

Again, call out impressions as you go or note them down to report at the end. Keep going as long as the majority feels actively involved.

Mind Linking

Esoteric and occult circles have traditionally held that psychic powers can be greatly enhanced in a group, just as multiple batteries properly connected produce more power than a single one. It is said that a sort of psychic power circuit can be achieved when all minds move in harmony with each other.

To test out this idea with your group, place the flasher in the middle of the room and have the entire group pulse out the same image to a single receiver in another room. Start with a number or other image to be sure everyone's visualizing the same things. Once the group feels in harmony, send anything—images, words, scenes. Put an appropriate picture or token object on the flasher. Or simply cover the flasher with colored paper—blue is one of the best colors—and use it as a focal point to help each member pulse his thoughts in rhythm with the whole.

If the group is teleflashing a picture or a reproduction of a painting, make it a vivid scene—something with outstanding details and a strong emotional theme. Emotion adds power to any telegraphic message.

After the group has teleflashed a picture to the receiver for sixty seconds or so, mix the target in with two very different pictures. Call the receiver back into the room. Show him the three pictures and ask him to select the one that matches his telepathic impressions most clearly.

If the receiver immediately spots the right picture, your group has a good psi current flowing. If the receiver picks the wrong picture, try to discover from his telepathic impressions which details have gotten confused in the sending and attempt to correct this the next time you teleflash this picture.

In exploring the group mind, see if you can determine who receives best from the group. Try to find out which members boost the group's sending power the most. Who is absent when power lags? Who is present when messages pulse clearly? Eventually, by having group senders and group receivers practice what they do best, you may work up a powerful group-communication system.

For a variation, divide the group into pairs of senders and receivers, preferably pairing people who've shown good rapport with each other. Each sender pulses a *different* picture to her or his receiver-partner. Each receiver tries to draw an impression of what is being sent. It's interesting that with a variety of pictures involved, a receiver generally picks up the picture meant for her or him and not the one intended for another receiver. In these experiments you'll soon discover that some people find it infinitely easier to lock telepathically onto a complex picture/thought, while others do much better on a simple shape.

This sort of experimenting helps show you that telepathy can be selective. A human receiver, just like a radio receiver, can apparently tune to different channels. In this vein, you may have noticed in other experiments a problem similar to the sliding effect on FM radio reception when you slide off the desired band and pick up other stations. Telepathic thought pollution most generally occurs when there is one sender and a number of receivers. You may find that you are consistently coming up with a wrong impression or image that is held by another receiver. You are getting his thoughts instead of the sender's. People claim it helps to put an imaginary circle around yourself and state that only the sender's communiqué will get through it. If you find this happening often with another receiver, you may have uncovered a telepathic twin, a person with whom you have natural psi rapport.

Kinetic Telepathy

Can you control another person's movements telepathically?

Scientific tests indicate that some people can. In the Soviet Union, ten objects were placed at random around a laboratory. A good telepathic receiver was locked into this insulated room. Then, from a distance, a strong sender, while watching his receiver on closed-circuit TV, attempted to direct him mentally to the target object, much as a missile is guided by remote control. In another experiment conducted decades ago in Holland, scientists attempted to telepathically influence a psychic to place chess pieces on selected squares of a chess board. Both the Soviet and the Dutch scientists succeeded in commanding action by telepathy. There have been many other such successful tests—most of which, however, required well-honed psychics. Your group can begin to train themselves in kinetic telepathy by playing some simple games.

Number the sides of a bridge table: one, two, three, four. You will try to telepathically command a receiver who is circling the table to stop before a specific side. Choose the target side while the receiver is out of the room. When he returns, blindfold him or just ask him to keep his eyes shut, then spin him around two or three times. Start him at side one of the table and have him begin to walk around it. The receiver should circle the table once, guiding himself if necessary by touching the edge of the table. When he arrives at side one again, begin pulsing your kinetic telepathic commands. The group gazes at the receiver and silently, mentally, forcefully, wills him to "go forward, forward," or to "stop! stop!" All senders should try to feel the forward motion or pulling back in their own muscles as they communicate. Kinetic telepathy takes a little getting used to. But some people who have trouble picking up telepathic images seem to be able to tune more easily to the kinetic impulse.

Sometimes the desired movement comes to a receiver in picture form. But most say they seem to feel a force propelling them forward or pulling them back, rather like the feeling of a slight undertow in the ocean.

Eventually try guiding motions generally. Mentally command a receiver to sway right, left, forward, or back while standing still. Have him walk and turn left, turn right, or raise one arm or the other, squat down, reach upward. With the whole group sending, try guiding a receiver to a specific spot in the room. Let him take his time. Try to correct any wrong turns in his course. Have him call out when he feels he's arrived at the chosen spot. You might try guiding him toward a hidden ashtray or other object. (This could be a prize if you're playing this as a game.)

Though often investigated in Europe, kinetic telepathy has been generally ignored in the United States. See if your group can help close this gap.

Telepathic Action Images

Once your group feels at home with kinetic telepathy, try flashing out action images.

The sender chooses an action—such as swimming, climbing a wall, dancing, galloping along on a horse, throwing a ball. He may use a picture, if he wishes, and start imaging, pulsing out his action. The sender should try to feel the action in his whole body as though he were actually performing it.

In one group a woman imagined herself skating, hands clasped behind her back. One receiver said he felt like rolling from side to side, another kept leaning right, then left. A third member "saw" a bright, colorful, fast-moving skating scene from above. It's intriguing to see just how an idea comes through to different people.

Psychic Clock

As a change of pace, your group might play Psychic Clock. Learning to tell time telepathically in this competitive game could help sharpen your telepathic rapport with a specific individual.

Divide into sending and receiving pairs. All senders gather around the flasher with receivers scattered about the room, or perhaps grouped in another room. Using a spinner or other means, senders choose a time and position the hands of the clockface on the flasher. (See page 130-31 for clock construction and randomizing procedure.) Each tries to send the *correct angle* to his particular receiver. Receivers note down the time they pick up.

The scoring for Psychic Clock is similar to the point system in a British parapsychology experiment in which a clockface was used. Score twelve points if the exact time gets through telepathically. Score six points for a mirror image—for example, three instead of nine, if nine is the target number. Score four points if a receiver gets the hour on either side of the target time—if he gets eight, for instance instead of the target number nine. If a receiver is consistently an hour off, he should wait longer until the correct angle stabilizes in his mind.

After a few rounds, switch and have senders become receivers. It is not known as yet why people seem to be more successful telepathically with one individual than another. Perhaps it is something physical, just as we have different blood types; or perhaps it has to do with emotional and psychological makeup.

It is known that childhood friends and members of a family seem to have an enhanced telepathic hookup. And it also seems that people may be eased into a telepathic communication if they practice together and establish a warm rapport. You can have fun with Psychic Clock as you attempt to locate a telepathic twin.

You can try Psychic Clock with two teleflashers. Senders use one. Receivers gather around the other teleflasher, using it to focus concentration.

Photoflash

Some psychics maintain that there is a sort of psi connection between a person and his or her photo. One group of English scientists claim that they found that when a light flashed on a man's photograph and a group tried to communicate this telepathically, the man, who was thousands of miles away, registered a strong physiological change on monitoring machines—at the exact time the light flashed on his picture.

Can you tell when someone is thinking about you, aiming a powerful thought at you?

You can test this out with your group. Have one person leave the room and lie down in a comfortable position. He should have a watch or clock and paper and pencil. Put his or her photo on the teleflasher, but have the teleflasher light off. At random times throughout an eight-minute segment, turn on the flasher and have everyone concentrate on the pulsing photo for one or two minutes. Note the times. See if the receiver can determine at which minute the light is flashing on his photo and the group is aiming their thought at him.

Telepathic TV

This is a classic telepathic experiment. You can try Telepathic TV with two—or two million—people. Tell the members of your group that you're going to send them a mental picture at nine o'clock sharp for the next three nights. You will transmit for exactly five minutes on the teleflasher. You want to see how many of them can mentally grasp your thought. (If you're a night owl, try sending around midnight or the midpoint in the hours of darkness on the particular night.) At first, you and your friends might decide to use a tele-set: numbers, letters or images. Choose the target randomly.

When you next meet, each person brings slips of paper with the images he received each night. Check them out. You may find that some people are being precognitive—i.e., looking into the future and always picking on Monday night the image you send on Tuesday night. This happened in a classic telepathy test in London. So try to keep track of all guesses over a period of time. (You might also find someone with retrocognition—i.e., telepathically seeing the past, picking up consistently on Tuesday night the image sent on Monday.)

Eventually, try sending a picture of any object or scene and see what impressions your receiving stations pick up out of the mental airwaves. If you want to be more scientific about checking the power of your mental broadcasting, have receivers write the image or the impressions they receive on a postcard and mail it to you as soon as possible. After teleflashing, mail yourself or someone else a card on which you've noted your broadcast. The postmark gives dated evidence that cannot be changed at a later time. (Don't use letters, the postmark is on the envelope, not the notations inside.)

These are just a few ideas for informal experiments to prime the group pump. Once you and your friends get moving, you'll be able to design your own experiments, following this trail and that, in the endlessly fascinating realm of mind.

A word of caution: Be as imaginative as you like, but don't do anything that would harm anyone or abrogate another person's will. If you've demonstrated the reality of psi, it might be reasonable to listen to those who've known and used such powers through the millennia. All warn against using this ability to harm or to violate another's will, even if "it's for his own good." To put it in other than high-minded terms, to refrain from walking out of a third-story window is not noble, it's sensible. It may be that the mind works on laws as definitive as those of gravity and if you break a "law," though it may take longer than plummeting from a window, you'll eventually be brought up hard.

Remember as you get together with your friends, the key to development is regular practice and the steady building of rapport. If the group is serious, read some of the books and journals listed on pages 297-98. You may not become a collection of famous psychics, but everyone should develop a greater awareness of the subtle currents of thought and feeling running through everyday life.

12

Genuine Games with a Psychic Twist

Anyone at all—both those experienced with psi and newcomers to the art of telepathy—can play these games. You don't have to be telepathic to score. The winning odds in each game have been carefully calculated on the basis of mathematical probabilities, so that everyone stands a chance of winning. But . . . games are designed to especially reward the good telepathic sender and the good telepathic receiver. You can use your psychic ability to beat the laws of probability, break the bank, or win the jackpot. Of all the teleflashing experiments, we probably had the most fun when a hard-core group of five, augmented by others from time to time, spent many weekends working out the games. After all, they say your work should be play.

The games have been set up to play with a teleflasher to help enhance telepathic transmission. However, they can certainly be played without the flashing light, if senders don't feel they need an assist to help concentrate and power their thoughts. For some games you'll need a deck of playing cards or poker chips and pads of paper. The rest of the equipment—flasher, symbols, spinner, or dice—is the same as used in the earlier experiments.

Playing tips

It may be helpful, not to mention sporting, before plunging into a game and plunking down bets to familiarize new players with the teleflasher and the general method of communicating. A brief demonstration is in order if players have had no experience with telepathy. Emphasize that the flasher makes mental contact easier. (See page 126 ff.)

Come for the filter...

A PRODUCT OF
Lorillard

KENT

WITH
THE FAMOUS MICRONITE FILTER

DELUXE LENGTH

© Lorillard 1975

...you'll stay for the taste.

DELUXE LENGTH

K·E·N·T
WITH THE FAMOUS MICRONITE FILTER

A lot of good taste that comes easy through the Micronite filter.

18 mg. "tar," 1.2 mg. nicotine av. per cigarette, FTC Report Oct. '74.

Position the teleflasher so receivers can't see material being sent or the spinner or dice. You might set up a piece of cardboard as a shield. Check the lighting of the room to be sure the teleflashed images and colors do not reflect on the ceiling or elsewhere. If a sender wears glasses, be particularly sure reflections can't be seen in them.

Receivers may sit comfortably anywhere they choose or may even lie down as an aid to relaxation during transmission. Let each person do whatever seems to work best for him or her.

Keep the atmosphere relaxed, *not* formal or experimental. And may the best telepathist win!

Games as Fund-Raisers

For groups looking for ways to raise money to finance psi research projects, some of the following games are good fund-raisers to include as part of a psychic fair or psychic ball or other function to which the general public is invited. The games are designed to be played with small groups of up to ten or so people, rather than with a throng. A different booth or area can be set up for each type of game—one for bingo, one for rummy, and so forth, so that a large number of people can be divided up and can take turns at each type of game. For a public event on a psychic theme, such as a psychic fair, the various games may also serve as a possible way of providing strangers to ESP with a subjective psi experience and as a way of getting them generally interested in the field. Each player chips in a certain amount of money to play each game. The prizes for winning players can be books about ESP, donated prizes, or small cash jackpots.

Psychic Roulette

Use your psychic ability to beat the bank and the laws of probability. In Psychic Roulette, you bet according to how powerfully you feel that you have received a telepathic impression from the sender. (All betting games can be played for small stakes or simply for points.)

Rules of Play:

1. Use individual pads of paper for players to note bets and have poker chips on hand (or substitute pennies, nickels, etc.).
2. Psychic Roulette Chip Values
   Red Chips   = 25¢

Blue Chips	=	5¢
Yellow Chips	=	2¢
White Chips	=	1¢

3.   Each player receives or, if you are playing for money, buys from the Bank:

2 Red Chips	=	50¢
7 Blue Chips	=	35¢
5 Yellow Chips	=	10¢
2 White Chips	=	5¢

$1.00

4.   Players rotate as sender, each teleflashing three times.

5.   Play with one tele-set, for instance, letters. The sender uses dice or a spinner to determine an image, and a blue or yellow color. Suppose the arrow stops at letter B and the color blue. Place blue paper and the Letter B on the flasher.

6.   The sender transmits color for a few seconds, then the letter. He wants to transmit strongly, because he is rewarded for every correct bet placed by the receivers.

7.   Start slowly. But as soon as possible, to keep the game moving, try not to teleflash for more than twenty to twenty-five seconds.

Betting

1.   A player draws a line through the center of his piece of paper, labeling one side ''Color'' and the other ''Image.'' After each transmission, he notes his choice of color and image and covers these with his bets. Conceal your choice from other players.

2.   Players must bet a minimum of two cents on a color and two cents on an image. If a receiver feels that telepathy is coming through loud and clear, he may up his bets to any amount. And he may bet on more than one image at a time if he wishes.

Winning

1.   Winning receivers always retain their wagers. For receiving the correct color, the Bank pays an amount equal to that wagered.

2.   For receiving a correct image, the Bank pays receivers four times the amount bet.

3.   All incorrect bets go to the Bank.

4.   The sender collects from the Bank one cent (or point) for each player who receives the right color and five cents (or points) for each player who receives the right image.

Switched-On Jackpot

Like many games, this one begins with players anteing up a pot. Everyone gets a hand in the action. But you'll need extrasensory betting power to bet on the right image and color and break the telepathic jackpot.

Rules of Play:
1. Draw a cross on a large sheet of paper dividing it into four squares. Label squares, *Yellow, Blue, Image,* and *Sender's Pot* respectively. Put this paper in the middle of the playing group.
2. Use either number, letter, or symbol tele-sets along with the colors blue and yellow. Rotate as sender, each teleflashing three times.
3. Players receive (or buy) a dollar's worth of chips from the Bank. (See Psychic Roulette for values of chips.)
4. The sender selects the winning color and image, puts them on the teleflasher and transmits for about twenty to twenty-five seconds.

Betting:
1. Before teleflashing begins, each receiver antes up: one white chip (1¢) on Yellow, one (1¢) on Blue and two (2¢) on Sender's Pot. He antes a blue chip (5¢) on the Image square.
2. After the teleflash, each player notes on a sheet of paper which color and image he received. Then the sender reveals the winners.

Winning:
1. Players with the correct color divide the chips in the corresponding Color square.
2. Players with the correct image divide the chips in the Image square. Any player who receives the correct image must win at least four blue chips (20¢). If there is less than that in the Image square for a winner, the Bank pays the difference.
3. The sender receives from Sender's Pot one white chip (1¢) for each player who gets the correct color at any time, and three (3¢) for each player who gets the correct image.
4. The Sender gets all chips in Sender's Pot when:
    a) Two or more players receive the correct color.
    b) All players receive the correct color.
5. Unclaimed chips remain to build up later jackpots.

Bazow Bingo!

Playing strategy combines with telepathic prowess to make Bazow Bingo! a fast-moving group game—with a psychic twist. Bazow, of course, comes from a lucky shake-out of the letters we used.

Rules of Play:
1.   Make up Bingo cards on paper or cardboard following the patterns in Figure 9.
2.   Each player receives or buys a Bazow Bingo Card from the Bank. Money paid to the Bank is the Jackpot.
3.   Before starting, each player takes a penny for use as a marker.
4.   Each player puts chips over the letters BAZOW on his card. These are free spaces.
5.   One person acts as sender for the entire game.
6.   The sender spins or rolls a die for the first number, either 4, 5, 7, or 8. (One on a die would stand for telenumber 4, two for telenumber 5, three for 7, and four for 8. If five or six on the die comes up, roll again.) The sender puts the correct number on the flasher and transmits telepathically for about fifteen seconds. Keep this game moving at a fairly fast clip.

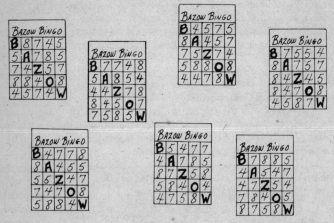

FIGURE 9.

Sample cards with randomized numbers for telepathic bingo.

7.   After a teleflash, each player puts his marker (penny) on the number he thinks was sent. The sender calls out the right number.

8.   If a player is wrong, he removes his marker.

9.   . Players who get the correct number remove their marker and put chips on two boxes containing the target number. Chips may be put on a number anywhere it appears on the Bingo Card. (With large groups or with experienced players, cover only a single number on the card at a time.)

10.   When a player gets five chips in a row (up and down, straight across, or the non-BAZOW diagonal) he has BAZOW BINGO!

Payoff:

The sender receives one-quarter of the Jackpot (if there is one). If he's gotten BAZOW BINGO! across in five or fewer teleflashes, he receives one-third. The rest goes to the Player-Receiver who got BAZOW BINGO!

Tele-Bingo

Here's a more difficult variation. There are no free spaces. The sender first telepathically sends one of the four numbers then one of the five letters (BAZOW), alternating numbers and letters throughout the game.

If you have a group of telepathic aces, play for a Full House, i.e., covering all the squares on the card.

Switched-On Rummy

A form of psychic rummy—the object is to discard all the cards in your hand.

Rules of Play:

1.   Each player is dealt five cards from a full deck of regular playing cards.

2.   One person remains sender for the entire game. He rolls a die. Odd numbers signify the Ace of Diamonds and even numbers the Ace of Clubs. Put the choice on the flasher—use cards from a separate deck or draw the symbols. Send about twenty seconds.

3.   If a receiver feels the black Ace of Clubs is being teleflashed, he discards a black card. If he feels it's a red Ace of Diamonds, he puts down a red card.

4.   The sender calls out the right color, and all players turn over their discarded cards. The cards that correctly match the telepathically sent color remain on the table. Wrong cards go back into their players' hands.

5.   Repeat until one player has discarded all his cards. The first player to do so wins the game.

Psychic Finesse

Can you silently, mentally transmit the image of a specific playing card to your partner? If you can learn to, you may be playing some interesting bridge games in the near future.

Rules of Play:

1.   Play with a fifty-two-card pack of playing cards, paper, and pencils.

2.   Psychic Finesse can be played with four, six, or eight people.

3.   Players pair off. Select eight cards—the Ace, King, Queen and Jack of Clubs and Diamonds—from a pack of playing cards.

4.   The senders—one member of each duo—shuffle the eight cards and place the top one on the flasher. Each sender simultaneously tries to mentally communicate the card to his partner, who acts as receiver.

5.   Senders do one round of five transmissions, flashing each card fifteen to twenty seconds.

6.   Reshuffle cards between each teleflash transmission.

7.   After each transmission, receivers indicate what card they think was sent. (Jot down the card, or have extra cards to hold up.)

Scoring:

1.   Correct suit scores   = 2 points
     Correct picture scores   = 4 points
     Correct suit and pictures = 6 points

2.   After one round of five teleflashes, the receiver of each pair becomes the sender for five more telepathic tries. At the end of the game the pair with the high score wins.

Telepathic Bridge

This game is bridge with an assist for those with a telepathic rapport. If there's any moment a bridge player would like an assist from his partner, it's on the opening lead. And that's just what Telepathic Bridge gives you.

Rules of Play:
1.   Play with a fifty-two-card deck of playing cards.
2.   Deal a bridge hand to the four players. Bid, following the usual rules of bridge.
3.   Once the bidding determines which is the defensive pair, the defender not making the opening lead leaves the table and becomes the sender on the teleflasher. (Position the flasher so that no one else can see what image is pulsing out.)
4.   The sender attempts to telepathically signal his partner one of five things: to lead Clubs, Diamonds, Hearts, Spades, or his longest and strongest suit.
5.   As teleflash material, the sender uses: four of Clubs; five of Diamonds; seven of Hearts; eight of Spades, to signify suit, and the King of Spades to signify longest and strongest suit.
6.   After fifteen seconds or so of teleflashing, resume normal play.
7.   If a receiver has no cards in the teleflashed suit, he will then lead according to his own judgment.

Flash Poker

In Flash Poker, hands are dealt telepathically by a sender to all receivers. The player who can pick up psychically the highest hand dealt, in the correct order of transmission, stands the highest chance of winning the poker pot. However, because the standard rules of betting for five-card poker are also used, the intriguing element of bluffing is retained.

Rules of Play:
1.   In this game you will choose the numbers one through twelve at random. Convert a spinner for this purpose, or number cards and shuffle them, or number pieces of paper, chips, or bottle caps to shake in a bag. (Dice will not work as the number one must have an equal chance of showing.)
2.   Determine in any way you wish, which player will be the first sender and which the first opening bettor. Thereafter, these positions rotate clockwise among players.
3.   Use the table below to determine which numbers signify each hand. The Suggested Poker Hands are quite distinctive from each other. Assemble the four hands from a pack of cards and give them to the sender.
4.   The sender determines which poker hand from the above table will be sent first. He places the previously assembled hand on the

Spinner Number	Rank and Designation of Poker Hands	Probable Frequency of Hand	Suggested Playing Cards in Poker Hands
12	Four of a Kind	1	Four 4's and one 7
10 or 11	Full House	2	Three 8's and two 3's
7, 8, 9	Flush	3	A,K,J, 5, and 2 of hearts or diamonds
1,2,3, 4,5,6	Straight	6	10,9,8 of spades, 7, 6 of clubs

flasher and pulses out the hand for about thirty seconds. He should concentrate on the hand as a whole and also on the individual cards.

5.   Each receiver writes down the name of the poker hand that comes to him telepathically. Players should not reveal their choices to other players.

6.   The sender removes the first hand. He repeats the entire procedure two more times, making a round of three hands dealt telepathically. (The same hand may, of course, come up more than once in a three-hand round.) The sender writes down the names of the poker hands in actual order of teleflashing, while each receiver writes down the hands in the order he telepathically received them.

Betting:

1.   Each player receives, or buys, one dollar's worth of chips from the Bank.

2.   Betting begins after all three hands have been flashed.

3.   Each bettor bets on the highest hand he thinks was dealt regardless of the order received. He circles this hand on his list of three.

4.   Betting proceeds according to the standard rules of betting for poker. For example, the opener begins the betting by placing three cents in the pot. He may, of course, check (if his telepathic reception was weak). The next player either (1) calls (i.e., matches all raises subsequent to his own previous bet) or (2) calls and then raises the previous player's bet or (3) drops out. And so on around the group. Betting continues until all players have called or dropped out, and there are no more raises. As in regular poker, it is perfectly legitimate to bluff.

Winning:

1.   After betting is completed, the sender calls out the name of the

highest-ranking hand he sent, as listed in descending order in the table.

2.   If only one player had the correct hand, he wins the pot provided he is still active, i.e., did not drop out of the betting.

3.   If more than one active player received the correct hand, the winner is the one who received the hand on the correct transmission—that is, on the first, second, or third hand in the order actually flashed. (Check the receivers' slips against the sender's record.) ·

4.   If there is still a tie, divide the pot equally.

5.   If no active player received the highest hand correctly, the entire pot goes to the Bank.

6.   If one player succeeded in bluffing out all other players, he, of course, does not have to show his slip and wins the pot whether he received the hand correctly or not.

7.   The sender gets two chips from the Bank for each player who correctly got any poker hand in the proper order whether or not the player stayed active in the game. As an added bonus, he also receives from the Bank ten chips for successfully sending telepathically four of a kind, and five chips for a full house received by anyone in the correct order.

Paranormal Parimutuel

Rules of Play:

1.   This game is played with a clockface. See page 130-31 for construction and randomizing procedure.

2.   Each player receives or buys one dollar's worth of chips.

3.   Players take turns as sender, each running one race.

4.   The sender randomly selects the number of the winning horse from twelve numbers. He turns the hour hand on the tele-clock to the selected win number (the minute hand always remains at twelve), transmits the number and *also the angle of the hands* for about thirty seconds.

5.   Each receiver notes the number he feels is the win horse. (Divide a sheet of paper into three columns: win, place, show.)

6.   The sender next picks and sends the number of the place horse and then the show horse. If the same number comes up more than once, try again to have different horses for win, place, and show.

7.   By placing chips on the three columns, players may bet on any

or all of the three horses. They may bet on more than one horse in any category.

8.   After all bets are down, the sender calls out the correct win, place, and show numbers.

Winning:

1.   If a player has picked the winning horse, the Bank pays ten times the amount wagered.

2.   If a player has picked a horse that places, i.e., comes first or second, the Bank pays *five times* the amount wagered.

3.   For a show horse—one that comes in first, second, or third— the Bank pays *three times* the wager.

4.   All wrong bets go to the Bank.

5.   The sender receives four chips from the Bank for each person who received the correct win number. He gets chips for each person who received the correct place number, and one chip for each person who received the correct show number.

Note: Paranormal Parimutuel can be played with a field of six horses instead of twelve. Use only the right-hand side of the tele-clock face. The sender rolls a die to pick a number from one to six. The Bank pays one-half the amounts noted above, but not less than one chip.

Bet Your Hunch

Practice in predicting horse-race winners might help improve your profits at the racetrack. Bet Your Hunch is played the same way as Paranormal Parimutuel—except there's no sender. This requires precognition similar to predicting the winners in a real-life horse race.

Rules of Play:

1.   Players put bets on the numbers they feel psychically will be the win, place, and show horses.

2.   *After* all bets are down, any one player spins or otherwise chooses three numbers in succession and calls out the actual win, place, and show horses.

Winning:

1.   Players who correctly predict the win number receive twelve

times their bet from the Bank.
2.   Place bets pay six times the amount wagered.
3.   Show bets pay four times the amount wagered.
    Extra Tip for horse-race games:
    To add to the enjoyment and perhaps to help add an extra clue in the telepathic transmission of winning horses, the twelve (or six) horses can be given names. Use any names that appeal to you—names of famous horses or even the names of people you know.

Psychic Detective

Could you use telepathy to tell who picked your pocket or pocketbook in a crowded bus or subway? The sender in this game plays the role of a witness who saw the pickpocket in the act. But he is afraid to finger the thief by speaking up out loud. The only way you can get your money back is by linking telepathically with the mind of the fearful witness.

Loot:

Each player forfeits a penny. This is the pickpocket's loot and is put aside until the end of the game.

The Plot:

1.   Have as many slips of paper as there are players. On one slip write WITNESS, on another write PICKPOCKET. Fold all slips. Shuffle the unmarked and the marked pieces together and have each player draw one.
2.   The player receiving the paper marked WITNESS declares himself to be the sender. The pickpocket must not reveal his identity in any way.
3.   All players write their names on the slips they chose and hand them to the sender-witness so he learns who the pickpocket is. Remember, the sender-witness is a timid soul. The only way he can tip off the victims is by thinking hard about the pickpocket.

Solving the Crime:

1.   The witness puts the pickpocket's name (written on a slip of paper) or his photograph on the flasher. (If you wish, each player can be assigned a number or letter beforehand.) The sender tries to broadcast the pickpocket's name for a minute or so, to all receivers.

2. To avoid drawing any suspicion on himself, the pickpocket must be sure to act like all other receivers.

3. At the end of the teleflash, each player jots down the name of the person he thinks picked his pocket.

Winning:

1. Players who identify the pickpocket get their stolen loot back.

2. If at least one player is correct, the sender gets his penny back.

3. The pickpocket naturally keeps the money belonging to all players who were not able to use their psychic powers to catch a thief.

Something Fishy

It's often said that when you do something wrong, you can't help thinking about it. The murderer returns to the scene, the cat burglar contemplates his cache of gems, the embezzling bookkeeper can't help thinking about his ledger. In this game, two players have done Something Fishy. Other players try to tune in on a guilty conscience.

Rules of Play:

1. Play with Fish and Clover Telesymbols, paper, and pencils.

2. Have as many slips of paper as there are players. Mark two slips with an X; fold and shuffle with the unmarked papers and have each player draw one slip. X marks the guilty persons. The two culprits must be careful not to reveal themselves in any way to each other or to the rest of the group. All players retain their slips of paper.

3. In turn, every player goes to the teleflasher and transmits about thirty seconds. Guilty players must send telepathically the Fish telesymbol—something is "fishy." Innocent players send the Four Leaf Clover, signaling that they are lucky enough to have a clear conscience.

4. After each transmission, players note down whether or not they think there is Something Fishy about the sender.

5. After all have sent, each declares which two players he felt had guilty thoughts. All players show their slips of paper, revealing the culprits. Points can be awarded to those who can psyche out guilt on the mental airwaves.

Across a Crowded Room

Can you switch on your ESP to draw someone across a crowded room to your side? In the game of Across a Crowded Room men and women try to attract each other telepathically. Players also try to tune in to those special vibrations to see if they can tell who is giving them psychic attention.

Rules of Play:

1.   Men and women separate into two groups. The men's group and the women's group take turns sending and receiving. To begin, one man leaves the room. He is the receiver. Each man in turn plays the receiver.

2.   Assign a number to each woman. Use dice to find out which woman will be the first sender.

3.   The sender puts in the teleflasher the name (written on a piece of paper) or a photograph of the man alone in the other room. She concentrates on him completely. She calls him mentally, over and over. She visualizes him coming to her.

4.   The rest of the group—both men and women—concentrate on the name of the woman sending, not on her male quarry.

5.   After a teleflash lasting a minute or so, the sender leaves the teleflasher and the receiver returns to the "crowded room." He must home in on and identify the woman he thinks called him telepathically.

6.   Keep score of the best psychic senders and also the players who can most often tell which woman or man in a group has psychic designs on them.

7.   Let the group decide the proper reward for the high scorers at the end of the evening. The best psychic senders may want to go on to try their attention-getting psi talents on waiters in restaurants. By and by psi may catch his eye.

Section Four

13

Energy Tracking

"The discovery of the energies associated with psychic events will be as important, if not more important than the discovery of atomic energy." So proclaimed Dr. Leonid L. Vasiliev, an internationally known Russian physiologist, holder of the Lenin prize and the father of Soviet parapsychology. It's a big statement and with it Vasiliev sounded the keynote of Communist psi research. They are hunting energies, searching for energy in PK, dowsing, Kirlian photography, psychic healing, telepathy, cosmobiology, hypnotism, even in miniature Cheops pyramids and perhaps in other less public research. The aim is to understand the laws of the energies involved in psi events, to control and use them. When we first became involved with Communist parapsychology almost a decade ago, the talk of energies sounded strange. In America the emphasis rested almost exclusively on the psychological and statistical approach to psi, often with the stated or unstated implication that psychic things lived wholly in the realm of mind or the immaterial, that they possessed no measurable link to the physical. Today that attitude has balanced out and Westerners are searching the energetic as well as the psychological elements of psi. The attitude has broadened for many reasons. The antithesis between mind and matter no longer seems as unbridgeable as it used to. And in part the search for energies itself has helped propel us into a new world view—or probably that should be a new *cosmic* view, for it seems that our connections are cosmic in proportion. Growing understanding of ourselves as beings of energies in a sea of energies is bringing a new concept of the nature of man, not man alienated, apart, a sort of stuttering of nature, but man connected, influenced and being influenced by everything about him from the grass beneath his feet to the planets above his head. Of course, it is a very venerable idea, the old mystic idea that all is one. It's beginning to get some hard scientific backing.

As we track energies in this section, the search sometimes acts like alternating current, following a known energy then reversing into the unknown. Researchers into psi and related fields are un-covering new, previously unimagined activities of known energies. At the same time a growing number of people are saying there is something else, another form of energy, officially, at least, undis-covered. This "other" energy is seen as very basic, all pervasive, and a link between mind and matter, unlike other energies partaking of both the mental and physical world.

Here again is a very ancient and a very modern idea. People have been claiming to discover this "something else" with almost monotonous regularity through history. If you were investigating this supposed force in ancient China, you would speak of *Ch'i*, the postulated energetic basis of acupuncture. If you were experiment-ing today in Prague, you would probably say that you were working with psychotronic energy, exploring the fifth physical interaction.

A genealogical chart including early practitioners and a few latter-day discoverers might read:

Ch'i	Anton Mesmer
Prana	Baron Karl von Reichenbach
Mana	Professor Blondlot
	L. E. Eeman
Vital Fluid	Dr. Wilhelm Reich
Universal Fluid	George de la Warr
Odic Force	Eloptic Energy
N-Rays	Di-electric Bio-
X-Force	Cosmic Energy
Orgone Energy	Psychotronic Energy
Prephysical energy	and Bioplasma
ancient Chinese	T. Galen Hieronymous
ancient Hindus	
Pacific civilization and,	Dr. Oscar Brunler
in part, ancient Europe	various Czech and Soviet
alchemists	researchers

These are just a few of the more illustrious ancestors. The energy had been discovered, christened, and nurtured by a great many others. If you're serious about working with energies, you might try to fill in some of the other names, learn what you can about cousins and lines of descent. With a little selective breeding of your own you might wind up with a progeny possessing all the most desirable family traits.

To help recognize this energy of a thousand names, if it should appear, some of the commonly agreed-upon features include:

- It permeates all things to a greater or lesser degree.
- It accompanies sunlight and probably other forms of light.
- It has properties similar to known forms of energy but is a distinct energy. It accompanies magnetism but also appears separately.
- It is polarized and can be reflected by mirrors.
- It emanates from the human body and has been particularly noted at the fingertips and the eyes.
- It can heal or, used negatively, can harm living creatures.
- It can be conducted by such things as copper wires and silk threads.
- It can be stored in inanimate materials such as water, wood, and even stone.
- It can fluctuate with cosmic and weather conditions.
- It can be controlled by mind.
- It can cause things to happen at a distance and enters into the dynamics of many paranormal phenomena.

This other energy sounds as if it could be the one that moved Vasiliev, usually a cautious scientist, to make such a strong statement. More important than atomic energy? It's not hard to get an inkling of what he meant when you remember that this supposed energy is claimed to be both cosmic and at the same time intensely personal, something that all of us possess yet few have learned to control consciously. Those who have supposedly learned, such as the great gurus, healers, PK psychics, are able to work "miracles."

Switching to the nonpersonal pulse of this force, it's interesting that the new name for it, surfacing today in America, is "free energy." "Free energy" brings kaleidoscoping thoughts of energy crisis, crop failures, pollution problems. Might there be some solutions in the realm of that often-discovered "other" energy for the tightening problems of today? Might this generation, pressed by necessity, bring *mana*, odic force, N-Rays into the mainstream?

It's still a very open question. Anybody can join the hunt. Is there or isn't there "something else"? If there is, who knows—you might be the one to bring home the bacon—which is one name it hasn't had.

PK—A Force on the Loose?

In the early seventies, a young woman Intourist guide in Leningrad sat in a hotel dining room, busily translating for two Americans who were entertaining a Russian couple. Suddenly the guide let out a yelp of alarm. A piece of bread was inching its way slowly but surely across the table under its own steam. The young woman hadn't before experienced the PK feats of her countrywoman, Nina Kulagina (Nelya Mikhailova). The Americans, Elsie and Bill Sechrist, were a lot more accustomed to paranormal events. They had a long-time association with the Edgar Cayce Foundation and Elsie had worked directly with the great psychic.

As the guide discovered, there seems to be a force on the loose, one that first alarms, then amuses, then quickly begins to fascinate. It's a force that moves things from afar, that causes forks and precision-built screwdrivers to bend like soft wax, a force that apparently allows people to interfere at a distance with mechanical and electrical equipment and to alter magnetic tape. If there is a cycle in the appearance of psychic talents, PK—often called mind over matter—would seem to be in top swing. More and more people are surfacing seemingly with some PK ability. A growing number in America and Russia claim they are training themselves to generate and direct the force.

Though they certainly are not the only ones with ability, right now two people, Nina Kulagina and Uri Geller, a young Israeli, hold a special place in PK research. Both are particularly talented, both have drawn the interest and research of high-level experts in the pure sciences.

What good is it to bend forks and screwdrivers, as Geller does? Apart from amusement, why pass the bread by willing it across the table? The factor that has drawn a blue-ribbon roster of scientists both in public and behind the scenes to puzzle over Kulagina and Geller is the idea of an energy. As many point out, if there is a force that can interfere with equipment, our technologically nurtured society had better find out about it. Is it another form of energy? Can we learn to control machines at a distance with it? What does it tell us about the connection of mind and matter or about healing?

PK investigation has come into its own with the new emphasis on psi energies. There's too much to it to condense into the space allotted in this handbook. Regrettably, even accounts of the major talents must be foregone. To toss out in capsule form the unfolding story of Uri Geller would make for a totally unbelievable paragraph. Yet Geller has demonstrated his ability at bona fide research labs such people as Dr. Edgar Mitchell and Dr. Andre Puharich, neurologist, inventor and long-experienced psi researcher. He is the subject of ongoing research by physicists Dr. Harold Puthoff and Russell Targ at Stanford Research Institute. Geller is apparently a genuine talent.

Since we last wrote about Kulagina (see *PDBIC* for lengthy story) many Westerners have watched her work—Dr. Thelma Moss, Dr. Herbert Puryear, Dr. Montague Ullman, Dr. William Tiller, to name just a few. A few interesting items about her influence on organic matter—on people—have come to light. In scientific tests in Leningrad, Kulagina supposedly was able to control the heart of a frog, make it beat faster or slower and finally to stop it on command. Electrocardiagraph recording showed a reaction similar to that of an electric shock just before the heart stopped. Soviet researchers also claim that she can influence the hearts of people—she once did this at a medical institute, providing quite an interesting first-person experience for the hostile skeptic. She can cause blisters to appear, then disappear on her own skin—she can also bring out blisters on someone else in the room at a distance.

In spring, 1973, Benson Herbert, director of the Paraphysical Laboratory, after completing regular scientific tests with Kulagina put his arm at the mercy of her PK. He had tried this on a previous occasion, experiencing a sensation of extreme heat. This time he asked Mrs. Kulagina not to let go no matter how he complained. She held his arm lightly above the wrist. Herbert began to feel a strong heat. "I am aware, of course, that suggestion alone is capable of producing such effects, including red marks on the skin; however, ample experimental evidence exists that in the case of Madame Kulagina, the phenomenon is objective . . . it felt like acute physical pain, and I had to clench my teeth and beat my forehead with my free hand in order to continue with the experiment." After about five minutes, Herbert collapsed on a couch and Kulagina let go.

Shortly afterwards, Herbert remarks he heard a groan and looked up. Kulagina held a small flat camera against the arm of Manfred Cassirer, Herbert's associate, her hand touching only the camera and not his skin. "Cassirer complained of the heat and asked to be released after a few seconds."

Mrs. Kulagina has control of her force and can also heal. Her demonstration for Herbert points out the danger of a person attempting to heal who has not gained good control of such an energy. Fortunately, Kulagina only produces this reverse healing for scientific demonstration. As one Russian researcher remarked, she is regarded almost as a heroine by some, for she has continued to put herself at the disposal of science at great physical cost to herself because she believes it is her duty to do all she can to elucidate the dynamics of her ability.

Soviet investigators have pursued organic PK to concoct unusual experiments with biogenerators. Two frogs' hearts, surgically removed, are put into solution to keep them alive. Drs. S. Sarychev and A. Nikandrov in repeated tests set up two metal hemispherical mirrors, reflecting each other. Then the hearts were put so that one was in the focus of one sphere and one in the other mirror. Electrocardiographs measured heartbeats. Soon the stronger heart put the weaker under its control, according to Soviet reports. There is an organic PK, or biocommunication, with one heart gaining beats, the other growing weaker. Apparently a number of Soviet scientists are exploring this sort of basic organic influence at a distance. With regard to the mirror arrangement, Russian researchers wonder if people placed in similar surroundings would more easily influence each other.

A PK Training Method

Dr. V. Pushkin of the Psychology Institute of the Moscow Pedagogical Institute, Dr. V. Adamenko, and Edward Naumov have all worked on training people to do PK. One of Pushkin's most apt students, Boris Yermolayev, can supposedly cause a book to hang on its own in the air. Alla Vinogradova, a Moscow child psychologist, is a successful trainee who has demonstrated her growing talent to many Americans. A variety of training ideas and insights have come from this work with Alla and others. Here are some of them if you want to try your own hand at PK.

Try to relax beforehand, perhaps do a simple relaxation exercise. Then begin to build up a strong feeling that you can and will move the object. While working, an air of sharp expectancy helps.

Begin with light, easily movable objects—something that rolls. The Russians often use light metal cigar containers. A cigarette will do, pingpong balls, even a lipstick top.

Become familiar with the objects, try various kinds, pick the one you like best and stick with it for some days.

Put the object you want to move on a di-electric surface. The

Russians use a transparent plastic cube table. You can simply use a sheet of plexiglass or other plastic about an inch thick attached to short, three- or four-inch legs. The surface must be dry. And don't start off in damp, humid weather.

Your skin must be dry, too. Concentrate on sending energy down through your arms into your fingers. Sweep your hand back and forth above the object; keep trying. It took Alla a day of trying to begin to move objects, others take longer.

Ability is supposedly greatly enhanced if you work in bare feet and are grounded—i.e., have a wire or metal chain around your wrist that is connected to ground.

Trainees improve with practice. If you get movement, see if you can learn to control it, to start and stop an object, spin it around. Try heavier items and nonrollables such as wooden matchsticks, or move to regular surfaces such as wood tables. See if someone else can move an object once you've put your "charge" on it. A number of Americans have been able to move cigar cases after Alla had worked with them. She was also able to check their ability by holding her hand above the object.

What Alla and others in Russia and here have learned to do is a beginning. They are not working on the same level of energy or power as the naturals, Kulagina and Geller. But they are learning to control at least the electrical forces of the body and possibly more. Almost all observers including the Russian investigators remark that electrostatics are involved in Alla's brand of PK. Yet they all note, too, that she has trained herself to go beyond simple electrostatic force, something else comes into play. For instance, objects are repelled not attracted by her hands and she can sweep her hand over two identical objects moving only the one of her choice, then switch and move the other. Alla is apparently slowly learning to use some sort of force, perhaps you can, too.

How does it feel to do PK? Kulagina undergoes great stress and has developed serious medical problems from exercising her PK. Kulagina told Elsie Sechrist that she feels a strong energy like a prickling sensation begin to move up her spine to the base of the brain. She has also said that she knows when she is going to move an object because she feels pain and her blood pressure rises. One of the cardinal aims of PK training is to teach people to manipulate the force without undergoing the ravaging physical stress that hits Kulagina. Uri Geller, who seems to show no sign of undue stress, remarks that he feels like a channel, that he is a conduit through which the energy flows. In this, Geller sounds like many famous healers who say that they are like antennae, drawing in and channeling energy. Alla feels energy gathering in her solar plexus and sometimes in her brow.

In an interview in the magazine *Technika Molodyezi,* she remarked, "I think that many people could learn to do these experiments. It is necessary to control your thoughts and your body. Above all, you must believe in the possibility, and by this you may develop healing powers also. I feel all the energy of my body concentrating at one point, and I then direct this energy by volitional act into my fingertips." For a new Soviet theory on the forces behind PK see page 189 ff.

Experiments in Od

In 1851, Baron Karl von Reichenbach, a well-known German industrialist, physicist, chemist, and discoverer of creosote, published a series of articles entitled "The Od Force, Letters on a Newly Discovered Power in Nature" in the *Universal Gazette* of Augsburg. The articles detonated a "deep sensation" in Europe, which was precisely what the Baron wanted. He took this unusual route for a scientist, he said, to appeal to the German public against the injustice of professional academics who rejected certain of his findings without examining them, who simply used their "authority" rather than argument or proof to dismiss an important discovery he'd made.

"Pray, test this for yourself," Reichenbach urged over and over, outlining simple experiments. He later recorded that hundreds of thousands of the public did just that and supported his findings. What were multitudes of Germans and later French, English, and Americans seeking in lab and at-home experiments? A flaming, colorful, new form of energy—Odic force. Reichenbach claimed he had uncovered a distinct natural energy, which he christened Od after the ancient German deity Odin, signifying an all-pervading power.

Od streams forth in greater or lesser degree from everything, according to Reichenbach—from people, plants, metals, magnets, crystals, sunshine, moonlight. Like other forces in nature, Od is polarized. There is positive Od, yellow-reddish in color, and negative Od, blue in color. As in magnetism or electricity, unlike poles attract and like repel. Supposedly you are Od positive on the left side of your body and Od negative on the right. Positive Od directed to your left hand will feel lukewarm and vaguely unpleasant because like forces repel. Negative Od will feel cool and pleasing because unlikes attract. The reverse effect happens with the right hand. However, sensations on the left side seem much stronger than those on the right.

The only instrument Reichenbach possessed to detect his new energy was the human nervous system. He used sensitives. Yet he was no occultist. In his nineteenth-century world a center of gravity had shifted from the church and the scholastic community to come to rest in science, and Reichenbach was wholly a child of the new perspective. If the actions of Odic energy seemed reminiscent of the accounts of sorcerers, water diviners, old nurses' tales, so much the better. Such phenomena, Reichenbach remarked, could finally be shaken free of the obscurities of mysticism and superstition. They could be explained by natural laws and put to work to benefit society. Reichenbach truly stands as the father of the modern approach to those "energies associated with psychic events" that so intrigued Dr. Vasiliev.

In light of contemporary research, it may be that Reichenbach's so-called Odic force relates in some way to the recently discovered phenomenon of bioluminescence. Using supersensitive photomultipliers, scientists have discovered that all things, both living and nonliving, have a glow. (See page 72 ff.)

Sensitive people can both see and feel Od, according to Reichenbach. With a bit of practice these people serve well to unravel the workings of the energy. He was not a sensitive himself, which perhaps made him a more objective experimenter. However, sensitives "exist aplenty," said Reichenbach; about one person in three can learn to detect Od. His lengthy list of traits that may indicate sensitivity—dislike of yellow, desire always to sit in the aisle seat at a theater or at a table, light sleeping—can remind you of trying to choose one from column A and two from B. Probably the best way to determine if there are sensitives in your vicinity is to attempt Od experiments. Reichenbach did remark that his sensitives could see a nonluminous stream of energy pouring from the fingertips when in dim light they extended their arms and hands against a dark background. A lot of people today claim they see this effect. Any of them might be good candidates for an Od experiment.

Od Sensation

Do all experiments with the left hand. Instructions come from Reichenbach's findings in literally thousands of tests with hundreds of subjects. He generally repeated each test fifty to a hundred times.

Place a bar magnet crosswise over the corner of a table. Put the left hand two to six inches from one end and hold it there for some minutes. Then place your hand near the other pole. Can you detect any difference in sensation? The south pole (Od positive) should give the sensation of a lukewarm breath of air, unpleasant and becoming increasingly exhausting and noxious-feeling to the arm. The north pole (Od negative) gives a cool refreshing sensation.

If you do sense something, turn the magnet around randomly so you don't know which pole is which to determine if your sensation is more than suggestion. (Also scientists have found that some people can sense magnetism.)

But is it more than magnetism? Reichenbach's multitude of sensitives found Od always came along with magnetism; however, it also could be found on its own, they claimed, in nonmagnetic substances. Reichenbach used spars of mountain crystal, gypsum, positioned as the bar magnet. The end of the crystal that grew uppermost felt cool and pleasant to the sensitive left hand; the end that had been embedded in the earth wafted a lukewarm, unpleasant breath. An even more simple experiment involves running a copper wire thirty feet or so from one room to another. At random times the experimenter holds the end of the wire. The sensitive holding the other end tries to sense when Od is flowing, i.e., when a human hand is in contact with the wire.

Sun, Moon, and Water

The sensitive stands in the shade under a tree and extends a long glass tube or even a wooden stick into bright sunlight. The end of the tube in the sensitive's hand rather than feeling warm, as one might eventually expect from the sun, supposedly feels cool—negative Od is flowing with the sunlight. The reverse effect happens in moonlight. Test the same way at full moon. The glass or stick should feel warm and rather loathesome. A glass of water left in the moonlight will seem distasteful to a sensitive. Glasses of water can also be put for some time on Od poles of magnets and crystals. The negative pole produces a light, slightly acid, refreshing drink for the sensitive. The positive pole produces a drink that Reichenbach said could on occasion even cause severe nausea if completely quaffed by a highly sensitive person. Od, then, supposedly bubbles over and transmits to or transloads itself into other substances. Substances such as water are not changed chemically Reichenbach reports, they simply pick up a charge of Od, of identical polarity.

Seeing Od

Patience is mandatory, but apparently well worth it if you do succeed in seeing Od flaming spectacularly in a dark room. Reichenbach repeatedly cautioned that a totally dark room with no light seepage was necessary to cleanse perceptions so Od could be seen. A fine sensitive should begin to see something within an hour, more moderate talents in two, three, or even four hours. What do they see? Perhaps the major reason this famous chemist kept plugging in such an unorthodox field was that so many different people of the widest variety all reported seeing the same things.

You can use the bar magnet or crystal. Sensitives supposedly see a rising flame of light, smoking and sparkling, blue from the Od negative pole, and yellow-reddish from the positive. You can also point a horseshoe magnet upwards. Using one of a hundred-weight power, Reichenbach recorded it eventually lit a six-foot circle on the ceiling and the light column "was described as exceeding beautiful and delightful."

Reichenbach often ran a copper wire from sunlight into the darkroom. Sensitives saw light effects. If you want to try, attach a small piece of tinfoil, copper mesh or wool to the end of the wire in the sun. Eventually move it from sun to shade. Can anyone see or sense with the hand a change in the other end in the darkroom?

Other experiments in the dark room include striking crystal glass or ringing a bell; examining metals or a lump of coal; conducting Od through such materials as glass, copper, silk; observing chemical reactions, solution, dissolution, decomposition—or as Reichenbach sometimes did, uncorking a bottle of champagne and un-stoppering a vial of iodine.

All of the above supposedly give light effects. Don't tell your sensitive what to expect. If you are the sensitive, note down reactions and eventually check them against Reichenbach's notes. If you see an Odic flame, try deflecting it, crossing it with another flare, or try blowing on it.

Plants and People

Take a blooming plant into your darkroom. Reichenbach reports one famous botanist, a moderate sensitive, after a time in the dark suddenly exclaimed as if terrified, "It's a blue gloxinia!" He was right. At first a faint gray mist appears, then the light grows brighter, with the plant's generative organs and flowers eventually shining most brilliantly. People can also be seen, first as a gray luminosity, then shining more brightly with their right negative sides of bluish cast and the left of reddish cast. Run your left hand over the left side of a sensitive or simply point your fingers or make passes in the air. A vaguely unpleasant warm sensation supposedly occurs. At least the sensitive should be able to determine when you are pointing at him. Do this in the dark or in the light behind the person's back and try it at various distances, keeping in a straight line.

Od and Direction

Part of the supposed energy effect in pyramids seems to be related to the structure's orientation. (See pages 195-96.) A discovery of Reichenbach's may or may not have something to do with this. Examining the reddish or blue energy flaming from a magnet, good sensitives also claimed to see within the light all the colors of the spectrum in proper order, though somewhat muted by the predominant color of the pole. Reichenbach placed a pointed cap of iron atop a bar magnet. (The magnet measured a square inch at the end.) The flare grew more slender, brighter, but still the spectrum of color persisted. He placed a cap with four vertical teeth, one at each corner, atop the magnet and at last was able to separate the colors. Blue flared from one tooth, yellow, red, and whitish-gray from the others. When he turned the magnet, rather than following the teeth the colors attached to the teeth in the new position; in other words, blue always shone to the north, yellow to the west, red to the south and whitish-gray to the east. Experimenting with an electromagnetic mock-up of the globe, Reichenbach found the same effect and also colors attached to other compass points, such as green for northwest. Orientation, then, very definitely seemes to affect the behavior of Od.

How would Od behave in a properly oriented pyramidical structure? If you have a fine sensitive handy, it would make an interesting experiment.

Although many experimenters seemingly corroborated Reichenbach's observations, the world found little use for Od detected by sensitives; people were too dazzled with the marvels of other energies that flowered into electric power, X-ray, radio. Some of the Baron's mountainous data may be explained by known effects today. Other parts of his labyrinthine studies can perhaps still provide clues to that "other" energy. Looking backward, it's easy to see his work as the prototype for many later investigations, such as those of Blondlot and Baraduc in France, Wendler in Germany, Eeman in England, to cite just a few, investigations that metamorphosed into today's accelerating hunt for a form of energy that interacts in special, so-called psychic, ways with human beings. If you're interested in the genealogy of the hunt and some of the experiments used along the way, a paper presented by Dr. Redjak and Engineer Drbal at the 1970 Prague Psychotronic Conference is a good résumé: "From Mesmer to the Fifth Physical Interaction and Biological Plasma," *Journal of Paraphysics*, No. 1, 1971.

Many of Baron von Reichenbach's observations fall into psychic areas—the aura, healing, to name the obvious ones. Reichenbach believed he'd explained the healing effect of magnetic passes made famous by Mesmer. Magnets would work equally well, he said, because the force transmitted was really Od.

So-called magnetic passes are being investigated by the psychotronic research group so ably led by Dr. Zdenek Rejdak. What Reichenbach would call Od, the Czechs now contemplate in terms related to bioplasma. Hypnotism can be induced by verbal and nonverbal suggestions. It will, however, only be completely understood when also considered as an energy transfer, according to some of the Czech researchers. (The American Dr. Leonard Ravitz from his researches also says that hypnosis might be considered an energy-field effect.) Passes involving a supposed interchange of bioplasma is a third method of hypnotic induction, they maintain. Vladimir Masopust, a psychotronic researcher specializing in this sort of hypnosis, claims that energy may be either transmitted or drawn from the subject by passes or by putting the hands on the body in circuitlike positions. In a sample experiment of magnetic induction with a Czech soldier, Masopust reports the soldier gained 340 grams while he himself lost 360 grams. He also reports heightened ESP—telepathy and clairvoyance—in the subject. Whether this differs in intensity from psi sometimes experienced in regular hypnosis remains to be seen.

Reichenbach also believed he'd solved the mysteries of dowsing when he found that the friction of moving water produced positive Od. He trained sensitives to rely on Odic sensation to detect underground water and identify hidden metals.

If you're interested in any of these fields or in the energies associated with psi or if you think you can sense Od, it might be a good idea to examine the foundation of research that the Baron built so painstakingly. His books can be found in some older libraries. You can also obtain reprints from Health Research, PO Box 70,

Mokelumne Hill, California 95245. His major work is *Physico-Physiological Researches on the Dynamics of Magnetism, Electricity, Heat, Light, Crystallization, and Chemism, in Their Relations to Vital Force.* Other books include *Reichenbach's Letters on Od & Magnetism. Somnambulism & Cramp.*

Dowsing

Today, almost a century and a half after Reichenbach, dowsing is beginning to emerge into the world of propriety. The US government commissioned a study of water dowsing by the Water Research Lab, College of Engineering of Utah State University. They reported positive results. The Marines successfully employed dowsing in Vietnam; for the first time in America a course in practical dowsing is being taught in an institute of higher education at Edison Community College in Fort Myers, Florida. Soviet geologists are rigorously studying and using dowsing as an adjunct to their profession, and major American companies are beginning to admit they've employed dowsers for years to locate such lost items as buried cables. Extensive, decades-long European experimental research in radiesthesia (a broad term covering all forms of dowsing) is finally beginning to be translated for the English-reading public. Dowsing in its many manifestations, from simple water locating to medical diagnosis to the far fringes of map dowsing at a distance, are of cardinal importance in the search for new forms of energy as well as the understanding of previously unanticipated effects of known energies. Dowsing, with its many interconnected facets, is so large that it seems to demand a book of its own and unfortunately we will have to omit more than a mention of it here.

Reichenbach decided that dowsing has to do with positive Od because he noted that his sensitives reported noxious, unpleasant sensations when they located underground water or minerals. Reports coming in from contemporary researchers tend to bear out the old Baron's observations as far as earth dowsing goes.

Evelyn Penrose, the famous Australian dowser, whom the government of British Columbia credited with helping to open up the province's mineral resources, maintained that she sometimes was overcome with a sickening, unhealthy feeling as she sensed underground deposits.

High-level investigations of noxious "soil radiations" carried out by doctors, physicists, and geologists have been going on for some time in Europe, particularly in the Germanic countries. Evidence suggests that certain dowsing zones (a place where the rod reacts to the earth) have deleterious effects on the health of plants, animals, and humans. Probably the best place to get at least a little data on this in English would be the American Society of Dowsers.

In Prague at the 1970 symposium of the Section for Research into Psychotronics, which is part of the Society for Applied Cybernetics, two Czech engineers, Frantisek and Jiri Boleslav outlined their reconfirmation of dowsers' reactions to magnetic and electromagnetic fields. They also explored dowsers' reactions to seemingly unknown waves from underground water. They call these WU (water undulation) and, like others, see it as an irritant. The Boleslavs are working on ways of blocking the dowsing reaction to these waves. In other words, they are trying to shield the dowser's body so it does not react to these underground radiations. The Boleslavs claim shielding success with the use of wire mesh and rings of copper wire. With shielding they are exploring the dynamics of dowsing, but they also believe that their work can have very practical medical benefits. Simple shielding might be developed, they say, to protect highly sensitive and sick people from irritating environmental influence.

In this aim the Boleslavs are not so unusual as they may sound in this country. They are working within a growing field of research in Europe, the study of the effect on human health of changes in the atmosphere (often called bioclimatology) and also of the influence on our bodies of the earthly environment beneath us. For one reason or another, this inquiry, which ties into accident prevention, preventive medicine, and medical therapy, is not as well known in the United States as in Europe. (One collection on bioclimatology in English: *Medical Climatology*, Baltimore: Waverly, 1964.) The Boleslavs' paper, along with others presented at the 1970 Prague Symposium, can be had in a booklet from the Paraphysical Laboratory, Downton, Wiltshire, England.

So it seems that Reichenbach may have been correct when he concluded that dowsing for underground water involved an irritated reaction on the part of sensitive individuals. For current information on equipment, practical dowsing and scientific research of the field contact: The American Society of Dowsers, Danville, Vermont, 05828. Society for the Application of Free Energy (SAFE), 103 G Street, NW #B-809, Washington, D.C. 20024

How to Make a Dowsing Rod

The simplest rod to construct is the old American standby made from coathangers. Take two thirty-four-inch lengths of coathanger

wire and bend each eight inches from the end to form an L-shape.
Hold one in each hand, with the twenty-six-inch rods extending in
front of you, parallel to each other and about three inches apart.
These pointers should either swing wide apart or cross in an X over a
dowsing zone.

Another make-it-yourself device is an adaptation of the aurameter dowsing rod created by the well-known California dowser, Verne
Cameron. The use of this rod was suggested by the German
physicist Ottmar Stehle and passed on to us by John Boyle of
Detroit. All you need is a six-foot length of copper or aluminum
wire approximately one-sixteenth-inch diameter, a wood or plastic
handle, cylindrical in shape, and a small weight, such as a fishing
sinker. Coil the wire around the handle until you have about one and
a half feet of wire remaining. Make three loops about two inches in
diameter (resembling a loose spring) in the wire extending from the
handle. Add the small weight to the end of the wire. (See photo
#22.)

An inexpensive device of somewhat similar design, called the
Vibroscopic Divining Rod, may be ordered from Venture
Bookshop, PO Box 249, Highland Park, Illinois 60035.

Organic Light and Messages of Sickness and Health

"Everything is therefore lucid, all and everything!" Reichenbach once rhapsodized. His sensitives were objective reporters.
Science isn't rhapsodic at least by the time it gets into print, but for
some decades scientists have known that a faint light, a
luminescence, does shine from all living things. We have sunshine,
moonshine, starshine—and now humanshine. Sensitive photomultipliers detect this bioluminescence. It seems feasible that this
subtle light was part, though not all, of what Reichenbach's human
sensitives detected. They may have been, as Dr. Shafica Karagulla
terms it, people of higher sense perception. If you're waiting in the
dark for your plants or friends to shine forth, it's comforting to know
that they do indeed glow. Dr. Boris Tarusov and his colleagues of
Moscow University have determined that plants modulate their
light, sending out signals full of meaning for the knowledgeable
interpreter—ajvance warnings of disease and even predictions for
the future yield of crops. (See pages 70-71.)

Light shines from living things signaling interior changes. In a
different way, light is apparently also signaling something far more
astonishing. It's carrying information from one group of living cells
to another *at a distance.* Three Soviets have found that cells com-

municate through ultraviolet light. Sickness, they state, can be transmitted by rays. This is a discovery pointing to the one-day possibility that health can be programmed by radiation. There are implications here for psi certainly, and researchers should be aware of the discovery; but the uncovering of a new form of biological communication has far broader ramifications. It is "an important step towards establishing the foundation of life," experts of the USSR Council of Ministers declared when the finding was officially listed in the State Register of Discoveries.

Vlail Kaznacheyev, Simon Shchurin, and Ludmilla Mikhailova, working in the science city of Novosibirsk, carried out more than 5,000 experiments to arrive at their revolutionary conclusions. The adventure began when they placed two vessels with quartz bottoms end to end, thus forming a wall of quartz separating the living cell colonies that were in each vessel. They infected one colony with a virus—the other fell sick almost at the same time and died of the same disease *though it had no virus*. Something transmitted a sickness pattern to the healthy cells; it would have to be a new kind of disease carrier, some sort of radiation. The three scientists extended tests at the Institute of Clinical and Experimental Medicine and the Institute of Automation and Electrometry, both part of the Siberian branch of the USSR Academy of Sciences.

Using quartz containers that allowed only ultraviolet radiations to pass, they tried various means of killing a cell colony: lethal radiation, chemical poisons, more viruses. Each time, the uncontaminated, shielded sister colony sickened with the same symptoms produced in the first. It wasn't simply harm that was transmitted but the identical sickness. Disease, it appears, can be programmed at a distance.

Obviously there's a long leap between cell colonies and the human body, but Soviet scientists believe the communication principle holds. A bright future for diagnosing before symptoms appear is now open, they say, because different diseases emit different patterns. There is also potential for new ways of halting disease without cutting or poisoning the body. Radiation may be used to interrupt the flow of photons carrying the deadly information. A few chemical preparations have been found to disrupt the "broadcasting" of some diseases. You probably own a bottle full of one such preparation—a substance gleaned from the old witch's willow—aspirin.

That light rays emitted by cells can carry highly specific information should be of interest to investigators of PK with plants and organic substances. And for those concerned with plant emanations, the Soviets point out that the work of Gurvich is supported by this discovery. (See page 29.) Research has focused on waves carrying data concerned with sickness; rays may well carry other sorts of information. These emanations could form part of the basic physical process involved in psychic healing and laying-on-of-hands. Psi investigators have noted that although some energy does seem to pass from healer to patient, it doesn't seem to be enough to effect a cure directly. Perhaps, they remark, it carries information that helps program the body to heal itself.

It's fortunate that the three Soviets performed so many careful experiments; when they first announced their conclusions, most scientists could not believe that organic radiation carried activating information. But the proof held. Perhaps "messages" from healers flow in part on ultraviolet rays, perhaps on some other sort of radiation—at least a principle of communication seems to have been discovered.

Swinging out from this basic idea which is the one thing scientifically established, one thinks of the many claims by esotericists and unorthodox scientists that vibrations, that different frequencies, have something to do with sickness and health. Claims spring from a multitude of directions. Color therapy is enjoying a rebirth of interest with therapists saying that one can cure certain ills by beaming specific frequencies of light, i.e., colors at the body. Zeroing in from a different stance is the work of George Lakhovsky, a famous but much-ridiculed scientist in the thirties. Taking a buckshot approach, he believed in beaming broad bands of electromagnetic frequencies at a patient, hoping one would effect the needed regulation and cure. (See *Waves That Heal* by Mark Clement.)

More comprehensive is the medical perspective of the late and great psychic Edgar Cayce. Cayce often spoke of the attuning of forces or vibrations within the body to restore health. And he repeatedly stated that mind was highly interactive with these inner energies. ". . . All healing of every nature is the changing of the vibrations from within—the attuning of the divine within the living tissue of a body to Creative Energies. . . . Whether it is accomplished by the use of drugs, the knife or what not, it is the attuning of the atomic structure of the living cellular force to its spiritual heritage."

Cayce often prescribed the vibrations or emanations of a specific substance, such as gold, for curative effect. The gold itself is not swallowed, rather its "emanations" are transmitted into the body. The psychic gave instructions for the construction of a simple appliance that anyone could use to conduct the supposed energy into the body. The great wealth of medical commentary given by Cayce is being actively researched at the A.R.E. Clinic, headed up by Gladys and William McGary both experienced MDs. A journal devoted to the work of the McGarys and other doctors exploring and explaining the use of Cayce's various medical pronouncements is now available: *Medical Research Bulletin* (monthly, $9.00 per year); A.R.E. Clinic, 4018 North 40th Street, Phoenix, Arizona 85018.

If you are interested in the medical aspects of psi energies generally, you might contact the Academy of Parapsychology and Medicine, created by physicians and scientists to "provide a catalyst for the study of all forms of paranormal and unorthodox healing." This group sponsors symposia and lectures for professionals and laymen and also publishes proceedings. The Academy of Parapsychology and Medicine, 314A Second Street, Los Altos, California 94022.

Another new research institute concerned with the healing has been started by the United Church of Religious Science in memory of their founder, the widely known philosopher and teacher, Dr. Ernest Holmes. They plan "a continuing program of scientific research into spiritual healing, to further refine, improve, and discover new techniques of spiritual healing that everyone can use." Membership is invited. Address: Ernest Holmes Memorial Research Foundation, PO Box 75127, Los Angeles, California 90075.

The "Magnetic" Effect of Healing Hands

"I am a Franciscan nun, but I kicked the habit." With this good-humored remark Sister Dr. M. Justa Smith often begins her lectures to scientists and laymen interested in psi. Just as she is a nun who wears modern dress, she is also involved with the modern concerns of science; she holds two master's degrees, one in mathematics, one in physical chemistry, and a doctorate in biochemistry. Formerly Chairman of the Natural Sciences Concentration at Rosary Hill College in Buffalo and now with Roswell Memorial Institute, one of the most prestigious research centers in the country, Sister Justa has carried through two first-rate series of experiments that relate to the search for energies. One series is a model of the serious scientific approach to psychic healers; the second, perhaps of even more intimate interest to all of us, involves the food we eat and is a test you might be able to duplicate.

Sister Justa mulled over Dr. Grad's experiments at McGill University, which showed the healer Oskar Estabany could speed the healing of wounded mice with the laying on of hands. Grad also found the solution Estabany had held in a stoppered flask could spur plants to grow faster. Something that promoted healthy growth seemed to be emanating from the healer's hands and it could be transmitted through liquid. Was there an accepted scientific method besides Grad's to confirm this?

Most biochemists will tell you that all metabolic reactions in a cell are catalyzed by specific enzymes. When enzymes behave properly, the cell runs smoothly. Sister Justa reasoned that if Estabany's healing hands did indeed have a curative effect, it should show up on this basic enzyme level.

Serving as research director for the Human Dimensions Institute, she invited Estabany to her lab to put his hands around sealed flasks containing trypsin, an enzyme that was the subject of her doctoral thesis. After some very careful testing of the "treated" enzyme with spectrophotometry she found Estabany did have something going for him. He was able to affect an enzyme; he could measurably increase the activity of trypsin. Most interestingly, the effect of Estabany's laying on of hands was strikingly similar to the effect of a strong magnetic field on the enzyme solution. Yet no magnetism could be detected around Estabany's hands.

It's hard to resist saying shades of Baron von Reichenbach, but Sister Justa thinks in more contemporary terms and turned instead to a statement by the famous Dr. Michael Polanyi. Life, he maintains, cannot be explained by the current workings of physical and chemical laws. Sister Justa asks, "Might he be suggesting an unknown field of force or energy which is perceptible but not yet measurable, and the existence of which is denied because it is, as yet, impossible to explain? Perhaps Polanyi is referring to a 'Psi field.' "

Sister Justa eventually tested three other psychic healers able to influence basic enzyme activity. It turns out that different enzymes are influenced in different ways by healers, but all in a curative direction that would seem to promote health in an organism. Working within the accepted structure of science, Sister Justa has added solid evidence that something other than suggestion emanates from a genuine healer.

For scientific description and data see "Professional Paper No. 2, Paranormal Effects on Enzyme Activity," *Human Dimensions*, Vol. 1, No. 2.

Live Food and "Dead" Food?

Life force—it's an idea at least as ancient as China. And recently it's surfaced in the battle cry, Live food versus dead food. If you are at all party to the warming debate over natural food versus processed food; natural vitamins compared to synthetic compounds; organic gardening as opposed to chemically improved gardening, you really ought to know about another ongoing series of investigations of Sister Dr. Justa Smith. If you're just interested in psi and other energies, there may be something in the work for you, too.

If you were in Sister Justa's lab and she presented you with one of a number of round colored pictures and asked you what it was, you might say "a sunburst mandala in muted colors."

As a second guess you might try "an American Indian design," for the radials fluting out from the center look very much like delicate brown-tipped feathers. Actually it's a picture or chromatogram of natural vitamin C.

Sister Justa produced a collection of them as she built on the work of another scientist, Dr. Ehrenfried Pfieffer, who in the 1950's found a very clear difference between natural and synthetic vitamin C. By clear we mean that *anyone* can see the difference between two chromatograms of the vitamins. Pfieffer used a technique of chemical analysis called paper chromatography. Roughly this involves slowly filtering a water-soluble substance through a specially treated round of paper which produces a colored pattern.

What does synthetic C look like? A dull circle of two rings. After duplicating Pfieffer's work, Sister Justa attempted to define the difference she'd found, keeping in mind that there is an organizing principle or pattern in all of nature. Vitamin C in its natural state, of course, contains elements that are removed in isolating ascorbic acid. One of these, Sister Justa determined, is protein enzyme, which accounted for part of the beautiful pattern. What else was in play remained to be seen.

Sister Justa and her assistants made chromatograms using two fresh green vegetables; the radiant fluted pattern appeared. She tested four very well known fruit-flavored breakfast "drinks." Dull circles of one or two rings showed. She also tried pure frozen orange juice. Once again a sunburst pattern came through—advertisers may have more going for them than they know, singing of the "sunshine drink." Sister Justa tested organic composts and produced a variety of very lovely sunburst pictures resembling mandalas in soft green, brown, and blue tones, no doubt the most aesthetic view of fertilizer we've ever seen.

There seems then to be what we might call a natural or live pattern. Nature apparently leaves her own trademark on products. It seems to disappear when we take things out. How about when we put things in? To natural vitamin C, Sister Justa added two ingredients that most of us can read on any box we open in the kitchen—the preservatives BHT and BHA. BHT completely wiped out the sunburst effect, leaving only a platelike circle. BHA very much weakened the pattern.

If anyone ever tells you that there is no difference between natural and processed food, natural and synthetic vitamins, you can tell him there is a difference. That's what these experiments prove—a difference. No one is saying good or bad, more research is needed before that can be said in a scientific sense. It might be an opportunity to test your intuition. In Sister Justa's lab we've looked through a bookful of chromatograms; lovely, striking, they might be worth making for artistic reasons alone, to capture a unique portrait of nature. But they also seem eminently worth duplicating for the "difference." In the difference there may lie some clues to further insights into the forces of nature.

Considering why Pfieffer's extensive research is so largely ignored, Sister Justa remarks it may have been caused by the "rather mysterious, nonphysical explanation Dr. Pfieffer offered for the difference in organic and inorganic matter, as we demonstrated by his chromatograms. He very simply stated that the difference was due to a 'life force,' neither apologizing for the expression nor attempting to define it."

Relatively simple to perform, easy to evaluate, germane to contemporary concerns, these chromatograms would make good science projects in a school or college laboratory. They could be done at home; however, to get accurate results absolute cleanliness must be observed, which seems to call for the sterile conditions available in a lab. For the chromatogram technique developed by Pfieffer see the journal *Bio-Dynamics*, No. 50, spring, 1959. Reprints of Sister Justa's paper, "Further Research into a Chromatographic Technique for Vitamin Analysis," which includes color and black and white pictures, may be ordered from Human Dimensions Institute (4380 Main Street, Buffalo, New York 14226, $1.00).

Other Leads

Those seriously attempting to crack open further secrets of natural energies should perhaps at least become familiar with the work of three contemporary scientists, most particularly with the theories of Dr. Nikolai Kozyrev, one of the three or four leading astrophysicists in the Soviet Union. We have written of Dr. Kozyrev elsewhere; to put it very simply here, he states that he has discovered a new energy, which he terms Time. "Time links us all and all things in the universe," Dr. Kozyrev once told us. Time is an *energy* and it is this energy that maintains the phenomenon of life in the world, in Dr. Kozyrev's view. Unlike many other energy and time theorists, Dr. Kozyrev can demonstrate his idea experimentally in his laboratory at Pulkov Observatory in Leningrad. These experiments are a continuing success.

Dr. Kozyrev's theories, like his mind, move with great sweep and depth. The cosmology he is developing includes a place for such supposedly paranormal things as PK and even levitation. These and other manifestations of psi, he believes, will be explained with thorough understanding of the energy of Time, an energy that does not propagate, but which is immediately everywhere.

Some American psi scientists are attempting to incorporate Kozyrev's ideas into their research. The Paraphysical Laboratory in England has conducted experiments that appear to confirm some of Kozyrev's findings. Dr. Kozyrev's most recent publication about his work appeared in 1972 in Prague under the imprint of the Czech Academy of Sciences. A review in English is in the *Parapsychology Review*, Vol. 3, No. 3, 1972. A translation of one of his technical papers was done by the US Department of Commerce, Joint Publication Research Service, 4th and Adam Drive, SW, Washington, D.C. 20443. "Possibility of Experimental Study of the Properties of Time," JPRS 45238, May 2, 1968, $3.00. For other information see *PDBIC*.

Another work that touches on time as energy and on the physical basis of the operation of psychic powers is *The Single Reality* (Dodd, Mead and Co.) by Preston Harold and Winifred Babcock. This book, which features an introduction and summary by the well-known philosopher Oliver L. Reiser and a preface for scientists by Robert M. L. Baker, Jr., has caught the attention of many new-wave psi researchers. Paperback $2.95; hardcover $7.95 from: Harold Institute Books, PO Box 11024, Winston-Salem, North Carolina 27106.

There are two publications that might hold some new testing angles for energy researchers. The first, available only in German at the moment, is *Research in Shackles. Electro-Gravitational UFO Phenomena; The Riddle of Electro-Gravitation* by "Rho Sigma." Don't let the pseudonym put you off too much. The author, a member of the American Institute of Aeronautics and Astronautics, has worked for NASA and the aerospace industry. Before that he was at Peenemünde, the famous German rocket-research center during World War II. He has written for various psi publications during the years.

The gist of his book from what we are told is: There is an unlimited quantity of energy in the universe waiting to be tapped. The basic discoveries have been made that would lead to a new use of electromagnetism, giving us gravity-free flight. But this data has been both ignored and suppressed. The author urges a fair reexamination of earlier scientific work and includes references and American source material. If you're curious, it's *Forschung in Fesseln. Elektro-Gravitation UFO-Phänomene: Das Rätsel der Elektro-Gravitation*, published by Ventla Verlag, Weisbaden, Germany, 1972.

Another somewhat out-of-the-way publication should perhaps be assessed by those interested in experimenting with new uses of energy. "This treatise presents newly discovered unique and startling properties of one of our induced electric fields. . . . Its unusual properties are possessed only by gravity. While it is too early to claim complete identification of this field and the gravitational field, the similarities are amazingly alike." The author was a reputable scientist, the late Dr. W.J. Hooper, professor of physics at Principia College. In 1969 and 1970 he presented two papers to the American Physical Society on his many years of experimental work on the "motional electric field" and the motional-electric-field generator. To summarize Hooper's thesis in a sentence is unfair, but it could be easily checked out by other scientists following experiments laid out in his *New Horizons In Electrical Magnetic and Gravitational Field Theory*.

Why bother? As Dr. Hooper clearly saw, if he is right in his basic discovery, it might well lead to free, nonpolluting power from the earth's gravitational field and could possibly bring us closer to attainment of antigravity. After reading the description of Dr. Hooper's field, it just might be of interest to compare it with recent data on the energies of PK. Hooper's treatise may be ordered from: Electrodynamic Gravity, Inc., PO Box 1976, Sarasota, Florida 33578 ($5.00).

Biogravitation, a fluctuating force generated by human beings, may be responsible for PK, according to Moscovite Dr. A. P. Dubrov. Studying PK psychics such as Boris Yermolayev, Dubrov drew on Einstein's General Theory of Relativity to postulate that certain types of brain activity have the ability to curve space to conform to the curvature of an object. Reportedly, some Soviet scientists are already considering two possible implications of biogravitation: It may be a basic life force that enables complex organisms to function; *it may also be the material form of human mental activity.* If Dubrov and his collaborators can verify their theory, it would give us a handle on PK. More importantly, it would begin to set out in scientific terms how the human mind can directly change the material world.

You may also be able to probe energies with detectors that are probably in the room with you right now—your plants. "Staggering as it may be to contemplate, a life signal may connect all creation," Cleve Backster declared after his discovery of primary perception. As outlined in Section One, this life signal may be carrying us to new understanding of energies apart from the electromagnetic spectrum. Plant sensing systems are already being put to use—some to rather startling use.

14

Cheops Revisited

Experimenting with Energies of Shapes

Inching over the monumental Great Pyramid of Cheops at Giza, investigators have had their hands and tape measures full, determining the geometric, mathematical, astronomical wonders of the structure. We don't know of anyone taking time off to lay out his dull razor blade in the King's Chamber to see what would happen. But a slew of plain blue blades are reposing inside ranks of scale-model pyramids springing up and facing north in the United States and Europe. Experts are still not agreed on what the original pyramid builders had in mind. The latter-day ones are seeking an energy, perhaps a couple of energies that seem to render dull razor blades sharp again, preserve perishables, and now, it is claimed, produce a host of unusual effects.

The adventures of the modern-day pyramid explorers working in the cool of their own home have prompted features on blade-sharpening pyramids in the likes of *Esquire*, the Toronto *Star*, the Los Angeles *Times*, and *Enroute*, Air Canada's in-flight magazine. Pyramids seem to be in the air in more ways than one. Author U.S. Anderson started a fund, Pennies for Pyramids in hope of eventually erecting a very large replica; while thousands of Americans have been swapping their pictures of pyramids neatly etched on the back of US one-dollar bills for scale models made of cardboard or vinyl.

American researchers, like their counterparts in Czechoslovakia who sparked the current interest in pyramids, are well aware that a razor-blade-sharpening pyramid is a funny idea. Yet most insist that the model Cheops is a good experimental tool in the investigation of "other" energies—what the Czechs and now some Americans call psychotronic energies. If your interest is psi energies, the pyramid might be an ideal "instrument," simple to make and requiring no psychic ability on the part of the experimenter. If nothing more, when you decide to tape four cardboard triangles together you may wind up with a useful, not to mention unique, household appliance.

The Great Pyramid at Giza, reaching forty stories into the air and covering thirteen acres, is hard to think of in terms of a household appliance. But there are some who consider it a kind of appliance, a very useful structure for the society that created it.

A precise scale model of the hemisphere; a tangible exposition of pi, the golden section, the theorems of Pythagoras; an almanac showing the year down to the extra .2422 of a day—a catalogue of the knowledge of the physical world incorporated into the Great Pyramid would pack a book. Recently Peter Tompkins has filled a contemporary gap with *Secrets of the Great Pyramid* (Doubleday, 1971). Tompkins traces the centuries-long exploration of the Pyramid and sets out in intelligible fashion the staggering mathematical comprehension scientists now agree is reflected in the Pyramid. Dr. Livio Catullo Stecchini, an authority on ancient measurement, adds extra data to the last millimeter. If you are seriously involved with pyramids, some sound, in-depth knowledge, such as Tompkins provides, of the Great Pyramid and its sister structures along the Nile might stand you in good exploratory stead. (See Tompkins bibliography for more books on pyramids.)

Though one of us had earlier circumambulated the Pyramid on camelback, it was not until we arrived in Prague and met engineer Karl Drbal that we began thinking about the energetics of pyramids. Drbal, who catalyzed much current research, in 1959 secured Patent #91304 for a Pyramid Razor-Blade Sharpener, and little plastic red and white pyramids soon appeared on the market in Czechoslovakia. Drbal's basic interest is in studying unusual radiations and the so-called waves of form, long of concern to European radiesthesists. We have detailed the account of his pyramid work elsewhere (see *PDBIC.*). Briefly he told us how he had drawn from the experiments of Frenchman Antoine Bovis.

As the story goes, the observant Frenchman, while examining the Great Pyramid in Egypt, noticed that small animals had wandered in and died in the structure. Rather than decomposing as one might expect, they had instead mummified. Mummies plus pyramid added up to an experiment Bovis performed on returning to France. He built a scale model of the Great Pyramid and put a dead cat inside, one-third of the way up from the base at the level of the King's Chamber. The cat dehydrated and mummified. So did dead fish and other organic matter with a high decay rate. Bovis concluded there must be something about the shape and alignment of the Great Pyramid that prevents decay and causes dehydration.

Antoine Bovis was deeply interested in unexplained radiations of all kinds and published *On The Radiations of All Substances* in the early thirties. From his long research, he eventually developed the biometer, which supposedly measures radiations of an unknown form of energy. The French government commissioned him to employ his device for the detection of adulterated foods and wines. In the US, Dr. Oscar Brunler further refined the biometer.

Other Europeans took up Bovis' pyramid work, particularly Drbal. Finally, many North Americans have joined in, seeking new applications of the pyramid, from charging metal plates to studying its effect on septic tanks. That there is a lot of working interest afoot certainly came home literally to John B. Boyle of Detroit. Beginning as an at home experimenter, Boyle became increasingly absorbed in pyramids, finally forming the Astral Research Co., which markets experimental pyramids to help support his widening investigation of energies associated with geometric forms.

"Immediately, we found ourselves in an extremely fortunate position, since we received correspondence from people in all walks of life from almost every country in the world!" Boyle told us. "New information, theories, and ideas poured in at a fast rate. We heard from astronomers, astrologers, mathematicians, physicists, philosophers, potential inventors. We soon learned that the era of the 'kitchen table' inventor had survived from the days of Edison and Marconi."

Boyle remarks upon the variety of perspectives shown by people who got in touch. Ottmar Stehle, for instance, a German scientist with NASA on a National Academy of Science Fellowship, stopped off to talk with Boyle before returning to Berlin. Stehle says pyramids are geometric shapes that focus energy fields. Not such an odd idea, he points out; this is what TV antennae do. Stehle, whom we've also met, seems a likely candidate to come to terms with "other" energies; actively grounded in contemporary science, he can also move out with his own dowsing ability and knowledge of European radiesthesia. A man with a very different approach to pyramids—a mathematical one—who also found Boyle was George L. Brandes of Nevada. "I am convinced," Boyle writes us, "that we must take a long hard look at Brandes' hyperspace theories, for it is in this area that we will find the answers to increase and harness the pyramid energies. Experimental science follows closely on the heels of the pure mathematician.''

Meanwhile, in Canada, Eric McLuhan turned out to be as eclectic and future minded as his famous father, media expert Marshall McLuhan. ''The medium is the message'' is the dictum of the elder McLuhan and the younger became intrigued with the medium of shapes, particularly the pyramid. While teaching at the University of Wisconsin and then at Fanshawe College in London, Ontario, McLuhan has confirmed to his own satisfaction the sharpening and mummifying power of the pyramid and has since done his best to draw experts from a cluster of fields into the study of the pyramids.

The consummate generalist, McLuhan believes—and we agree—that only an interdisciplinary approach will crack open the enigma. What the Egyptologist may miss the engineer might notice; what an expert in crystallography might overlook a musician might spot. McLuhan showed the floor plans of some pyramids to an acoustical engineer. ''It blew his mind,'' McLuhan remarks. ''The plan looked exactly like a speaker system.''

Pyramids, we've been taught, were tombs; yet there is little evidence of burials and no mummies have been found in pyramids. Tombs or not, it seems likely the pyramid was seen as having a variety of benefits. The Great Pyramid was about the same scope of undertaking for Pharaonic Egypt, McLuhan notes, as the space program for the United States.

After he and several scientists experimented with various model pyramids, trying to isolate the wavelengths and frequencies of pyramid energies, McLuhan has some basic observations.

Most experimenters agree that for the model pyramid to work well and for material to be dehydrated or blades sharpened, the material must be placed one-third of the way up at the king's chamber level, and the pyramid must be aligned north-south. In McLuhan's view, this means several energies could be involved:

• The king's chamber, the major energy center in the pyramid, is also the center of gravity. This can't be coincidence, he says.
• The pyramid is aligned north-south, parallel to the earth's *magnetic* axis. This is no coincidence either, he says and would indicate that the energy waves involved are somewhat polarized. This coincides with the complementary theory of magnetism being somewhat polarized, he believes.
• The Egyptian pyramids are solid masses of rock with specifically

shaped cavities (chambers) hollowed out and interrelated in a specific way. These chambers are "resonant cavities," according to McLuhan—enclosed spaces in which electromagnetic energy may be stored or excited, something like hi-fi speakers.

In McLuhan's view, data on these three aspects, gravity, magnetism, resonance, as they relate to the pyramid, may hold the key to pyramid power.

It is his understanding that prototypes of the shapes and dimensions of the resonant cavities or chambers and their interrelationships were experimented with by the priests long before being incorporated in any pyramid design, and that many types of pyramid designs and alignments were tried. He considers the Bent Pyramid of Dahshur the most enigmatic and the best departure point for studying all the pyramids in the series.

Because he speculates that the pyramid, among other things, may produce a coherent magnetic field, he is trying to find a company to grow semiconductor crystals inside the magnetically "pure" pyramid environment—the idea being that they would prove superefficient, free of the effects of extraneous radiation. Semiconductors revolutionized electronics, bringing in miniaturization. Should McLuhan be right, could pyramid technology help lead to at least another semirevolution?

Many of the following pyramid experiments and suggested leads are drawn from what people have shown us, told and written us about their ad hoc experiments with pyramids. From Prague to Portland, a crowd of individuals report success with basic experiments; Czech psychotronic researchers continue to attest to them. But there are other people who report completely negative results. Who's right? Could they both be right? Perhaps you can find out something about the persistent, decades-long reports that there are some sort of energy fields associated with pyramids.

Groundwork

Make your pyramid model as close to scale to the Great Pyramid as possible. One need not become fanatic, but the more correct the proportions, the better the results.

Place your pyramid at least four feet from walls, radiators, TVs, radios, fluorescent lights, or any electrical appliance. It should not sit on anything metal.

Pyramids seem to work better with a base or bottom. This may be taped along one side making a convenient hinge arrangement.

Make an orientation mat by tracing the square base of your pyramid on a larger sheet of paper or cardboard. Draw a north-south and an east-west line crossing exactly in the center of the square, and extending out beyond the square so you can see the lines once you position your pyramid on the square. The area where the lines cross is directly under the apex. If working with a bottom, also draw a cross on that to let you know where to put material.

The most "active" section of the pyramid is supposed to be the bottom third. When possible, place experimental material in the king's chamber, or so-called focal-point position, in the middle of the pyramid, one-third of the way up to the apex.

Direct the middle of one triangular face north. Which north—magnetic compass north or true north? Some claim results with either. Although the Egyptians some 5,000 years ago did remodel temples to realign them with stars that had shifted position, no one would want to keep realigning the girth of the Great Pyramid to our wandering magnetic pole. The Great Pyramid in Egypt is oriented almost exactly to true north. If you would like to align your model with true north, you have to obtain the angle of magnetic declination—the difference between compass north and geographic north in your locality. Use geodetic charts usually available in libraries. These give the variance plus the annual rate of change of the magnetic pole since the map was drawn. Very roughly, the variance in Washington, D.C., is about six degrees west, Chicago one degree east, San Diego fifteen degrees east, and Vancouver twenty-four degrees east. In Washington then, geographic north is six degrees west of compass north, while in San Diego it is fifteen degrees east of the compass point. The simple route to finding variance is to ask a surveyor, geologist, or anyone in your vicinity who's taken a navigation course.

Cardboard is the easiest material out of which to make a pyramid. Plastic, wood, and even metal or layers of foil and cardboard are commonly used. Color of material seems to make little difference, nor does opacity; tests with transparent plastic succeed.

The basic testing model is the six-inch pyramid. Each side is an isosceles triangle with equal sides of eight and seven-eighths inches and the base of nine and three-eighths inches. For more exact models of the Cheops pyramid, it is best to work in centimeters. See Figure 10 for instructions on how to make pyramids of any size.

Pattern for Pyramid and Base

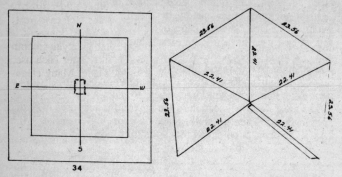

measurement in centimeters
(not drawn to scale)

FIGURE 10.

Cut or score the sides and assemble the pyramid with the flap on the inside, using glue or tape. It is easiest to measure in centimeters. Dimensions of often-used pyramids:

Height		Base	Side
15cm	(approx 6″)	23.5620	22.4190
31cm	(approx 12″)	48.6948	46.3326
61cm	(approx 24″)	95.8188	91.1706
100cm	(approx 3′3″)	157.0800	149.4600

To make pyramids of various sizes, a simple formula for determining the dimensions of the base and sides of the triangle is: length of *base minus 5% equals* length of *side.* Another often-used system follows more precisely the European dimensions, with the side measuring 4.855% less than the base of the triangle. This has been incorporated into a formula widely introduced to pyramid aficionados by Valerie Ann Olin. To make a pyramid of any height:

$$\text{Height} \times 1.5708 = \text{base of triangle}$$
$$\text{Height} \times 1.4946 = \text{side of triangle}$$

(1.5708 is half of pi; 1.4946 is half of pi less 4.855%. The formula follows from the idea that twice the height of the pyramid divided into the perimeter of the base (total of four sides) should hit as close as possible to pi.)

Razor-Blade Sharpening

The old-fashioned blue blades are the ones that deliver results. Place a blunt blade on a two-inch match box or other holder directly under the apex of a six-inch pyramid. Sharp sides face east-west, the ends north-south. Leave it there at least a week, longer if it doesn't prove ready. On removal, it should again give you smooth shaving. Replace blades under pyramid regularly after each use. Drbal claims up to 200 shaves with a single blade. Many clean-shaven pyramid builders speak of using a single blade for a month or two and claim marked difference between treated and control blade shows most clearly after four weeks' use. Drbal observes that the crystallinelike structure of the blade edge tends in time toward its original form. The pyramid, he feels, enhances this tendency. Put a blunt control blade aside for the same length of time as the one in the pyramid. Keep on shaving one side of the face or one leg with the control and one with the treated blade. It is claimed that dull kitchen knives or dull scissors can also be sharpened with appropriate-sized pyramids.

Mummifying

Just about anything that goes bad is a candidate for the king's chamber. The most commonly preserved items are eggs (in and out of shells), sprouts, flowers, vegetables, hamburger, and whole meat. Put an equal portion aside as a control; you might also cover it with a square cardboard box. Samples are usually left under the pyramid for one to eight weeks.

Not all American pyramid builders are recent devotees. If you're interested in psi, you probably know of two earlier investigators, the late California dowser Verne Cameron, and his friend Max Freedom Long, expert and writer on the ancient Hawaiian art of Kahuna. In 1953 Cameron put two ounces of raw pork, which was about half fat, under a four-inch pyramid. He set the structure "in a bathroom where it was hot, steamy, or draughty by spells—not conducive to preservation of foods, certainly. In about three days the pork had a faint odor, but it lost this, and in about nine days was completely mummified." He reported that the pork remained "perfectly edible after several months. A large chunk of watermelon [placed in a pyramid] dried down to the texture of a dried apricot but is still sweet and good."

More recently a Toronto group put ten pounds of porterhouse

steak under a two-and-a-half-foot pyramid. After several weeks the dried steak tasted delicious when fried and eaten, they report. This suggests a unique way of beating rocketing beef prices if you care to convert your garage into a Cheops pyramid. At least when the electricity goes off, the pyramid doesn't go out.

Vegetable spoilage is also supposedly retarded in larger pyramids. You might try storing flower bulbs in one to prevent mildew. And mildew control generally could provide a chance for practical experiments. In the area of slowing chemical processes, a Czech scientist, Jaroslav Mrkvicka, suggests that the fermentation of beer might be retarded if bottled in pyramid-shaped containers.

Rather than worry about the shape of their beer, members of the Toronto Society for Psychical Research decided to run basic dehydrating and sharpening tests. Neither succeeded. They compared photomicrographs of blades that had been lodged under two cardboard pyramids for seven days with a control blade. As might be expected all showed a natural tendency for jagged peaks on the blade edge to round off. But pyramid blades showed no extra enhancement. It might be interesting to see what, if anything, would show if blades were used for four or five weeks, one always returned to the pyramid, the other set aside. The Torontonians conclude that claims made by some enthusiasts that anyone can get dehydration and sharpening effects with the pyramid weren't supported by their investigation.

If the pyramid does work at all, why doesn't it always work? Dr. Tiller at Stanford studied the blades in his pyramid experiments with an electron microscope. "The first time we tried, it worked; the second time it didn't." Possibly, Tiller remarked to an audience at Drew University, his trouble with the pyramid was an instance of the difficulties of working with "other" energies generally. For instance, testing a dowser, identifying samples, Tiller found that accuracy vanished after two or three trials. Now he's worked out a protocol to allow body and material polarities to return to "normal" at the end of each test. This has increased reliability. In his varied probes of energies Tiller concludes, "Whatever this force is we are tremendously interactive with it." He feels that it is just within the realm of possibility that this interaction negated his pyramid test, because after initial success he and his cohorts focused strong attention on the second experiment.

If pyramids sometimes demonstrate an energy, someone will have to unravel why it happens sometimes and not others, for some people and not others, and perhaps in one place but not another. For anyone familiar with the history of psi research generally this plaguing on again off again, for you, but not for you, sort of snag is hardly new.

Pyramid Effect versus Green-Light Effect

Engineer Drbal has done further investigation of meat preservation by testing out light waves instead of the waves of form. He hung two pieces of meat on threads about four inches apart in a normal room. He neither curtained the windows to keep out sun nor kept the lights burning all night. Normal conditions held sway *except* that Drbal keep a constant ray of green light on one piece of meat day and night. Supposedly the meat continually bathed in green light remained fresh when the other piece had spoiled. Numerous researchers including Verne Cameron have said the other energy behaves similarly to light. Reichenbach and, among others, Abbé Mermet, the great European expert on radiesthesia, maintained that the other radiation accompanied light. Can Drbal's green-light tests be duplicated? If so, what is it about the frequency of green light that would inhibit decay? And if Drbal is right about green light preventing decay, could a green light in basements or closets help prevent mildew and mustiness?

Yogurt and Milk

Some researchers assert that dairy firms in Italy, France, and Yugoslavia market yogurt and/or milk in pyramid-shaped containers to lengthen shelf life. If this is so—and if the pyramid containers do keep yogurt fresh for a longer time, according to Eric McLuhan—it would mean that more than one kind of energy is at work in the pyramid. For most of the effects described previously, for instance, razor-blade sharpening, the pyramid supposedly had to be aligned on a north-south axis; but as McLuhan points out, yogurt and milk containers couldn't possibly always be lined up north-south on store shelves. For some effects then, both shape and north-south alignment are needed, but supposedly to preserve yogurt, the shape alone has an effect.

To test this out, make a liquidproof pyramid and fill it with yogurt. Weigh it. Fill a different-shaped container with an equal amount of yogurt. Set both containers out at room temperature, but don't align them north-south and see whether or not the pyramid shape stays fresh longer. Try the experiment again with the pyramid aligned north-south and see if there's any improvement. Find out exactly how much longer the pyramid will keep dairy products fresh. What is needed in the current pyramid adventure is more repeated hard-nosed experimenting with charts of facts and figures.

Varied Claims

Claims for the various effects of pyramid power are widening to say the least. A host of these new entrants revolve on subjective judgment. The best way to separate fancy from possible truth is to test on your own. Water is supposedly enhanced by pyramid treatment. The most common claims include that the water tastes better, will increase the staying power of cut flowers, has a beneficial effect in fish tanks, and increases healthy growth if poured on seeds and sprouts.

To attempt to charge water, experimenters use a dish, glass, or pan that's little more than one-third the height of their pyramid and small enough in diameter to fit comfortably inside the pyramid. They fill the dish with water and leave it in the pyramid anywhere from a few hours to a day or so. Other experimenters use an aquarium-size container, put a plastic pyramid into it and fill the whole thing with water to the king's-chamber level.

An assortment of other common substances are also supposedly enhanced in the pyramid, tobacco, for one. To keep more or less steady as you go when doing this sort of experiment, use the jury approach. Can other people tell the difference between brand X and pyramid product?

Like many energies sighted over the years, pyramid force is said to boost plant growth. A pyramid placed on the earth above newly planted seeds for a few days is also claimed to enhance plant growth. On the other hand, it also seems to retard certain processes in organic matter. Can you reconcile these two effects? And can you work out a controlled test to rule out the possibility that it is thought—your positive expectation—and not some energy of the pyramid that is influencing plant growth?

Researchers in Toronto have found that placing an open pyramid over plants will double plant growth and produce healthier specimens.

Probing for Energies

If you are using your pyramid as an experimental tool, some of the avenues you might try include:

- Reflecting the energy by the use of mirrors. Does it follow the laws of light reflection?
- Shielding or cutting off the activating force. Place a pane of glass, metal screening, or other substance a few inches above the pyramid. Can you find any material that when made into a pyramid nullifies the usual effect?
- Seeking a polarity in the supposed pyramid energy. Is there a negative and positive? It has been suggested that there is a different sort of energy operating in the upper part of the pyramid. To get anywhere one would have to make the polarities visible by some sort of effect.
- Testing capstones of various material. No one knows definitely what comprised the capstone of the Great Pyramid. Edgar Cayce in one of his readings said it was made of an alloy of copper, brass and gold.
- Creating a pyramid from alternating layers of organic and inorganic material—in other words, following the orgone-accumulating pattern propounded by Wilhelm Reich. (See page 212 ff.)

Czech researchers feel that a form such as the pyramid acts as a resonator of psychotronic energy, the other energy. The effect doesn't seem readily explicable by the currently accepted laws of energy, but it might fall into place when the dynamics of such things as PK are understood. Benson Herbert, director of the Paraphysical Laboratories in England, of all people in the West probably has the widest understanding of psi-related scientific work in the Communist countries. Herbert speculates about the relation of architecture to poltergeists, which are generally considered a form of unconscious PK. He is mulling "the possibility of designing a poltergeist house, of such a shape as to encourage paranormal incidents, a kind of scientific 'House that Jack Built,' incorporating architectural features that I had seen in certain 'haunted' Scottish castles; I visualized these shapes as hypergeometrical sections." If Herbert ever gets up a house that sets PK flowing, it could certainly lead to entertaining house parties.

Pursuing the idea that pyramid energies might be similar to those involved with poltergeists and PK, you might try hatching up some cross-checking experiments. For example, Uri Geller has demonstrated on occasion a very marked influence on broken and unwound watches. Would the pyramid have any influence on the behavior of a watch wound or unwound, or a broken one? What about other energetic effects supposedly shown by PK psychics?

Psychotronic energies seem vulnerable to interaction with thought. It just might be interesting to see what a heavy dose of directed thought, once or twice a day, will do to pyramid experiments. This is not to say that all pyramid effects are PK, but there may be a shade of influence. Can concentrated thought retard or change usual effects?

Mapping the Pyramid Energy

Ottmar Stehle, who returned after his NASA stint to the Technical University of Berlin, explored the pattern of pyramid fields with a dowsing rod. Specific reactions occurred, he told us, at the apex, sides, edges and king's chamber. Stehle has also reported that in preliminary testing he found field reactions up and down the apex-base axis. These provoke horizontal motion in the rod and appear equidistant. He maps twelve in the Cheops model plus a circular movement at the king's chamber. In very informal dowsing with a few friends, we did get many of the reactions Stehle noted. The reaction to the side faces is particularly good to test as it is generally unanticipated. (Don't tell people what to expect.) Stehle registered seven counterclockwise circles, five vertical bobs, then seven clockwise circles. We did get the shift in motion but not such an accurate count—perhaps because no one who tried could be classed as a practiced dowser.

Horizontal and vertical motions evoked by pyramids suggest to Stehle and many others that two forces are involved moving at right angles like electricity and magnetism. Rotation implies a further factor concerned with space-time and gravity. Alignment to true north would appear to tie in with the earth's rotation and therefore elements of gravity and time. This leads some to ask if there is a link between any pyramid effect and Dr. Nikolai Kozyrev's proposition that time is an energy, energy that when understood will explain many psi effects.

Many experienced users of dowsing rod and pendulum concur that pyramids evoke reactions beyond any that might be expected by the materials involved. With the rod, of course, we again confront a detecting device that involves a human being in the circuit and is thus, by necessity, somewhat subjective. However, objective evidence of the accuracy of the information gleaned from Verne Cameron's dowsing rod remains in scores of wells, in plentiful supplies of drinking water and in hot springs that have turned arid California towns into resorts.

Cameron's further observations about pyramid energies include a dowsing reaction to the place a pyramid occupied on a surface after it is removed. He claimed detection too of an invisible pyramid of energy extending downward to ground with the model pyramid as its capstone. Cameron also found that when he placed a metal pyramid that was connected apex to tip with a metal cone on the earth, it wiped out his dowsing ability. In other words, he could register no reaction over a known source of underground water. To some this will sound like wiping out zero with zero. However, if we are dealing with real forces, if anyone could further elucidate this interference effect, it might lead to better knowledge of each force, and a potential shield against certain so-called psi effects.

Magnetism and Pyramids

Some people have tried putting bar magnets inside pyramids to increase the supposed energy effect. At first, set up a pyramid with no magnet; one with the south pole of a magnet (inside under the apex) facing north; one with the north pole facing north; and place a magnet, north pole pointing north, on a table without a pyramid. Dowse for any difference. And as always, don't tell one dowser what another registers. Other directions can be tried and tests set up with pyramids and magnets combined to see if mummification or desiccation is influenced. If possible, tests can be done with weak, pulsing magnetic fields.

Open Pyramids

Especially with larger structures, it is claimed that little influence is lost if you simply construct the frame of the pyramid without bothering to construct solid sides. There is a large area here for comparative testing.

Meditation Pyramids

Not only razor blades, but a good number of human beings seem to be sitting inside pyramids from Virginia to Oregon. Pyramids, it is said, enhance meditation and soothe the body. In a sense, the meditators have a long lineage of lore going for them. Just about every mystery tradition in the Western world, including those of Christianity and Judaism, holds that the pyramid was a place of initiation into higher knowledge. It is said that Sophocles, Plato, and Pythagoras studied with the keepers of the pyramid and became initiates. According to tradition, just as the builders incorporated their extensive knowledge of the material universe into the pyramid, so they also exhibited within it some of their understanding of inner things, of mental and spiritual laws. Details vary wildly but the skeleton of the esoteric story is that as a final initiation rite, a candidate was left alone in a chamber of the pyramid for a number of days during which time he experienced altered states of consciousness and enlightenment. (If nothing else, such an environment would provide sensory deprivation, which can induce alterations in consciousness.)

Contemporary meditation pyramids usually run from four to six feet either open-sided or closed. Frames are of wood or plumbing pipe. Some simply attach strong thick wire to the ceiling and floor, making the outline of the pyramid. If closing the sides with plastic or other material, you can use short legs at the corner of the base to allow air to enter. Some meditators try to position themselves so that specific chakras—energy centers of the body—are at certain points within the pyramid.

If you don't want to build your own people-size pyramid, you can order a ready-made wood and vinyl one over four feet high from Pyramid Products, Box 6386, Glendale, California 91205. (If you ever wonder what happens to boy geniuses when they grow up, at least one of them, Patrick Flanagan, the head of this company, has plunged into studying pyramids as energy generators. When he was seventeen, a decade ago, Flanagan received national publicity and scientific distinction for inventing the neurophone, a hearing aid that transmits electrical impulses directly to the brain. Since then he helped develop man-dolphin communication for the Navy and has come up with other inventions. Right now his focus is biocosmic energy, which, he says, "is the very essence of the life force itself.")

If there really is an energy active in model pyramids, exactly what its effect may be on the human body is anybody's guess. Engineer Drbal maintains that the pyramid and semicircle (like Buckminster Fuller's geodesic domes) are beneficial. Others point out that the triangular shape may have had something to do with the unusual powers supposedly raised inside the special teepee of the Indian medicine man. For those who like to prime their imaginations, there is a neat speculation we heard in Europe: Psychotronic energies may explain the riddle of the Sphinx. The seeker stood at a specific spot before the great Sphinx, put his question and waited. An energy focused by the Sphinx affected the person, expanding his consciousness. Whether this worked only when the Sphinx held its original obelisk against its chest was not explained.

Could a model pyramid really improve your meditation? No one else can answer that question for you.

Other Shapes: Cones and Coils

While checking a misbehaving electrical appliance in the late forties Verne Cameron made an accidental discovery. His dowsing rod indicated an energy above a metal coil, one similar to those on an electric stove. Yet no electricity was flowing in the coil. This launched Cameron on a decades-long investigation. He repeatedly got a dowsing reaction as if an energy were coming from coils.

Interestingly, Dr. Rejdak of Prague, tracing the history of the search for energy, has come across a coil-type "X" energy device patented some years ago by a German, Professor Oscar Korschelt. Korschelt had spent some years in Japan looking into the work of magnetic healers. As a result of his research, he developed an energy device consisting of "an electrical disc, nonconductive, disposed freely or in a stand, that has been provided on both sides with conductive spirals, interconnected in the center. One of the sides, the one that is exposed to the light, is meant as the energy's collector, and the opposite side serves as the irradiator of the energy." Rejdak reports that it was only because Korschelt was able to demonstrate that this device enhanced plant growth that he was awarded Patent #69.340. (German, we assume, but do not know for sure.) Once again, this work is reminiscent of the many accounts of energy collectors continuing from the days of Reichenbach.

Cameron eventually pulled out his coils and began experiments with cone shapes. Very briefly, he found by dowsing: A seeming ray of energy comes only from the tips of cones; cones have to be constructed of metal or covered with metallic foil; they *must* be right-angle cones; they should be suspended by the wide edge at least five feet from the ground. Cameron connected cones in series, running copper wire from tip to tip. The energy he claimed could also be conducted from a single cone with a wire. He generally used cones twenty-two inches across at the wide end, though other sizes will work. The effect is supposedly heightened if the open end is covered. In one instance, according to Max Freedom Long, he buried a wire from a cone a few inches underground and found it seemed to have an inhibiting effect on seeds planted directly above. This remains to be duplicated. One wonders if leads from cones would have any influence if directed at organic matter. Cameron noted too that the rays could in certain circumstances affect radio reception.

Understandably perhaps, scientists generally refused to look at Cameron's reports because the idea of an energy, but not a known energy, emanating from a simple shape seemed so nonsensical, particularly since it could only be measured with a dowsing rod. With the new interest in pyramids, people are again building cones and claiming dowsing results similar to Cameron's. The task now is to search for objective effects. Often called a master dowser, Cameron died before he was able to have his research on the waves of form extensively published. His fellow townsman at Elsinore, Bill Cox, is now attempting to remedy that situation. (See page 212.) Perhaps the time has come to check out and critically evaluate Verne Cameron's wealth of data on cones, pyramids, coils, and other material shapes.

Cameron, a fine working dowser, did his best at experimentation with limited funds and little or no scientific support. By now a number of established scientists, mainly in Europe, have conducted painstaking investigations of dowsing from a variety of academic perspectives, including monitoring changes in the dowser's bodily processes as he reacts to such things as electromagnetic force fields and substances in the earth. This sort of dowsing now appears scientifically verifiable. If someone with a good grounding in this scientific data were to explore the dowsing reactions provoked by shapes like the pyramid and cones, he or she might be able 1) to establish objectively whether or not something really is going on and 2) to begin to sort out by analogy to established data, some of the energetic reactions taking place.

Other patterns

For reasons not wholly comprehended, the ancients seemed addicted to pyramid building around the globe. Not all are exact replicas of the Great Pyramid. Eric McLuhan, contemplating the bent pyramid of Dahshur, south of Giza, exclaimed, "That's a two-frequency octahedron"—a mathematically perfect shape. As you might imagine, other people have said other things about the various pyramids of Egypt and about the pyramids found in other lands, Mexico and Cambodia, China, for example, and even the United States (near St. Louis). Is anything afoot, active, and resonate in pyramids of different dimensions? Do they, as McLuhan suggests, represent different models put forth by an unknown technology? According to papers sent us by Alexander Abramov, a Soviet specialist in the history of science, the three pyramids at Giza are arranged in special geometric relation, called the *abaka* in ancient Egypt. Is there anything to be gleaned from the relationship of structures or the repetition of this grid in other locales?

Model experimental pyramids are hollow, their progenitor is as solid as granite with a few cavities and conduits. Does it make a difference? What would happen with an exact model? The Great Pyramid has a pit about one-third of the distance below the base, just as the king's chamber is one-third above. The pit may well have been used for astronomical sighting. Yet it has caused others to construct two pyramids placing them base to base in a diamond shape.

Theories about what causes the effects in pyramids range far and wide. For instance, Jaroslav Mrkvicka, a Czech specialist in communications systems, is working on the connection between information theory and geometry. Most speak of resonance with a coupling to some universal force via dimensions and orientation. McLuhan talks of magnetic and gravity waves; others view the pyramid as a prism, focusing an energy with a very long wavelength. Those of a mathematical bent, such as George Brandes, who published *Calculus of Organizers* in 1963, moved into mathematical theories of hyperspace for explanation. Although we have not had the opportunity to go into them, Brandes' ideas, communicated to us by John Boyle, sound an interesting note particularly because Brandes has developed graphics to help one grasp his mathematics. It could well be, too, that a theory in contemporary terminology could be built from the reams of empirical data gathered over the past century by European radiesthetists.

Probably the best way to check your own theories is with objective tests that show your ideas in action. Whether you are the theoretical sort or not, it isn't hard to feel the fascination the mysteries of the pyramids have exerted on humanity for centuries. As the ranks of pyramid builders increase, the claims for what the structure can do are running rampant. It's almost impossible to separate any kernels of fact from the proliferating foliage of fancy except by repeated experiment. If nothing else, contemporary pyramidology is immensely entertaining.

To move completely into the wild blue yonder from the orthodox point of view, there are four often-repeated assertions that intrigue many people. The first is that the ancients used pyramids to produce water, operating on the fractionating-column principle. Others maintain that within the pyramid and related shapes lies the secret of antigravity, in other words, levitation. Numerous individuals, mainly in California, assert that pyramids were constructed at strategic locations in the ancient world to help balance the forces, the stresses and strains, of the planet. Author U.S. Anderson and the engineer/psi investigator Ralph Bergstresser advocate erecting large pyramids on or near such things as the San Andreas Fault. Finally, there is a speculation whose advocates are international. The pyramids they say produced an energy that served as a powerful homing beacon. For what? For aircraft.

It appears to be a shade more respectable these days to entertain the speculation that highly advanced science and technology may have existed on this planet at some earlier time, either home grown or imported. Simultaneous with our own advent into space has come the idea that sudden advances in earth's previous civilizations may have been seeded by beings with superior knowledge from outer space. The American astrophysicist Karl Sagan and the Soviet astronomer Dr. Iosif Shklovsky have outlined such a thesis. In a much more free-swinging manner, the visitation idea has, of course, been spread far and wide by Erich von Däniken's *Chariots of the Gods?* series. Electronics expert L. George Lawrence's own research also prompted him to think about extraterrestrial intelligence. (See pages 42-43.) Before hearing of von Däniken, Lawrence independently collected data that he claims supports the general visitation theory.

An excellent proponent of the idea that advanced cultures of old were at least in part home-grown, is Charles Berlitz. His ongoing research is global in scope. And being a Berlitz, among the many solid clues he stitches together pointing to lost civilizations are those of language. (See *Mysteries From Forgotten Worlds*, Dell, 1973.)

That Russians might have similar ideas about lost civilizations isn't surprising. What is curious is that they are hotly debated by scholars and scientists. Dissertations appear on the subject in the Soviet Union; new translations of ancient writings and archeological finds are often checked from the superior-knowledge point of view. Soviet mathematical physicist M.M. Agrest recently remarked that we may have reached the point where we could recognize messages left by such highly advanced people. Scientists, he urged, must look for such clues on a worldwide basis.

A delightful example of what can happen when you take a clear-eyed look at ancient leftovers is an experience of Ivan T. Sanderson's vis-à-vis a small gold trinket. Sanderson, one of the most meticulous and fair-minded investigators we have ever known, had a penchant for coming up with delightfully disconcerting bits and pieces of the world, which stubbornly refused either to evaporate or explain themselves within the cannons of orthodoxy.

A little gold trinket, known to have been crafted at least a thousand years ago, now resides in the Columbia National Collection. Everyone who thought about it at all assumed it represented some creature, probably an aquatic one, a skate or ray. But Sanderson, biologist and naturalist, knew his creatures. The more he looked at an exact blowup of the trinket, the more he had to admit the disconcerting fact that the features did not look animal. They looked mechanical. Various experts, unhampered with the knowledge of whence the artifact had come, after taking into account a host of features, more or less concurred that the trinket seemed to be a model of a flying craft—perhaps one of the latest Delta-wing types. All of which entices to speculation. (For the full account, see Sanderson's *Invisible Residents*, World, 1970.)

The effect of the model pyramids is another spur leading more people than an antiquarian might realize, to start looking at ancient architecture from the perspective of a technologist and skimming ancient symbols and decorative art with the eyes of circuit-diagram readers. Of course, it is extraordinarily easy to read anything into anything. Still this new approach to museum going is a good deal more broad than that of the Freudians of other days who sought circles and perpendiculars in the world's art.

Did the builders of the Great Pyramid know that their architects' models might preserve bits of meat and potatoes? More seriously, did they possess knowledge of another energy? Sir Flinders Petrie, considered the father of modern scientific archeology, was a nonesotericist who did original scientific studies at Giza. Like other Egyptologists he attempted to figure out how the Egyptians built their pyramids with their supposed low-level, heave-ho construction techniques. Eventually he came across a two-ton portcullis in the pyramid of Chephren in an untenable position as far as the theory of direct manpower goes. Petrie had to conclude that the builders must have known of some construction method unknown to us. Perhaps it was an ingenious device. Or perhaps they used some energy other than mechanical power. It is not altogether irrational to suppose that people who it now appears purposefully built a structure memorializing the exact dimensions of the earth and correct calculations of its movements in space might have known another thing—or two.

There are far too many groups selling small pyramids to list. If you don't want to build your own, check ads in psychic publications or inquire at a metaphysical bookstore. However, as a partial reply to the many people who ask us where they can locate other pyramid experimenters and compare notes, depending on your approach, you might find something of interest in: *The Pyramid Guide, A Bi-Monthly Newsletter*, $4.50 per year, short features, plus a broad-spectrum forum for correspondents to exchange results of pyramid research. Editor Bill Cox also has Verne Cameron's books and devices available. El Cariso Publications, PO Box 176, Elsinore, California 92330. (For basics, ask for list of early issues.)

Astral Research Company markets experimental pyramids. This group is headed by John P. Boyle, who has accumulated data on experimenters across this country and in other countries working on generators and pyramids. PO Box 583-A, Detroit, Michigan 48232.

Karl Drbal's licensee in the United States is the Great Pyramid Company, which sells six-inch cardboard pyramids with compass and directional board, Box A, 81/60 248th St., Bellrose, New York 11426.

Generators and Accumulators

An energy, but not one of the recognized ones, can be condensed, some claim, by juxtaposing layers of organic and inorganic materials to make a blanket or sandwich. The theory behind this sort of accumulator is similar to theories behind the pyramid experiment—that there is some kind of cosmic energy accompanying solar radiation reaching the earth. The inventor of the energy blanket and similar accumulators in box shape was, of course, the internationally known psychoanalyst Dr. Wilhelm Reich, who believed he had discovered a new form of universal energy. He called it orgone because he felt it was connected with all organic life. Dr. Reich believed every living thing is immersed in this energy, which is the basic life force. The energy blanket was alleged to concentrate this unknown life energy, which is supposedly present everywhere in the atmosphere. Once orgone energy is collected, according to Reichean experimenters, it can be used in various ways.

How to Make an Energy Blanket

To make an energy blanket you'll need several pieces of organic material such as wool or silk. For a simple basic blanket 2' × 3', you'll need about two yards of 36'' wide material. Cut it into three sections of about two feet each. You'll next need two or three cartons of fine steel wool (inorganic material), available at most department stores or hardware stores. Spread out the steel wool evenly all over the first rectangle of wool (or silk) material; put a second piece of wool (or silk) material on top and also cover it with a layer of steel wool. Top off the heap with another layer of wool (or silk) material. Then sew all around the edges to hold all the layers firmly in place. Blankets can be made like hero sandwiches—with as many alternate layers of wool and steel wool as you wish—and they can be made in larger or smaller dimensions. Some people have put together energy blankets of regular full-size wool blankets and made them more than five layers thick. A small portable version can also be made the size of a pocket handkerchief.

The energy condensed by the blanket is said to depend to some extent on the weather. Sunny days are supposedly best for accumulating blanket energy. Rain, fog, and smog are said to interfere with the accumulation process and the effect of the blanket is supposed to be minimal when the weather's bad. The blanket is said to be strongly affected by lightning storms during which an excessive charge may build up. Reich thought such an excess could damage organic substances. Reich and other experimenters felt that the blanket helped people build up their energy if they were run down; and by strengthening resistance, the blanket helped people overcome colds and various aches and pains. Putting the blanket on for an hour was supposed to overcome exhaustion and tension and induce a feeling of well-being and relaxation. Two or three applications of the blanket for an hour each per day were supposed to clear up a cold in forty-eight hours. Reich cautioned that a person taking any kind of medication or drug should not use the blanket. After some months of applying the orgone blanket, the energizing effect is alleged to get weaker as a person can be built up only to a certain point.

Does the blanket really accumulate energy? Trying to assess objectively whether a person's aches and pains disappear because of the blanket or for some other reason is difficult. Perhaps tests can be devised to see whether or not the blankets do have an energizing effect.

A small pocket-size energy blanket can be made up, and a small control blanket of the same dimensions can be made of alternate layers of wool and paper. Place a handful of bean seeds under each blanket for a few hours, then sprout them. (See plant section.) See if the seeds under the energy blanket grow faster and have more vitality. Another angle is to place an energy blanket on the soil and a control blanket on a similar patch for a couple of days. Then put an equal number of seeds in each patch and see which batch grows faster. Put an energy blanket over a bowl of water. Water is supposed to be able to accumulate orgone energy also. Then try watering one of two plants with the treated water. An energy blanket could also be placed under or over a plant to see if its growth is enhanced. Try placing a slice of fresh meat or cheese under each blanket and after several days see if there's a difference. Some people are trying experiments with the pyramid form made of energy blankets to see if it enhances the pyramid's effect on desiccating meat or whether the two energies cross one another out. Combining ideas from other sections of the book and your own ideas, you may come up with some objective evidence that juxtaposing organic and inorganic materials in layers, like a battery, may have some sort of energy effect. The ideas of Baron von Reichenbach may be helpful in assessing the type of "odic" charge on wool, silk, and steel wool. For more information on the energy blanket get Reich's small book, *The Orgone Energy Accumulator—Its Scientific and Medical Use*, 1951, available from Health Research, Mokelumne Hill, California 95245. As this book goes into print, we have just received Professor W. Edward Mann's excellent account of Reich's researches of energy. Mann's *Orgone, Reich and Eros* (Simon & Schuster, 1973) provides intriguing information on embattled energy explorers through the years.

And if you are seriously interested in generally pursuing a new form of energy, you might try to find out all you can about Reich's experiments and theoretical formulations. The blanket was really a tidbit cast up by investigations cosmic in proportion. Dr. Reich believed that he had found *the* Cosmic Life Energy. His experimental observations jibe with those of many other energy researchers from Reichenbach to Soviet PK investigators. He concluded that this energy, controlled, could be eminently beneficial to man kind, that it had practical application of the widest sort—from rainmaking to orgone energy motors, to counteracting atomic energy.(Could atomic tests affect the "other" energies, sending them ricocheting through the planet?) Reich, almost everyone agrees,was a genius and an extremely difficult personality; whether or nothe was right about orgone remains still to be seen. He died in thefederal penitentiary at Danbury, Connecticut, in 1957, jailed because he refused to allow an FDA injunction against the rental of his accumulators for therapeutic purposes. On principle, Reich refused to argue his case legally. He would not admit that a court of law or government agency had the right to decide on scientific discoveries.

Reich's discovery of orgone and the disaster it eventually called down upon him from various strongholds is described by his wife, Ilse, in *Wilhelm Reich, A Personal Biography*, Avon, 1969. Reich's works on psychology and sociology are being reissued at a fast clip. However, not many include much on the energy aspects of orgone. Reich's voluminous reports on the energy, including the annals of the Orgone Institute and the *Orgone Energy Bulletin*, are very hard to come by because the FDA destroyed most of them. Science did not recognize another form of energy, orgone. The FDA decreed Reich's claims fraudulent and went into the book-burning business—not so very long ago, in the latter half of the fifties.

Reich's experience should perhaps serve as a caveat. Many believe that psi-related research carries enormous potential for curing today's incurables. Inherent, too, in some of the work such as Kirlian photography are probably better means of diagnosis to replace some of the current enervating and torturous procedures. There are possibilities, too, for effective preventive medicine.

Medicine and psi, the links are there. But it is best to resist understandable temptation and stay out of strictly medical areas in ad hoc psi research. Certainly don't start advertising cures or treatment. There are two good reasons for this: First of all, many of us have a little medical knowledge but not enough to know what we're doing in the round. The so-called paranormal facets of heal-ing opening up now are genuine and exciting, but the energies and physical interactions that come into play are not yet fully com-prehended. If something has the power to heal, treated wrongly or ignorantly it may also harm and it already has in a few in-stances.

The second good reason for turning your experimenting to other pastures is simply that if you found a "cure," it would probably be your undoing. During the last hundred years, even highly accredited doctors and scientists who claimed to have found from their experiments a means of healing through other than accepted channels have fared poorly, to put it gently. This probably sounds ultracynical—like saying "whatever you do, don't find a cure for cancer"—which is not quite the point.

If you are genuinely interested in bringing in new forms of healing, in seeing practical results on a wide scale, there is something you can do that could be very valuable. You can experiment in the paranormal, become familiar with it. You can show others, you can spread information, particularly solid scientific reports. You can help change the climate of understanding. Only when the climate shifts will claims such as those of Reich and many, many others avoid dismissal by fiat. They can be evaluated intelligently and developed if anything promising should turn up.

Psychotronic Biogenerators

As a bridge from the cosmic to the personal in the energy area we might follow some observations of T. C. Lethbridge, naturalist and archeologist, for thirty years director of excavation for the Cambridge Antiquarian Society and for the University Museum of Archaeology and Ethnology. Lethbridge has done much study of the ancient stone rings in the British Isles, the most famous of which is Stonehenge. It was another circle, cheerfully named the Merry Maidens of Cornwall, that literally jolted Lethbridge into speculating about the accounts of mana or special sort of energy that have come down to us from many parts of the ancient world including England.

"For untold generations it has been believed, especially by the devotees of the old witch religion, that by means of exciting people to execute wild circular dances, power could be generated and stored in stones and trees." Lethbridge says that when he put his hand on a stone in the largely undisturbed Merry Maiden ring, he received something very much like an electric shock. He thinks it at least possible that the charge came from human beings. If you do your wild circular dancing "in rings formed of stones with gaps between them, you have a form of dynamo." To understand why this experienced archeologist thinks anyone may have wanted such a dynamo, see *The Sons of God, A Fantasy?* Routledge & Kegan Paul, 1972.

The idea that dancing activates paranormal powers is widespread and is perhaps seen most consummately in the Sufi whirling dervishes. Lethbridge's other proposition that humans can transfer some sort of energy to inanimate matter is another idea with a long and sometimes bizarre pedigree.

It appears in its most contemporary shape as the Pavlita generators in Czechoslovakia. Modern sculpture? Archeological find? Machine parts? Glance at the photo section and see what you think they look like. Many psychotronic researchers maintain that forms such as the pyramid operate on a *cosmic* psychotronic energy, while the generators are involved with a form of this force which is a *bio*energy. In other words the charge comes from living things. That there is both a cosmic and biological pulse to this X force has been noted by most energy researchers from the most ancient to the most modern. Since we have written about them in *PDBIC* and still do not possess the precise directions on their construction, we will not go into the generators in depth here. By now, a number of Americans, ranging from a movie producer to an atomic physicist, have watched Robert Pavlita and his daughter Jana demonstrate at least a few of their generators. Pavlita also demonstrated the generators for the First International Congress of Parapsychology and Psychotronics, June, 1973, Prague.

Robert Pavlita, who holds various patents relating to the textile industry, which is his field of professional endeavor, maintains that he is a technologist, too, when it comes to his generators. His claim is not proven certainly, but as research into the energies associated with the body expands, Pavlita's seems to have edged further into the realm of possibility. Briefly, the devices supposedly accumulate a bioenergy, store it, and redirect the force to produce various effects. The secret is in the shape and juxtaposition of materials—which is perhaps not as mysterious as it sounds. Whether you see at night, fry an egg, or electrocute yourself when you switch on the electricity depends on whether you are using an appliance shaped like a light bulb, a frying pan, or an electric chair.

Supposedly, Pavlita switches on his appliances by transmitting or inducing energy: through his gaze, often in conjunction with a staring pattern on the device (again, the idea that force comes from the eyes); by fingering and touching the devices in a certain scheme (again, the idea of polarity); and by other unrevealed methods.

The Pavlita generators reputedly produce many phenomena that psychics also elicit, implying a common energy. (For uses see photo section.) Psychotronic researchers believe they are working with a real force, and warn that like any energy it can be dangerous when mishandled.

At this date what can one say of the Pavlita generators? One might say that if a creative person searched even half the reports describing an "other" energy that have appeared just since the days of Mesmer and Reichenbach, it wouldn't be too surprising if he could concoct devices that produce unusual effects. There may not be anything to the generators. Maybe Pavlita is a ringer, an inventor with strong PK abilities. If there is something to the devices themselves—or perhaps more correctly to the combination of person and device—we would guess that Pavlita is right in calling himself a technician and that his generators are the first spawn of a new technology. They would be, then, rather crude prototypes needing much research and development to be converted to wide practical use. Would investigation be worthwhile? Was it worthwhile to develop apparatus to put other energies to work?

One can't blame Pavlita for withholding his secret, for he believes that there are patent concerns and the possibility of commercial application. It is noteworthy how many of those who contact us about Pavlita are consulting engineers and university scientists. They don't seem to be in a conversational mood either. And, as always, in a field of unknowns there are rumors, sensational and otherwise, about powerful interests suddenly beginning to sniff at the whole field of other energies as reflected in PK, dowsing, and psychotronic generators. Whether that's true or not, there does seem to be a dawning awareness in many quarters that psi—particularly in its energetic aspects—is coming in as an applied science.

Pyramids and generators—if nothing else they've led to a new interest in shapes, which fits well with a time when various thinkers are toying with geometric and holographic models of life and world. We suspect, too, that in the coming decade you'll be hearing a great deal more about investigations of the effect on body and mind of specially designed shapes combined with color and probably sound.

In this section we've traced a few approaches to so-called psi energy. If you're on the trail, don't overlook some of the areas we had to leave out. Eyeless sight phenomena are important, so are types of PK that we omitted. The huge domain of dowsing certainly holds keys to the understanding of energy. Also there is the scientific study of astrobiology already revealing that we resonate to more energies and things in the universe than we might have imagined. (See "The Sun and Us," and "The Lunar Beat" in *Natural Birth Control*, Bantam, 1973.)

Quite obviously the hunt for what is now often called "free energy" is heating up. It doesn't take much imagination to figure out why in a world of energy crisis, pollution, food shortage, sickness. (For what it's worth, a few years ago one Czech researcher told us that gasoline treated with psychotronic energy would give better mileage. Unfortunately we don't know what kind of generator he used.) Perhaps it's time for our native love of gadgets, of tinkering and experimenting to take a whirl at psychotronics, now that we really need the energy—any energy. There may be a lot of plums to pull out of the unknown. The field is open for homesteading, for discovery and practical invention.

To say it again, energies are neutral, the good or ill is in the use. Unlike other forces, the energies that we've been talking about apparently interact in special ways with mind and body. It would seem, therefore, that the creation of a body of knowledge about these energies would be of at least passing personal concern to everyone.

"The discovery of the energy associated with psychic events will be as important, if not more important, than the discovery of atomic energy." If Vasiliev is even half right, people other than pure psi researchers and ad hoc experimenters will prove interested. The more people who have knowledge, the less likely it will become the preserve of a single vested interest.

Section Five

15

Your Tape Recorder—A Tracking
Station for Paranormal Voices?

"The medium is the message" says media expert Marshall
McLuhan, referring to the impact the electronic media have had on
society. Today his dictum may apply in some quite unexpected
areas. For the past fifteen years, research has been conducted in
Scandinavia, Europe, and Britain into the conundrum that the
electronic "medium" of the tape recorder is manifesting paranormal "messages." For centuries human mediums have claimed
to bring messages from the beyond. Now some scientists claim
electronics receptors can pick up these broadcasts from other
dimensions. The tape-recorded paranormal sounds are believed to
be voices of some sort. Quite apart from the questions of who is
speaking and how do they get recorded onto magnetic tape is the
apparently well-documented evidence that paranormal sounds of
some kind have been tape-recorded under the strictest test conditions.

Moreover, as you will see in Chapter 16, anyone can check out
this phenomenon for himself or herself with a tape recorder—which
is exactly what has happened throughout Europe, Britain, and
Scandinavia, where in recent years thousands of people have
personally experienced the voice phenomenon. Before getting into
the how-to, it's helpful to have some of the scientific background.

The whole issue of tape-recorded paranormal voices might be
dismissed as self-delusion and a bizarre fad were it not for the
careful research and painstaking investigation of many distinguished scientists and researchers over the past decade.

The most sophisticated electronic techniques have been used to
analyze the voicetape phenomenon, including voice printers,

videotape recorders, oscilloscopes, all the resources of radio-frequency screened labs, designed to suppress all forms of electromagnetic interference with tape-recording. Still, voices marginally in the human frequency range, speaking recognizable words (analyzed in visible speech diagrams) appear mysteriously on tape-recordings done inside labs shielded from all known forms of interference. The research has now come to involve scores of outstanding scientists, sound-recording engineers, and electronics specialists in numerous countries; and outside the scientific sector it is known that even the Vatican has become involved.

The accumulating scientific evidence points to two stunning conclusions. The human mind may have the ability, in some unknown way other than speaking, to impress language directly onto magnetic tape at a distance. Or, more startling still, the conclusion reached by the pioneers of the voice phenomenon: The so-called dead are attempting to make contact with us through the electronic medium of tape-recording.

A hundred years ago, people in America strained to hear the first faint, indistinct voices reaching them over the stovepipe wire and tin cans of the early telephones. Do we stand on a similar frontier of communications today, as thousands of people strain to hear through their tape recorders the first indistinct transmissions of paranormal voices addressing them personally from some unknown dimension? Has the dream of inventor Thomas A. Edison at last been realized—the development of electronic instruments to communicate with entities in the "next world"? What is one to make of the mounting scientific data on the paranormal voice phenomenon?

Dr. Walter H. Uphoff of Colorado, one of the first Americans to investigate the European research and duplicate it in the US, counsels about the "voices": "Do not be in a hurry to *accept* or *reject* evidence of paranormality. Let the evidence accumulate until a certain explanation becomes more or less plausible. If it is true, you cannot make it go away. If it is not true, you cannot make it come into being."

Basic Evidence

Are these paranormal voices just tape-recorded scratches and scrapings onto which listeners project imaginary words? The eminent European psychologist and parapsychologist Dr. Hans Bender, Director of the Institute for Border Areas of Psychology and Psychohygiene of the University of Freiburg (Germany's government-supported university institute for parapsychology), headed teams of scientists who conducted several investigations and voice-print analyses of the tape-recorded paranormal sounds. The teams included, among others, physicist Dr. B. Heim, Director of the Institute for Field Physics at Northeim, Dr. Friedebert Karger of the Max Planck Institute, Dr. Jurgen Keil of the University of Tasmania Institute of Psychology, engineer N. Lemke of Munich. The voice prints were analyzed by engineer Jochem Sotscheck, Director of the Research Group for Acoustics of the Central Office for Telegraphic Technology of Berlin. In the summer of 1964 Bender and several colleagues went to Sweden to meet the discoverer of the voice phenomenon, Friedrich Jurgenson, and to conduct initial tests. These early tests were successful and they returned in May, 1970, with a whole battery of equipment—an oscilloscope, various types òf tape recorders, special directional microphones, videotape recorders—for several series of tests over a number of days.

Analysis of the voice prints showed the paranormal sounds were indeed voices. Visible speech diagrams confirmed the words spoken. The frequency range of the recordings was within the range in which normal voices would be recorded and they showed the signals common to regular voice recordings. The "voices" also registered on the oscillograph as visible impulses filmed by the videotape recorder. After analyzing the voice prints of the paranormal voices at his Berlin lab, Jochem Sotscheck described results as "most encouraging."

Voice-phenomena recordings are done with a tape recorder and microphone set up in the usual way and using factory-fresh tape. No sounds are heard during recording, but on replay, faint voices of unknown origin appear to have been recorded. An alternate method is to connect a radio to a tape recorder and tune the radio between stations.

During one of the tests in Sweden, Bender had thought to himself the name of a friend of his, Brigette Rasmus. On replay of the tape recorded at that moment, a voice was heard whispering "Rasmus."

"I was the only one present who knew this name," says Dr. Bender. "The visible speech diagram shows that the word is objective and furthermore the analysis of the Berlin specialist, Jochem Sotscheck, makes susure that I cannot have whispered it." Several tape recordings done at the time all register the same word but analysis showed the sound did not originate from Bender's area of the room.

During another session, all present agreed to remain silent and

motionless for a full minute without so much as moving their lips.
They could observe on the oscillograph what was happening inside
the tape recorder. Thirty-eight seconds into the minute as they sat
silently, the oscillograph showed marked deflections indicating the
tape recorder was activated. On replay they heard a voice whispering in English with an American accent, "Stop as you like."
Several more words followed plus "One pause," pronounced in
German.

Could it have been a freak radio pickup? It seemed unlikely,
considering that the statement was relevant to the situation. In
addition an electronics engineer had supervised the recorders for
radio interference the whole time and found no radio pickup had
occurred. Did one of the group speak? It seemed improbable in
view of the tense mutual control, and neither the Swedish nor
German participants could speak English with an American accent.
Moreover, throat microphones would have revealed whispers of
any of those present.

In July, 1971, new experiments began with a surprise. The
German team en route to Jurgenson's country house, Nysund, lost
their way driving in seemingly endless woods; at the same time, one
of the group, Gisela was stricken with a very severe toothache.
Meanwhile Jurgenson waited impatiently for the German scientists
and finally decided to try a recording session on his own. Replaying
the tape he was intrigued to hear the German words—"*Sie kommen
bald. Zahnarzt. Zahnarzt.*" (They will arrive soon. Dentist.
Dentist.) Jurgenson played the tape for the group the moment they
arrived while the unfortunate Gisela made arrangements to go to a
dentist.

Typical of results during this 1971 series was the inexplicable
voice of a woman recorded on a brand-new Sony cassette tape.
There was no woman in the house at the time. The voice said,
"*Peng*" (a German interjection used when some striking event
happens); it resembled Gisela's voice and was recorded at the
moment she was away in Stockholm getting her aching tooth treated
by Mrs. Jurgenson, who is a dentist.

The German scientists concluded that on the basis of the voice-
print analysis of the voice-tapes the sounds were genuine objective
acoustical events—not imagined fantasies of the listeners; genuine
words were spoken by the voices on the tapes; the people in the
room had not uttered the taped words; they were not radio-broadcast
fragments.

In the *Parapsychology Review* (Vol. 3, No. 5), Dr. Bender

concludes that *the paranormal origin of the voice phenomena is highly probable.* (For more details, see *Journal of Paraphysics*, Vol. 6, No. 2, and voice prints of the voices in *Carry On Talking*.)

Robert Crookall, the well-known British writer and parapsychologist, reports that Dr. Bender considers the voice phenomenon equal in importance to nuclear physics.

Where are the voices coming from? In Bender's view they may be PK emanating from the people present at a recording session. Investigation of the voices as a PK effect should come first, he thinks, before turning to other explanations.

Could all the German scientists have been mistaken? Could they have missed monitoring fragments of some ham-radio broadcast bouncing off the ionsphere and onto their tapes?

On March 27, 1972, the firm of Belling and Lee Ltd., at Enfield, England, conducted an experiment on the voice phenomenon at their Radio-Frequency-Screened Laboratory. Supervising the experiment was Peter Hale, physicist and electronics engineer. Hale is the foremost expert on electronic-screen suppression in Britain and one of the five leading experts in the West. Physicist and electronics engineer Ralph Lovelock was another of the investigators. Pioneer voice researcher and psychologist Dr. Konstantin Raudive also took part. The Belling and Lee Lab is used to test the most sophisticated electronic equipment for British defense and is specifically designed to screen out any form of radio signal. The lab's own equipment for recording was set up and factory-fresh tape was used in the tests. Again paranormal voices that should not have been there were recorded on tape. "In view of the tests carried out in a screened laboratory at my firm," states Peter Hale, "I cannot explain what happened in normal physical terms."

Ralph Lovelock asserts that the voice phenomena are probably not explainable by any electronic means. (For more of his analysis, see appendix of *Breakthrough* and the book *Carry On Talking*.)

Within the past five years, interest in the voice phenomenon has burgeoned in Britain and on the Continent as news of this new research spread.

In 1969 the Swiss Association for Parapsychology awarded their First-Prize award jointly to psychologist Dr. Konstantin Raudive, West Germany, and physicist Professor Alexander Schneider, St. Gallen, Switzerland, for their work on direct voice messages on tape recordings.

At Britain's Cambridge University, Trinity College announced in September, 1970, that the Perrott-Warrick post-graduate-Studentship for Psychic Research had been awarded to David Ellis, MA, for the investigation of the voice phenomena. Ellis held the studentship for two years.

In that same month in 1970, the International Society for Catholic Parapsychologists held a conference in Austria in the series known as *Imago Mundi* Conferences, devoting a major part of the conference to scientific papers on the voice phenomena. Papers were presented by Theodor Rudolph, a high-frequency engineer with the well-known Telefunken company in Germany; Professor Alex Schneider, a physicist from Switzerland; Franz Seidl, an electronics engineer from Austria; and Dr. Konstantin Raudive, a Latvian psychologist now living in West Germany, who has been a leading experimenter with the voices.

In England and Ireland, scores of TV and radio shows devoted programs to discussions and examples of the voice phenomena and it became a subject for heated controversy in newspapers and magazines. Clergy, scientists, and the general public argued over the voices and what they seemed to be saying and why they were saying it and whether they *should* be saying it. Spiritualists worried over the caliber of the sources of the voices.

Moreover, if the voices ought not to be manifesting on magnetic tape recordings, what could be done to stop them anyway? Where were these voices coming from? the public asked. Some scientists felt that language could be impressed on tape by PK. Some thought the voices might be from UFO's. Perhaps they were the voices of living humans in altered states of consciousness. Still others asserted that the voice phenomena could all be attributed to the United States Central Intelligence Agency! Others maintained they were the voices of the dead. Amid the swirling theological controversy over this element of the voice phenomena, a letter to *The Irish Times* pinpointed the crux of the situation:

"If these be the dead, and if it be indeed a sin to listen to them, is there any way, short of a couple of decades of the Rosary, of inducing them to get to Hell off the air?"

How had this whole thing begun?

Discovery of the Voice Phenomena

In the summer of 1959 Friedrich Jurgenson, the Swedish painter, operatic tenor, and film producer, set out to tape-record bird songs in the country near his villa in Sweden. On playing back the recording of bird songs he heard a quiet male voice discussing "nocturnal bird songs" in Norwegian. Sometimes, by a fluke, a tape recorder can pick up radio broadcasts. Was this a fragment of a radio broadcast? he wondered. It was an odd coincidence, he thought, for a broadcast about nocturnal bird songs to be picked up on his tape at the very moment he switched on to tape-record bird songs. Subsequently he tried several more recordings. Nothing could be heard while taping, but during playback, Jurgenson could hear voices of some kind on the tape that seemed to have significant information for him. It seemed less likely it was some freak radio pickup when they addressed him by name and conveyed personal information. Moreover many of the "voices" claimed to be deceased relatives and friends.

The "voices" taped further instructions on different methods of recording their utterances. For several years Jurgenson continued experimenting at his home, Molnbo, near Stockholm. In addition to Dr. Bender and Dr. Karger, he gained the cooperation of numerous other scientists. In 1964 Jurgenson published a book in Sweden, *Voices From the Universe* (with a record), which described his strange experiences with tape recorders. In 1967 his second book *Radio-Link with the Beyond (Sprechfunk mit Verstorbenen)* was published in both Swedish and German. He has presented his findings at numerous conferences in Sweden. Currently Jurgenson and Bender plan to have a research center on the voice phenomena set up in southern Europe.

During the last decade or so Jurgenson, who is now seventy, also became well known as a producer of documentary films which dealt mainly with Italy. For years Jurgenson has had very close connections with the Vatican, with many cardinals and with Pope Paul VI. Among the documentary films he produced recently is one about the life of Pope Paul VI. In 1969 Friedrich Jurgenson was decorated by Pope Paul VI with the Commander's Cross of the Order of St. Gregory the Great. Did Jurgenson acquaint the Pope, cardinals, and other church officials with his intensive work on the electronic voice phenomena?

In 1971 Jurgenson wrote British author Peter Bander, "Besides, and perhaps it is the most important aspect, I have found a sympathetic ear for the voice phenomenon in the Vatican. I have won many wonderful friends among the leading figures in the Holy City. Today 'the bridge' stands firmly on its foundations."

One can conjecture from Jurgenson's statement that the leaders of the Roman Catholic Church are familiar with Jurgenson's books on the voice phenomena and his tape recordings. Possibly, Vatican officials have even participated in voice-phenomena experiments.

No official statement has been made by the Vatican about the voice phenomena, but individual opinions have been expressed by various church representatives. For instance, Father Pistone, Superior of the Society of St. Paul in England, which controls most of the Catholic Church's radio and TV stations, stated on TV and in interviews that he did not see anything against the teaching of the Church in the voice phenomena. ". . . scientifically it has yet to be established that we are really dealing with voices from the dead. What we are faced with is a phenomenon; we need accept no more and can accept no less."

Father Pistone indicates that the Church would and must keep a close check on what was happening in the area of paranormal voice recordings.

The Vatican has given official authorization to Father Andreas Resch of Innsbruck, Austria, to conduct research into psi and paranormal recordings, and in 1971 Father Resch started a course in parapsychology at the Pontifical University of the Lateran, the Vatican's school for priests in Rome. Father Schmid of Argau, Switzerland, has also been authorized to collect voice recordings.

The research on the voice phenomena most accessible to North Americans is that published in English in *Breakthrough* by Dr. Konstantin Raudive (pronounced *Row*-dee-vay). Dr. Raudive is Latvian and was forced to flee his native country when the Soviet Union invaded and absorbed the Baltic republic of Latvia in 1945. Dr. Raudive and his wife, Dr. Zenta Maurina, fled first to nearby Sweden, then later moved to Bad Krozingen in southern Germany, near the Swiss border.

Dr. Raudive, now in his sixties, has both a literary and scientific background. He is well known in Germany as the author of many books and as a psychologist. He is a former student of both Dr. Carl Jung and Spanish philosopher Ortega y Gasset. He studied psychology in Switzerland, Germany, and in England, at Oxford. He taught at the University of Riga in Latvia and at one time edited a Latvian daily newspaper.

In 1965, while living in Sweden, Raudive met Friedrich Jurgenson and learned the various techniques for tape-recording paranormal voices, which Jurgenson had evolved according to the instructions of the electronic voices. (See Chapter 16.) Dr. Raudive's explorer's instincts were aroused, he says. From 1965 on, he has devoted his time almost exclusively to the phenomenon of the voice recordings, at first by himself and with his wife and later with the cooperation of physicist Alex Schneider of St. Gallen, Switzerland, and various engineers.

Raudive has now recorded well over 100,000 phrases spoken by the enigmatic voices on tapes. The recordings are carefully classified and stored in his library. Both Jurgenson and Raudive are multilingual and the voices they recorded speak in polyglot phrases, like "telegraphic word salads." (Phrases recorded by unilingual people tend to be in their own language although on occasion a person may receive a message in an unknown language.)

Messages are rarely longer than ten to twelve words at a time and in Raudive's and Jurgenson's recordings, an ungrammatical mixture of languages is characteristic making it less likely that the messages are fragments of radio broadcasts. In a typical recording, Raudive may be addressed by his full name or various childhood nicknames. The name of his birthplace may be given in a Latvian dialect—Latgalian. The compressed sentence may continue in Swedish, Russian, or German. The compressed voices are unlike any normal voice broadcasts. The speech is almost double the usual speed and the sound is pulsed in rhythms like poetry or chanting.

The voices sound a little like the early radio transmissions of the astronauts from the moon. The voices are audible over tremendous background noise and a rushing sound. It's a little like trying to hear someone over a terribly bad phone connection from a foreign country. Raudive and Jurgenson both emphasize it's a question of training the ear. Raudive feels the skill develops gradually. If a person has fine hearing and perfect pitch, he or she has a big advantage.

Raudive classifies the voices according to audibility as A, B, or C. The faintest C voices he doesn't bother to catalogue. The information obtained from these terse, pulsed voices is generally relevant to the individual doing the recording. No voices are audible during recording, only on playback.

Among the scores of scientists and researchers who have worked with Dr. Raudive are Dr. Gebhard Frei, president of the International Society of Catholic Parapsychologists and co-founder of the Jung Institute in Zurich; Dr. Hans Naegeli, president of the Swiss Parapsychology Society; Dr. Theo Locher, president of the Swiss Parapsychological Association; Dr. Alex Schneider, physicist; Theodor Rudolph, high-frequency engineer.

Dr. Raudive published his findings in German in a book called *The Inaudible Made Audible* recently translated into English and published by Colin Smythe and Taplinger under the title

Breakthrough. The book contains Raudive's how-to instructions, his theories about the voices and selections of his decipherings, analyses, and observations of some of the 100,000 or more taped phrases. In addition, to back up Raudive's own documentation, there are eighty-four pages of reports from experts who examined Raudive's material, listened to the original tapes, conducted further research of their own, developed new recording instruments to improve reception, and in general duplicated and advanced the research.

The editor of the British edition, Peter Bander, added a very helpful preface. A record put out by Vista Productions (see Section Six) gives a selection from the original Raudive voice tapes and provides some idea of what the electronic voices sound like, according to the different recording methods. Because of the polyglot nature of the original taped material, the great difficulties in accurately translating idiomatic expressions, and the often disjointed nature of the telegramlike phrases, the texts often have a resemblance to some of those multilanguage phrase books for tourists.

To add to the interpretative difficulties with multilingual phrases, the same phonetic pattern can sometimes have widely different meanings in different languages—a kind of Rorschach sound test for linguists. Sentences received are also often totally confused as if spoken in a dream.

Sometimes messages are very clear, but occasionally the tapings are like a kinetic ouija board running a gamut of alphabet sounds hard to attribute to any known language. Jurgenson reports that the significance of some of the apparently meaningless words he's taped is often discovered years later.

Critics of the voices complain of the banality of the messages on the linguistic loops of tape, though technical problems may be partly responsible for the brevity and distortion of statements.

The voices are always recorded on factory-fresh tape. There are voices of men, women, and children speaking in hurried snatches. Voice-print analysis confirms the voices are in the frequency bands associated with men's and women's voices. The voices identify themselves, give their names and hometown; they address the persons in the recording room by name; they respond to questions asked; comment on conditions in the room and on transmission conditions (storms cause static during "voice broadcasts"); they comment on who is present or not present in the room; they even discuss the clothes the experimenters are wearing ("He has a red pullover on''); voices are still recorded if the experimenter leaves the recorder running and goes out.

Direct interaction with the experimenters seems to eliminate the possibility that all the voices could be explained as fragments of radio broadcasts. It seems unlikely that a program out of the blue would address you by name. Could Radive be misinterpreting the phases or imagining they say something other than what is really there? At present the difficulties of interpretation are enormous owing to the static and noise accompanying the voices. David Ellis of Cambridge believes that on at least one occasion, Raudive mistook fragments of an English-language Radio Luxembourg program for German and Russian phrases of a different meaning.

Nevertheless, by now, hundreds of people have listened to the Raudive tapes and there is a high percentage of agreement among them that at least certain of the statements anyway seem to be correctly interpreted. Physicist Alex Schneider has pointed out that even if just one single voice pronouncing one single name such as ''Konstantin Raudive'' could be proven genuine and not some freak reception, the voice phenomenon would be established.

It may be that dogs, whose hearing range is greater than humans, hear the voice phenomena more clearly than humans. Peter Bander observed that his Great Dane, Rufus, would bark and bristle at the instant a voice spoke on the voice-phenomena tapes. Rufus ordinarily paid no attention to radio, stereo, or tape recorders.

Viennese electronics engineer Franz Seidl has developed what he considers greatly improved recording instrumentation. It seems as if the energy available for the sounds is extremely small and must be conserved by terse, telegraphic statements. In his work, ''Everything has been done to keep extra material off the tape,'' says Seidl. He has also tried the reverse experiment, trying to transmit messages onto the tape using powerful electronic sending gear. The tapes remain unaffected by the radiations produced. In addition he's found the same voice-phenomena messages have been received in independent experiments in different parts of the world. Seidl has found the paranormal voices helpful in detective work. He used the instruments to help a family try to find their daughter who had disappeared. Voices appeared on tapes giving information about her whereabouts.

British expert Ralph Lovelock, of Belling and Lee Labs, suggests it would be interesting to try voice recordings somewhere on the earth's surface where there are no significant levels of broadcast radiation—the middle of the Pacific for instance. It might also be valuable to experiment with the voice phenomena above the earth in an airplane. Height and speed may have an effect on paranormal phenomena according to medium Arthur Ford. In his book *Nothing So Strange* (Paperback Library, pp. 92-94), Ford reports on an airborne psi experiment conducted at night in a plane with a distinguished group of people aboard. The experiment took place in the late 1940's and dealt with direct-voice mediumship. Ford was present as an observer. The plane reached an altitude over 8,000 feet and Ford reports a multitude of voices, which were immediately recognized by those present, began to come through. High above the murky atmosphere of the earth's cities, psi perceptions seemed to heighten, Ford says, and psychic information came through very clearly. Would this be true of outer space, too?

Dr. Raudive states that he has twice been visited by American engineers connected with the space program who have carefully examined his work on the voice phenomena. He reasoned that if his relatively simple recording equipment produced voice phenomena, the highly sophisticated recording equipment on board space vehicles with the astronauts might be even more likely to produce voice phenomena. Raudive asked if he might hear any of the moon flight tape recordings and was told that those recordings would not be released for some years to come.

Because of the policy of silence on the space tapes, conjecture has spread that paranormal voices were registered in outer space. This idea may be totally unfounded. Many people in the space program are interested in psi research simply as private individuals and it has nothing whatever to do with their jobs. Nevertheless, Raudive considered the space engineers' comments and questions unusually pertinent.

Recent mass sightings of UFOs; assertions by Soviet scientists that they have picked up outer space signals; plus the revelation by US defense engineer L. George Lawrence that by using biotransducers, seemingly intelligent signals from outer space have been monitored in the US (see plant section), have led some to place more credence in the hypothesis that some of the voice-tape messages could even be from extraterrestrial beings. (See also *Saga*, November, 1968.)

In *Our Haunted Planet* (Fawcett, 1971), John Keel claims that thousands of Americans have picked up strange, inexplicable, intelligent signals on ham radio and civilian band radio on frequencies from VLF (very low frequency) to UHF (ultra high frequency). Keel maintains too that NASA space shots have been repeatedly troubled by anomalous radio transmission of strange voices in unknown languages, music, and noises.

Rolf Schaffranke, senior research engineer, at one time with the National Aeronautics and Space Administration, visited Dr. Raudive in September, 1969. He reports, ". . . The existence of the phenomenon can be considered established with the statements of three hundred independent observers who have listened to demonstration tapes and taken part in one or more of the sessions. . . ."

In a report in *Fate* (July, 1970), Schaffranke observed that Raudive was spending most of his lecture and royalty income to buy equipment and tapes for his experiments and putting in up to twelve hours a day on the work. Schaffranke cites and seems to concur with the review of Raudive's *Breakthrough* in the British *Journal of Psychic Studies*: "To call this a potentially epoch-making book does not seem out of place for the first scholarly work on a new paranormal phenomenon which holds out the promise of becoming a verifiable and repeatable channel of survival research." Unfortunately, Dr. Raudive died in 1974 before his book could receive wide recognition in America.

Does the Survival Hypothesis Explain the Voices?

"Everything I have read and heard forces me to the supposition that only the hypothesis of the voices belonging to transcendental personalities has any chance of explaining the full scope of these phenomena." So stated Dr. Gebhard Frei, a cousin of Pope Pius XII, a cofounder of the Jung Institute, and an internationally known Swiss parapsychologist.

Father Frei died October 27, 1967. In November, 1967, at numerous taping sessions, a voice giving its name as Gebhard Frei appears on tape. (One of these segments is included on the record of voices released by Vista Records.) Schaffranke claims that Professor Peter Hohenwarter of the University of Vienna positively identifies the voice as belonging to Dr. Frei.

Schaffranke was also intrigued by the visits to Raudive's studio of the celebrated Soviet writer, Valery Tarsis, author of *Ward Seven*. Tarsis was able to get out of the Soviet Union in 1966 and settled in the West. In February and November, 1967, Tarsis conducted voice-phenomenon experiments at Bad Krozingen. For some of them, Raudive is not present. Among the voices audible on the playback is one Tarsis identifies as his good friend Boris

Pasternak, author of *Dr. Zhivago*. (Pasternak died in 1960.) The voice speaks in Russian and comments, among other things, on Tarsis' escape from the USSR, the book Tarsis was then writing, and on Pasternak's friend Olga.

This same type of paranormal voice message keeps coming in from all over Europe—from both scientists and amateurs. Harald Bergestam of Stockholm reports in *Fate* (March, 1973), on a visit to Jurgenson during which he heard his own Hungarian-born wife speak to him in Hungarian on the voice tapes, addressing him by name. She had died four years earlier. Bergestam visited Claude and Ellen Thorlin of Eskilstuna, who have researched voice tapes for eight years. During an experiment, "We heard a man's voice saying clearly, 'I am living,' and he repeated this. The second time his voice was filled with excitement and happiness. We understood that he had just come to realize that although he had died he still lived. Another voice came on, a young woman's voice saying tearfully, 'They can hear us on the earth.'" Bergestam concludes, "A tape recorder is a dead thing, not an instrument of the emotions, and this technical vehicle can record voices from another world."

American scientist Dr. Walter Uphoff, after investigating Raudive's research in Germany, points out that when relatives or close friends are the ostensible communicators, the messages are often intimate and personal and unlikely to be fragments of a radio transmission. A frequent voice on the Raudive tapes is purported to be that of Margarete Petrautzki, who was secretary to Raudive's wife for ten years. Prior to her death, February 10, 1965, she had often expressed doubt about existence after death. Shortly after her death, a female voice sounding like Margarete's and identifying itself as Margarete on the tape exclaims with amazement, *"Bedenke, ich bin!"* (German "Just think! I am!") This voice can also be heard on the Raudive record.

Voice prints of "voices" purported to come from the same source always show identical patterns, according to Peter Bander. Voice prints are produced by a sound spectrograph, which traces on graph paper the distinctive sound patterns of a person's voice. The voice print is said to be as reliable as a fingerprint in identifying a person. One difficulty though in applying voice printing to many of the voice tapes is that the paranormal voices are imbedded in an enormous amount of noise and static, which distorts the voice quality.

Dr. Uphoff reports that Theodor Rudolph, a high-frequency-electronics engineer with Telefunken at Ulm, Germany, has been working on refining recording equipment for some time to avoid any probability of interference. Rudolph worked with the pioneers of radar in Germany, including Willy Messerschmitt, and later studied electronics in England and the US. With his improved equipment he is convinced that he has recorded the voices of his deceased parents and his brother, Otto, who was killed in World War II.

Reverend Father Leo Schmid of the Oensingen parish in the Swiss canton of Aargau, told of a taping experience where he became convinced that "the voice was unmistakably that of Monsignor Josef Meier, who died in 1960 and to whom I had asked to speak before the play-in began. . . ." In another recording a female voice says "suitable for a trip to the court" in the archaic Aargau dialect spoken in the region up until the end of the 1700's.

Father Schmid, an esteemed Catholic scholar, who has written extensively on theology, has been given the express permission of his superiors to collect the voices, and since 1969 has recorded more than 10,000 samples on tape. Father Schmid does his recordings in his church at around 2 A.M. Setting up the tape recorder some six feet away from himself, he meditates and prays. Paranormal voices have frequently been recorded at these sessions.

In Dr. Uphoff's opinion the voice phenomenon opens anew "the age-old enigma: What happens to man when he dies? Many questions remain to be answered, as Dr. Raudive is first to admit, but the evidence that is accumulating suggests that perhaps there can be 'electronic communication with the dead' as the subtitle of the [Raudive] book suggests."

Probably the most urgent, constant theme in all the voice-tape messages received so far from all parts of the world is—there's life after death: "We are the dead—we live!" Is this a PK effect on the part of a populace anxious to believe that life continues after bodily death? Or are these messages genuinely from intelligences in other dimensions? It's curious that back in 1936, theosophist Alice Bailey made the clear-cut prediction in *Esoteric Psychology* (p. 184) that electronic contact between the "seen and the unseen" would eventually be set up: "Through the use of the radio by those who have passed over will communication be eventually set up, and reduced to a true science. . . . Death will lose its terrors, and that particular fear will come to an end."

Strangely enough, one of the ways scientists register these paranormal voices is through a radio, by tuning it between stations and plugging it into a tape recorder to record and amplify the sounds. It was Bailey's opinion that the electrification of the planet and the mass of electromagnetic radiation emanating from our communications equipment (TVs, radios, etc.) would eventually alter the vibratory pattern of the atmosphere around the earth and thus facilitate the possibility of communication with other dimensions of life, which, she said, are vibrating on other energy frequencies.

Should the survival hypothesis be right and the voices on the tapes are those of people who have died, the fact that they are trying to communicate with the living may not be that unusual. An American psychologist and a Welsh physician both estimate that nearly fifty percent of normal people experience "seeing" or communicating with dead relatives or friends.

"People who have these experiences are not mystics or spiritualists, but secretaries, mailmen, barbers, and other practically minded persons," says Dr. Robert Kastenbaum, on the staff of Detroit's Wayne State University Center for Psychological Studies of Dying, Death and Lethal Behavior.

Dr. Kastenbaum bases his findings on a study of 140 persons— none of whom had any association with the occult. Some sixty-three individuals described an experience "which seemed at the time as though it involved communication with another mind, since deceased and invisible."

A similar conclusion was reached by Dr. W. Dewi Rees, who reported that of 293 widows and widowers he studied, 137 (or forty-seven percent) admitted to having experienced some form of communication with their deceased spouse.

Says Dr. Rees, "I am convinced from my study—probably the most rigorous and definite on the subject—that almost half of all widows and widowers receive messages from their former mates, even years after their death."

Survival research from around the world has generally shown that messages purported to come from deceased persons frequently reflect the culture in which they lived and its general organization and expectations. As Dr. Gertrude Schmeidler pointed out at a Symposium on Survival Research (*ASPR Journal*, April, 1965), messages from the dead in our Western society typically say something like, ". . . 'I am still with you and I love you.' But among the Atimeland of Alor, typical messages say, 'You are sick and suffering because you did not give me a death feast.' "

Many of the people allegedly communicating on the Raudive tapes describe the horrors of the war situation in Latvia, the Soviet takeover, the gruesome ways they met their deaths at that time. They reflect the bureaucratic organization of their own society on earth talking about "camps," "passports," "official passes," "customs officials," and types of red tape they must go through in order to communicate on the voice tapes. In messages alleged to come from dead persons from America, a "control personality" is described who organizes the group of people who wish to communicate.

Some spiritualists in Britain have expressed concern about certain messages alleged to be from famous and infamous people. Some of them feel that if the voice-tape messages are from beings in other dimensions, some of them might be tricksters who assume identities and are eager to create trouble. On the other hand, unlike mediumship, one can always press the stop button on the tape recorder.

It might be interesting to compare what the voices say with what various "personalities" have dictated about life in other dimensions through psychics. *The Seth Material* and *Seth Speaks* by Jane Roberts and *The Betty Book* and *The Unobstructed Universe* by S.E. White may contain helpful data against which to view the voice-phenomena messages. Of course the great central classic of psychical research is F. W. H. Myers' *Human Personality and Its Survival of Bodily Death*.

Controversy in Britain

Raudive's book on the voices created a stir in Germany. Before it could be published in Britain, the English publisher Colin Smythe wanted to be sure the voice phenomena existed. Colin Smythe tried a test recording on his own with his own tape recorder and on playback he heard a rhythmic sound like a voice, but could not understand what it said. He asked editor Peter Bander to listen to the recording. Bander replayed the tape many times. He too heard a rhythm—then a voice—quite distant but very clear. He was sure it was his imagination. A woman's voice said in German: *"Mach die Tür mal auf?"* (Why don't you open the door?). Says Bander, "As soon as I heard the voice I recognized the speaker; although the voice spoke terribly fast and in a strange rhythm, I had heard it many times before. For eleven years before her death I had conducted my entire correspondence with my mother by tape [London to Germany], and I would recognize her voice anywhere. And this was my mother's voice."

Bander was aware that Colin Smythe could not speak or understand German and was not the type of person to play deceitful tricks. He asked other staff members to listen to the tape and write down phonetically what they heard. According to Bander in the preface to *Breakthrough* they were indeed all hearing the same thing.

Smythe invited Dr. Raudive to England for further experiments. The tests proved successful and Colin Smythe decided to go ahead with plans to publish the book in English.

Meanwhile the Deputy Prime Minister of England heard about the Raudive book and Smythe's decision to publish it. He immediately objected to this material being released in English and wrote his good friend Sir Robert Mayer, who happens to be Chairman of Colin Smythe Ltd., that publishing the Raudive book in Britain would have serious repercussions if it did not get the backing of British scientists. Sir Robert Mayer agreed. The Colin Smythe Company would be compromised if they brought out a book that the scientific establishment scoffed at, he said. He insisted that the book would have to be dropped unless the publishing company could get British scientists to do a series of controlled experiments demonstrating the validity of the scientific data being reported by German scientists.

As authors we must admit to being surprised that the British scientific establishment should function as a kind of censor board for a publisher. It becomes a kind of self-defeating circle when, before foreign scientific findings can be made available for local scientists to examine, they must already have been investigated by local scientists, and they can hardly have been thoroughly investigated before they are translated and printed.

Colin Smythe Ltd. duly embarked on its program of experimental research into the voice phenomena. First they did their own experiments with electronics experts brought to company headquarters. Then they brought Dr. Raudive back to England for more controlled experiments, including the ones in the Belling & Lee Labs. (See page 227.)

The *Sunday Mirror* of London also financed and organized tests on the voices. From Pye Records Ltd., a major British recording company, they hired the chief engineers in charge of recordings and recording equipment. They set up a host of shielded electronic equipment for the tests, four tape recorders, and even specially protected tapes. Freak transmissions of any kind were ruled out.

Along with several technical experts there were more than a

dozen observers present, including Sir Robert and Lady Mayer. Raudive had no access to any of the equipment, which was constantly monitored by the recording specialists, Ken Attwood and Ray Prickett. Everything was set for a most interesting confrontation between the "voices"—and the publisher. The sound specialists assured the group seated around the table that it would be totally impossible for a sound wave of any kind to penetrate their fully shielded control equipment. The test began. The tapes rolled.

Only a few minutes into the test, one of the control devices began to register electromagnetic impulses. The sound engineers were baffled. It couldn't be happening.

After eighteen minutes the group began the playback of the tapes. There were at least 200 paranormal sounds, twenty-seven of which were extremely clear voices.

A male voice identifying itself as Artur Schnabel spoke in German on the tapes addressing Sir Robert and Lady Mayer and giving personal information. Sir Robert was shocked. The late Artur Schnabel had been one of their dearest friends. This seemed to be Artur's voice, and German was the language they'd always used together. Schnabel also referred to other friends of theirs, including Sir John Barbirolli the famous conductor, who'd recently died.

There were numerous personal statements involving others present too. "Kosti," a voice called. It was Raudive's nickname. His dead sister's name could be heard three times.

There was so much excitement, Peter Bander recalls in his absorbing book, *Carry On Talking*, that the session went on into the early hours of the morning. The recording engineers could not explain how sounds of any kind could have gotten through onto tape. Ken Attwood suggested the best way to investigate the mystery might be to try to improve the quality of the voices.

Sir Robert, who is ninety-two, said he would have to reorganize his ideas about life, but Lady Mayer said she had known all along. Sir Robert confessed, ". . . I am relieved at the thought that eternity does not mean being condemned to eternal inactivity." On the spot he decided Raudive's book must be published in English. He also felt if the chief sound engineers were baffled by the voices then the Deputy Prime Minister of England need have no qualms.

Peter Bander describes what happened next. Raudive's book, *Breakthrough*, was launched. Soon Britons were gaping at their TV sets in astonishment as a popular late-night interview host revealed a voice purporting to be his own dead mother was addressing him on tape. TV switchboards were jammed for hours with hundreds of calls. TV shows ran overtime. Clergy scrambled on TV to match up the "voices" description of the afterlife with various religious dogmas. British psychical researchers were rushed on TV to plunge into the controversy. A leading spiritualist told TV audiences that the future lay with new instruments capable of recording vibrations emanating from other worlds. Newspapers headlined Peter Bander's dog: DOES RUFUS HOLD THE SECRET OF THE VOICES FROM THE DEAD? And thousands of Britishers hastened to turn on their tape recorders and tune in on the "voices."

The Voice Phenomena in America

Essentially experiments along the lines of the voice phenomena have been anticipated for decades by American geniuses in the field of electricity such as Steinmetz, Edison, and Tesla. They were convinced that instruments could be devised to facilitate communication between different planes of existence. Over fifty years ago Edison revealed he was working on an apparatus to communicate with the next world. He told the *Scientific American* (October 30, 1920), "If our personality survives, then it is strictly logical and scientific to assume that it retains memory, intellect, and other faculties and knowledge that we acquire on this earth. Therefore, if personality exists after what we call death, it's reasonable to conclude that those who leave this earth would like to communicate with those they have left here. . . . I am inclined to believe that our personality hereafter will be able to affect matter. If this reasoning be correct, then, if we can evolve an instrument so delicate as to be affected, or moved, or manipulated . . . by our personality as it survives in the next life, such an instrument, when made available, ought to record something." In addition, he felt, such devices could confirm mediumship. Dunninger claims to have seen the apparatus built by Edison to talk with the dead. A General Electric engineer also claims to have worked on it and plans are still turning up. Whether the voice phenomenon is a realization of Edison's dream remains to be seen.

Several American researchers have checked out Raudive's work so far. Dr. Jule Eisenbud, author of *The World of Ted Serios*, listened to Raudive's tapes in Germany. Some think the voice phenomenon is the auditory equivalent of Ted Serios' thought photography. Dr. Karlis Osis, Director of Research for the American Society for Psychical Research, inspected Raudive's lab also. Osis, like Raudive, is Latvian and a linguist. He says he could hear twenty-six out of thirty voice texts clearly, but would differ on some interpretations.

American academic parapsychologists have shown little interest in voices—the reason perhaps being that according to a 1971 survey of the Parapsychology Association, few are interested in survival research. The European pioneers tend to back the survival hypothesis as the major one.

Across America we know of a handful of private individuals researching the voice phenomena, some of them with quite sophisticated equipment. Among the few groups—the Southern California Society for Psychical Research; the Society for Experimental ESP (California); and the Aquarian Research Foundation (Philadelphia).

Several of the SCSPR members have achieved encouraging results with this new form of electronic clairaudience. In 1972 a selection from the SCSPR tapes was played over the Hilly Rose Show on LA radio station KFI. Both voices and paranormal musical sounds were included. It was a program KFI remembers well, Hilly Rose told us, because coincidentally or not, the night the paranormal tapes were being broadcast, the KFI transmitter suddenly went off the air.

William Welch of the SCSPR presented some voice-tape phenomena at a psychic conference at California State University, Long Beach. Bill Cox of *California Scene Magazine* states, "Welch didn't press his point of view, he rather let the tapes speak for themselves, and I must say the demonstration was convincing. The Voice-Tape Tests are bringing us closer to a new threshold of psychic awareness," says Cox.

Frances Brown Zeff, president of the SCSPR, told us that voice-tape-recording takes lots of time and patience and that not everyone can get them. At first there are noises, very faint and of a whispering quality that are hard to understand. Later, sometimes, there are personal messages. Mrs. Zeff told the Los Angeles *Times* of her first experience with voice-recording at her Reseda home, in the presence of Bill Welch. "We had a blank tape until the end and then a word was spoken that sounded like 'home,' " she said. During another taping session with Attila von Szalay, Mrs. Zeff asked questions in three languages. An answer in German appeared later on the tape. There was a woman present who had recently lost her sister. The sister's voice was heard on the tape to say, "Now, dear."

Mrs. Zeff, who has an academic background in social work as

well as several other fields, feels that survival research and voice-tape research both can provide a valuable basis for counseling suicidal and depressed individuals, giving them some idea of what an afterlife might hold if they proceed with their intention to kill themselves.

Well-known musician, author, and psi investigator Stewart Robb, one of the directors of the Society for Experimental ESP, reported to the *Parapsychology Review* he has reason to believe he may have gotten the postmortem voice of George Bernard Shaw on tape. For some time now, Robb has worked with electronics expert Jay Miller, chief engineer of KEZY who has rigged up improved equipment for recording these elusive paranormal voices.

Author Susy Smith announced in 1972 the setting up of a Survival Research Foundation, which would have as its first project the investigation of the voice phenomena. Research director is electronics engineer Karl Romer. (PO Box 50446, Tucson, Arizona 85705.)

Dr. Walter Uphoff presented his firsthand report on the voices at the June, 1973, Harold Sherman ESP Workshop in Hot Springs, Arkansas. Douglas Dean of Newark College of Engineering and healer Olga Worrall were present, along with several others at an informal taping session with Uphoff at the hotel. "The voices recorded were extremely clear," Dean reports.

What to make of the voice phenomena? Based on the fifteen years of evidence gathered by eminent European scientists and other researchers, there definitely seems to be a phenomenon. At this stage of investigations, it's important not to rush to hasty conclusions. The source of the voice phenomenon has yet to be identified and proved conclusively. Because the voice phenomenon holds great promise of being a major breakthrough in psi research, the wisest course is to accumulate more evidence before hastening to accept or reject claims about the voice tapes. Further research will provide a better body of data on which to base answers. Application of new technological discoveries (mentioned in Chapter 16) may provide clarification of some of the mysteries involved. You may be the person who will succeed in finding the keys—conclusive proof of who the voices are, where they come from, and the validity of what they say.

The famous Irish medium, author, businesswoman, and publisher Eileen Garrett emphasized how urgent investigation of this area may be. She wrote in 1956, in her magazine *Tomorrow*, "Now the time may have come to apply . . . newly found techniques of research to the still-unanswered question: Have we gained, or are we about to gain knowledge that will help to solve the enigma of human life beyond death? This, we feel, is a challenge to all scientists who are engaged in that most momentous study of all: the nature of man. Psychologists and physicists represent only two categories of scientists who may be qualified to meet this challenge. The circle of research is closing. The work that began at the end of the last century needs to be taken up anew, in the light of added knowledge and with the tools of recently acquired techniques. No longer will man be satisfied with 'intimations' of immortality; he is seeking, and may be proud to state it frankly, a certainty of his own being.''

16

How to Record Voice Phenomena

On an average some six out of ten people who've attempted
tape-recording voice phenomena in Britain have been successful,
according to Peter Bander. As more people explore the technique,
improved methods have been developed. Following the Raudive
methods, we have tape-recorded voice phenomena ourselves. To
begin, we found it very helpful to listen to the Raudive record,
Breakthrough, put out by Vista Productions in London (see page
282) to accustom the ear to the unusual rhythm, speed, pitch, and
intensity of the voices. We include below Raudive's recording
techniques from *Breakthrough*, plus tips of our own and others,
including Richard K. Sheargold, a researcher for the Society for
Psychical Research (London) and a ham-radio operator for forty
years, and Art Rosenblum of the Aquarian Research Foundation
(Philadelphia), an electronics technician.

Preliminaries

Most researchers emphasize it may be several days to several
months before you succeed in recording clearly audible voice
phenomena. "The voices you are trying to receive are very weak,"
Sheargold asserts. "This cannot be overstressed. Although there is
always the possibility that you may be favored by a voice much
louder than usual right away, this is greatly the exception and you
must expect to exercise patience and perseverance." Sheargold
suggests you devote a regular time each day to listening to the voice
tapes for about half an hour. "Long sessions will only be tiring," he
points out.

Earphones

Earphones are considered practically essential. For months, Sheargold had tried unsuccessfully to duplicate the voice phenomena. Finally after consulting the publisher Colin Smythe, he got a pair of earphones and was at last able to distinguish the faint paranormal voices. Dr. Raudive feels it's a matter of training the ear. People who've heightened their hearing ability through training in music, for instance, are likely to be more successful. Each minute of recording requires at least fifteen minutes of replaying and intense listening.

Headphones are considered absolutely key equipment in trying to separate the voice from the background noise. If the voice is extremely clear, it can be listened to over the tape-recorder speaker or any hi-fi speaker. If the voice is very weak, the amplification of the background noise through the speaker drowns it out. Any tape-recorder or hi-fi dealer can advise you on the type of earphones suitable to your recorder. For small cassette machines, a stethoscope earphone set is available. Not only do the earphones assist in hearing the voices, but they may also preserve family harmony.

The noise made by the tape recorder is a loud rushing sound akin to "white noise." "Prolonged listening to this produces a very well known effect when voices tend to be heard which do not really exist," cautions Sheargold. This is like the conch-shell effect and of course no words can be deciphered. It's easy to distinguish the real voices from the spurious voices because the illusory voices cannot be repeated as often as is desired. Once you've gained some experience with distinguishing the real voices, the conch-shell effect is rare.

Tape

New tape should always be used for voice phenomena experiments. It should be good-quality, low-noise tape. The tape head on the recorder should be clean, free of magnetism and not too worn. If you pick up hum from power lines, recording can be done with a portable recorder inside a parked car.

Type of Tape Recorder

Any type of reel-to-reel tape recorder in good condition will do for recording the voice phenomena. It needn't be a technically elaborate or expensive tape recorder. People have successfully recorded paranormal voices even with small inexpensive battery-operated cassette recorders. For *playback*, the more elaborate machines have the advantage. The controls for treble, bass, tone, and volume allow the researcher to hear more easily. With earphones, the controls allow adjustment of the volume in each ear piece. Sheargold found that the older type vacuum-tube tape recorders suffer from hum to such an extent as to render them useless for this research and he recommends the quieter trans-istorized machines. Two-track machines are preferred, though good results have also been obtained with multitrack machines. A tape recorder with automatic level control during recording is not as suitable for voice phenomena recording, says Sheargold, unless the level control can be switched off.

How to Record

Dr. Raudive's various methods are detailed in his book, *Breakthrough*. Examples of the voice phenomena produced by each method are included on the Vista record. The initial methods were arrived at from suggestions given by the voices. Experts have devised new ones.

1. *Microphone recording*

This method involves using the tape recorder in the same way as for ordinary recording. Set the microphone a good distance away from the tape recorder so that it does not record the hum of the motor. Turn the volume to maximum and stand or sit some distance away. Make the initial identification announcement stating date and time of recording and who's present and ask for voices. (See later.) Then keep perfectly still. We've found it a good idea with this method to keep a complete log of *everything* said and of any extraneous noises during recording time, correlating if possible with the counter number on the recorder. Should additional voices seem to be audible on playback, you can at least be certain they're not some outdoor sound or anything anyone in the room murmured. Mike recording should be done in a quiet spot. This method is not so satisfactory in a location abounding with street and traffic noise or with people talking nearby.

Tape speed can be either 7 1/2 ips or 3 3/4 ips or the slower speed of cassettes. Record only two or three minutes at a time, making an announcement every minute or so asking for voices. Voices often tend to be heard immediately after your announcement. Playback takes so much time it's wise to keep recordings brief. (Art Rosenblum suggests that with the microphone set at a distance using shielded cable, a good low-noise preamplifier close to the recorder could amplify signals without increasing hum pickup.)

2. *Radio Recordings*

The radio is tuned to a spot on the dial between stations where only a rushing sound is audible. It should be a location free of any broadcasts and where stations won't suddenly fade in. It can be on AM, FM, or shortwave. We found that in major eastern North American cities it's hard to find any spot on the AM dial free of programming, so we've had to rely mainly on FM and shortwave. *Turn the radio volume down so the rushing sound is just barely audible.* You'll need a cable to connect the radio to the input of the tape recorder. (Cables are usually available anywhere tape recorders are sold or at any electronics store.)

First plug in the microphone and record an announcement in the regular way, then unplug the microphone and plug in the cable from the radio. The voice phenomena become audible on the tape above the rushing sound. Recordings can be done with the tape recorder turned up to around medium volume. Raudive says the voices clamor for radio recordings.

3. *Microphone-Radio Recordings*

Follow the same procedure as for microphone recording. Tune the radio between stations and turn down the volume so the rushing sound is scarcely audible. Use the microphone with the zape recorder in the regular way. Make the announcement with the volume low, then turn the recorder volume to maximum and place the microphone close to the radio. Record only two or three minutes.

4. *Microphone-TV Recordings*

We found empty TV channels also worked well and were less likely to pick up fade-in broadcasts. Same method as above, except TV is used instead of radio. Use either Ultra High Frequency channels or regular channels. We got better results with UHF. Tune into a channel that is not telecasting. Turn the TV volume so the rushing sound is barely audible. Make the usual announcement and place the microphone close to the TV set.

5. *Diode Recording*

A diode is like the little crystal sets from the early days of radio. It picks up all the electromagnetic frequencies in the immediate vicinity of the tape recorder. Basically it is just a little crystal of germanium and a piece of wire for an aerial. (See instructions.) Make the usual announcement on the tape recorder with the microphone—then unplug the mike and plug in the diode. A switch can eventually be used to switch from mike to diode. Turn volume to maximum for diode recording. Dr. Raudive says diode-recorded voices can be heard without difficulty even by the untrained ear, that diction is clearer and voices more natural.

6. *Recording Without Mike or Radio*

The tape recorder with fresh tape is turned on to *record* in the usual way, but *without* a microphone plugged into the input socket. Turn volume to maximum. Announcements and questions are asked aloud. A written log of the questions should be kept. Voices come through with material relevant to questions asked. This method overcomes the objection that the voices are broadcast fragments, but with this technique, it takes a very long time to get voices. Voices have also been recorded with the recorder set at *record* connected to another tape recorder set at *play*. So far no one has gotten voices directly on tape without running it through the recorder. The tape must pass through the recording head on the tape recorder and the effect might be through currents flowing in the recording head.

7. *Frequency-Transmitter Recording*

Dr. Alex Schneider has developed a method to exclude radio interference and the objection that the voices are broadcast fragments. Briefly, a noise generator or carrier-frequency transmitter is used with the tape recorder. (See *Breakthrough*, p. 340.) Some voices sound as though they were put together from the noise spectrum by some physically unexplained process of selection, says Schneider. Possibly recording could even be done with the microphone held up to various types of machines that give off a rushing sound or hum, he thinks.

General Notes

● Several tape recorders may be used in one experiment.
● Time of recording: Evening is more favorable. On several occasions voices have asked for recordings after sundown. The electromagnetic fields of the earth shift after sundown (see Kirlian photography) and these field may affect recording. Full moon is believed to be a more favorable time for recordings. This would also be an electromagnetic-field effect. Weather and atmospheric con

ditions affect voice transmissions—storms may cause interference. Planetary configurations may also play a role.

• Shielding—Benson Herbert of the Paraphysics Lab suggests that the whole apparatus should be screened to avoid picking up radio broadcasts—either regular or ham-radio transmissions. For the amateur home experimenter, if a small portable transistor radio and small cassette recorder are used, we found they could be somewhat screened by simply placing them inside a foil-lined bag and tightly closing the bag around the recorder, radio and cable.

Announcements

You will probably develop your own method. To begin it's helpful to identify recordings by first announcing the date, time and names of people present. Some researchers suggest you should start off something like, "Good evening, friends. The date is . . . and the time is . . . and I wonder if there is anyone there who knows me and who can speak to me using the microphone [or radio, or diode] *now!*" Recording is then done at maximum volume for thirty to sixty seconds. Some suggest you should ask for "friends in the beyond." Next you might ask for a particular person by name. If a particular voice has spoken before, ask for that person again.

"In my experience it is unwise to make long-winded announcements," says Sheargold. "It seems best for them to be short, clear, concise." Sheargold feels it is wise to observe politeness and to thank voices for information they provide. He believes sessions should be bright and cheerful but not frivolous. See *Breakthrough* for other announcements.

Raudive suggests that a calm, relaxed state of consciousness helps in the recordings. Others suggest a brief meditation before recording is helpful.

Peter Bander observes that although he feels silly talking alone to a tape recorder, this personal method of approaching voice-recording yields better results than simply switching on the machine. He suggests that one speak freely and naturally to those who wish to communicate via the tape and invite voices to manifest themselves. Questions can be asked leaving time in between for answers. If on playback, voices and statements can be heard, one can respond to them. After researching voice tapes for some time both Jurgenson and Raudive eventually got a specific broadcast "controller," who organizes the voices and acts as an announcer for them.

Playback

"Unless you have 'beginner's luck,' it is almost certain that your first playback will reveal nothing," Sheargold cautions. The recording must be played back over and over and over again. These supernormal voices are very quick, sharp, and rhythmic. At first you may detect only a metallic whir. Then on playback again, it becomes clearer, as the ear grows accustomed to the sound, that a voice is there. Then repeated playbacks help verify what it is saying.

Sheargold notes when using the microphone method that a voice will sometimes come so very quickly after your own announcement that it is almost like an additional word—probably a name. You will hear male and female voices and whispers. . . .

"It is impossible to generalize, but if, for example, you carry out all the outlined procedure every day for a week, you cannot hear anything at all, I would say that almost without a doubt you are just missing voices. It is useless to go on messing up huge totals of recordings yet hear nothing, and I would suggest it is better to spend a week listening to the recordings made during the first week than to continue recording if nothing is heard," Sheargold advises. Dr. Raudive feels a five-minute recording requires at least an hour spent listening.

Peter Bander suggests playbacks be done with several people present. He likens the rushing noise of the static to the sound of a waterfall between the speaker and himself and he must try to hear the voice above the noise. He has a junction box attached to his tape recorder and several sets of earphones plugged in. Each person is asked to write down what he thinks he hears. Afterwards they all compare. About half the voices can be identified after six to ten playbacks, he says. A quarter may take twenty playbacks or even thirty; the rest may take half an hour or longer.

Bander found continuous tape loops a great help in voice-recording and playback. He cuts a length of recording tape long enough to go around both reels and thread through the machine—on an average around thirty-two inches. He splices the ends together for an eight-and-a-half-second recording. The loop can play over and over, greatly simplifying playback. Drawback: A voice may be cut off in midsentence or not manifest within the eight and a half seconds. (Longer continuous tape loops and automatic repeating cassettes are available at many tape-recorder stores, and also from Edmund Scientific.)

When a clear voice is isolated on the recording, the message can be re-recorded on another tape recorder several times over to improve clarity.

Logging the Voices

A detailed log should be kept and tapes labeled to correspond. Otherwise you may end up with a jumbled collection of strange-sounding tapes. The log should include essential details: date, time, recording system (i.e., microphone, diode, radio, dial setting on radio), revolution-counter reading, track number, weather, astronomical or astrological data (i.e., full moon), announcements made and response if any. Other details can be added.

Obviously you must work out your own system, abbreviations, etc. "But without keeping a log," says Sheargold, "it is very difficult to refer back to any interesting response, or what is even more important, to follow any trends that may be observable." Comparison of logbooks may also show a particular configuration that leads to good reception.

General

Sheargold says, as does Raudive, that incipient mediumship on the part of the experimenter is not involved. He says, "This is a straightforward electronic experiment . . . I personally am not committed to any one explanation of the voices. They may be the voices of the deceased, or they may be due to some as yet unexplained action of the subconscious mind. That they are a fact in nature is beyond doubt. Our first aim should be to improve their strength and clarity by development of more suitable equipment."

Interpretation

Common sense and a good ear are absolutely necessary to interpreting the voice tapes. No doubt improved technical receiving facilities will eventually make the voices clearer and easier to interpret. At this state of development of the voice phenomena, members of the Swiss Society for Parapsychology, having spent several years researching voices, warn in particular about misinterpretation of the statements (*Parapsychology Review*, Vol. 3, No. 4). The Swiss asked ten specially selected, well-educated people to spend three days listening to a tape of twenty different voices culled from Raudive tapes. (The data doesn't state whether the participants had good hearing.) Agreement between the group's interpretation and original text for syllables was 16.9 percent; vowels, 38.2 percent; letters, 27.7 percent. Only on a few of the sample voice statements was there agreement of 50 percent to 80 percent.

Dr. Theo Locher, president of the Swiss Society, stresses great differences could be noted in what each person believed he had heard, clearly indicating how subjective judging by ear is. He states that in this case many of the original interpretations of the sounds on the tapes were surely false, "often induced by the working of his [Raudive's] own imagination or by what he had heard beforehand."

Experimenters must exercise great care that the voice tapes are not an auditory Rorschach test for them—a burble of sounds onto which they project their own impressions.

Interpretation is, at present, a bit of a bugbear with the voice phenomena. In previous centuries disciples accompanied "Holy Fools" across Russia and Europe and interpreted their babblings as messages from the beyond. Today there's a danger of a parallel, with people accompanying babbling tape recorders, interpreting scratches and confused voices as messages from the great beyond. A major goal in voice research must be to develop technology to make the voices clearly audible. It may be that some of this technology already exists and needs only to be applied to the voice phenomena.

Potential Technical Improvements

A recent advance has come in recording technology that might be of great help in eliminating background noises and distortions in the voice-tape material. Scientists in the space program have developed an electronic filter-amplifier device that can be hooked up to a microphone to clarify speech and eliminate distortions. It's used at present to diminish the static and background noise in radio messages from astronauts in outer space. In addition, it's recently been adapted to make the speech of children who have cerebral palsy understandable. These devices are being made by the National Institute for Rehabilitation Engineering in Pompton Lakes, New Jersey. The institute is directed by Don Selwyn.

In addition to devices to make the recorded voices clearer, there's also the new Laser Microphone Matrix developed by Pat Flanagan of Glendale, California, that allows a tape recorder to "hear" the locations of sound in its vicinity.

It may be that new techniques such as these could resolve interpretative problems and make possible longer and more coherent messages.

An even more important question, once having gotten a clear recording, is how accurate are the statements made by the paranormal voices? Are they the people they say they are? Could distortion have occurred in transmission? Psi transmissions of all kinds, telepathic, mediumistic, etc., are generally subject to distortion and displacement. Images are often confused. The same may be true of the voice phenomena. Arthur Ford has suggested that the atmosphere of the earth and electromagnetic pollution from machines in our cities can also be a distorting factor.

In view of these difficulties how can the validity of some of the things the voices are saying be assessed? Many voices assert they are famous people, statesmen, authors, philosophers, criminals, dictators. Hitler and Lenin are alleged to have come through on Raudive's tapes. Are they impostors? Even if the identity could be established by voice-print analysis, are the statements made by the voices correct? Some sound totally confused—even psychotic.

A discovery has been made recently in the technology of voice analysis that might possibly be of importance in analyzing the voice-tape phenomena. The device called the Psychological Stress Evaluator (PSE), and its inventors claim it detects the truth or falseness of statements by voice analysis. The old-style polygraph (lie detector) measured heartbeat, skin response, and breathing rate to determine the stress that accompanies lying. The new instrument, which some feel will make the polygraph archaic, was developed by two former lieutenant-colonels in US Army military intelligence: Allan Bell, an electronics expert, and Charles McQuistan, a polygraph specialist. Bell and McQuistan recently set up their own company, Dektor Counter-Intelligence and Security Company, just outside Washington, D.C. PSE evidence has been ruled admissible in four US court cases, and PSE's are coming into wider use in police work in the US and Europe. The inventors claim the PSE can determine whether a person is lying even over TV, radio, or a telephone.

Vibrations of the vocal cords and resonance of vibrations in the skull cavities produce two types of frequencies known to be present in the human voice. Recently scientists discovered a third frequency modulation in the human voice undistinguishable to the naked ear. The PSE works on the basis of it. This frequency is caused by muscle tremors and is always present in normal speech. In times of stress, such as when you're lying, this frequency modulation disappears from the human voice and the PSE chart shows when it's missing. The instrument can detect what human hearing cannot detect. A tape recorder, which is part of the PSE, records and replays a voice while a strip-chart recorder attached to the instrument prints out the analysis of up to thirty-two different characteristics of the human voice.

It would be an interesting project to have some of the clearest recordings of the voice-tape phenomena analyzed by an expert with PSE instrumentation.

One of the most controversial recordings Raudive got is one purported to be the voice of Winston Churchill (also on the Vista record). It says, "Mark you, make believe, my dear, yes. Winston Churchill." Is this somebody attempting to quote a statement of Churchill's? Is part of the statement missing owing to static in transmission? Is it really supposed to be Churchill? Incidentally, the topic of the statement—getting people to believe that the voice phenomena exist—is a constant theme among a great many of the voices. It could be that the Psychological Stress Evaluator might help not only in identification of the voices produced but also in separating out which parts of their statements are true, which are getting through correctly.

Other new techniques in PK research described elsewhere in this book, such as electromagnetic-field monitors, will be helpful for determining interaction between experimenter and tape recorder. (See Sergeyev Detector, pages 295-97.)

As Dr. Raudive says, "The decisive factor in studying the voice phenomenon is not the theoretical interpretation . . . but the empirical result, arrived at through experiment . . . verified under test conditions."

Points of Departure for Other Experiments with Voices

Conduct tests in airplanes, underground, on the ocean.

Would making more energy available for the voice transmissions increase volume and clarity? Would the energy focused by the pyramid help? Could recording inside a pyramid help?

Would a psychic pick up impressions of the voices who are speaking inaudibly during the recording time? On playback, the psychic's impressions could be checked out. Could a psychic impress his own name on tape without speaking? How could this be monitored and proved?

Do the electromagnetic fields of the experimenter and geographic location play a role? Would electromagnetic field detectors show changes during recordings?

Could animals detect the voices?

If the words spoken on the voice tapes are genuinely of paranormal origin, then by what technical mechanism are the sounds produced? Are words produced by modifying a sound carrier frequency? The English language, for instance, has forty phonemes or basic sound units, each one a set of frequencies with a certain sequence. The frequencies can be made up electronically and fed into a speaker to say anything in English with any accent, emphasis or pitch. The Ontario Science Center has a machine built by the Philips Company that can say "coffee" with a Dutch accent by manipulating electronic frequencies.

Would videotape produce phenomena similar to those produced on regular recording tape?

Would comparison of message content from experimenters in different countries show a pattern?

Could planetary conditions play a role—could astrological analysis pinpoint days giving best reception? It is known that specific configurations of planets—such as oppositions or squares of the heavier planets, Jupiter and Saturn—can interfere with the electromagnetic fields of the earth and with radio reception. At RCA, John Nelson pinpoints these oppositions and squares long in advance so that RCA can reroute radio transmissions through undisturbed areas. Does this same planetary configuration also interfere with voice-phenomena reception?

Would voice experiments in different settings, such as hospitals or historic houses, produce relevant material?

Cancer patients have been given LSD to ease pain before death (see *Harper's Magazine*, March, 1973), and describe unusual experiences. Are there similarities between their descriptions and those of the voice tapes?

In his experiments with Jurgenson, Dr. Hans Bender utilized several tape recorders located around the room. The voices seemed to be louder on two of the machines, implying that the voices might be localized in an area or coming from a specific direction in the room. If so, it might be possible to use an "electronic sound collector" (one type available from Edmund Scientific), which can be plugged into a tape recorder.

The above are just a handful of ideas that could be explored in relation to the voice phenomena. You will no doubt come up with others as you embark on your own investigations.

For those seriously interested in voice phenomena, some of the key material to get would be Konstantin Raudive's book *Breakthrough* and the record, *Breakthrough; Carry On Talking* by

Peter Bander; and the scientific reports by Dr. Hans Bender. If you know German, Jurgenson's book would be valuable. For where-to-find details, see Section Six.

The Diode Circuit

The circuit (see Figure 11) must be fully shielded (enclosed in a metal box, except for the four-inch stiff-wire antenna) to avoid hum from power lines and excessive interference from radio stations. Any (external) wiring employed must similarly be shielded. (The shield or box is connected to ground or to the chassis of the tape recorder, as is usually the case with the shield of the microphone cable—within the machine.) The diode is the type used by Richard Sheargold, and the circuit was originally printed in the *Aquarian Research Foundation Newsletter*, #32.

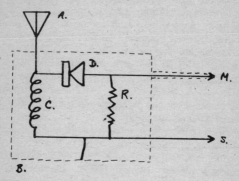

FIGURE 11.

The Diode Circuit

Components:

A. Antenna: four inches of stiff wire insulated from box and extending outside it.
B. Metal box large enough to hold other parts easily. Obtained in electronic-parts store.
C. Radio frequency choke, about 2.5 Millihenries. Cost: around 70¢.
D. Germanium crystal diode, such as type 1N191. Available at electronics store. Cost: around 35¢.

E.   100,000 ohm resistor—may be quarter or 1/2-watt size. Cost: around 15¢.

F.   Center lead of shielded cable. Connect to microphone jack or volume input of tape recorder. Cable should be no more than twelve inches long to avoid hum.

G.   Shield of cable. Connects box and grounded side of tape recorder input as well as resistor and choke as shown.

Total cost of all components is just a few dollars. If you are not adept at electronics yourself, you can buy the components at an electronics store and ask them for the name of someone who can assemble the diode. It can be assembled in an hour or so.

A ready-made Diode Detector as well as a demonstration tape of voice phenomena from Europe and America is available from: Para-Dimensional Researchers, PO Box 11288, Phoenix, Arizona 85017. See also: *Talks with the Dead*, by William Addams Welch, Pinnacle Books, 1975.

Section Six

Where to Find It

Information of all kinds, as everyone knows, has been exploding in the last decades with a hail of disconnected facts flying like shrapnel. The psi field, too, has had its information explosion and implosion. The detonation has taken a rather curious pattern for a subject that relates to all of us. A growing number of people of every stripe and education today know a great deal about psi, about research and practice. Cheek by jowl with them another crowd of people barely knows the meaning of the word telepathy. Every specialty of course tends to spawn its information ghetto, but psi is more than a specialty and a research project. It is a human potential and capability.

As an example of the cleavage of communication about psychic things generally, the cultural historian Dr. W. I. Thompson, formerly of MIT and now with York University, Toronto, observed in 1971 that interest in Edgar Cayce "amounts to a cultural syndrome, and yet I have encountered only one academic who was aware of Cayce." Thompson warns, "Our democratic society is so stratified that one level can be totally ignorant of what is going on in the other."

Apart from the larger problem of trying to come to any form of social consensus with this kind of isolationism, lack of communication can block benefits that may well come to all of us from the burgeoning research into psi. In order for alternate solutions to many contemporary problems to be tried in fields from crime detection to medicine to geology, people who are the decision makers have to know such approaches exist. To take a close-to-the-home example: What if your child or another member of your family were missing, as are thousands today in the United States; what if police methods have failed to find any trace? If you lived in Holland, your missing person might be successfully traced by a psychic working *with* police.

This perhaps suggests another do-it-yourself field wide open for the person interested in psi. You can be an active, creative communications channel. People in key positions may be unaware of the mass of serious research on psi, or they may have been given erroneous or even highly questionable "facts" that strike them as nonsense. Such people may well be open to new techniques gleaned from bona fide research if they are presented constructively, not as something to replace the accumulated understanding in any field, but as something to broaden and enhance their work. Why bother?

One academic who usually seems to pulse with what's happening, Marshall McLuhan, sees the current psychic boom as no coincidence. A media expert, he views it as part of a trend that is drawing everyone in the world closer together, making more conscious our interconnectedness. "Mysticism is just tomorrow's science dreamed today," he says. The speed and accuracy with which information spreads from such fields as psi research will help determine how soon the tomorrow McLuhan is speaking about becomes today.

And then there is the "facts as flack" problem. "If only there was an adequate, modern data bank of all psi related work, if only one could start information retrieval in a broad band of disciplines and pick out work that perhaps, unknown to its authors, relates to psi—then a great many of our current questions about psi might be answered and we could get on to a deeper round of questioning." This sort of comment is increasingly heard in psi circles. And it may well be that answers to some enigmas do exist, it is simply that no one has come along to connect part A with part B. A few groups are making a start at remedying the situation; but money, time, and canny and willing detectives are required. If you like to learn about a lot of different subjects, this mode of treasure hunting can be as exciting as it is worthwhile. But before you can connect with other fields, you have to know where you can find out what's happening in the psi field itself.

How to Find What's Hard to Find, but Worth Finding

"My library doesn't carry . . . Where can I possibly find information on. . . ?" These are phrases that most frequently turn up in our mail. It's a refrain that points up one of the major short circuits in the psi field today. Unless you live in a large center, it is often difficult to get current information on psi, particularly detailed reports of scientific and professional work. A short listing of some of the sources in English appear on pages 273-75. The information problem balloons almost out of management as soon as you begin looking for psi-related work in other cultures. We are most often queried on how did we find and how can others find publications from Russsia and Eastern Europe. We were somewhat fortunate in the information department because before researching *PDBIC* we had been writing and publishing for some years on Russian culture and so had a collection of hard-to-find Communist publications. But we still had to hunt others. What follows are a few sources and strategies that might pay off. Because of length restrictions in *Psychic Discoveries Behind the Iron Curtain* (a title chosen, incidentally, by the publisher), we were able to include only a partial bibliography. An extensive bibliography of psi-related work in the Soviet Union up to 1971 was put together by Edward Naumov and Larisa Vilenskaya. This 101-page bibliography (8 1/2'' × 11'') has now been translated into English by the Joint Publications Research Service. Order: *Bibliographies on Parapsychology (Psychoenergetics) and Related Subjects—USSR*, by Naumov and Vilenskaya, JPRS 55557, 28 March, 1972, National Technical Service, Springfield, Virginia 22151 ($6.00).

Some of the scientific papers listed dealing with Kirlian photography and bioenergetics are available in collected translation. *Bioenergetics Questions* (eighty pages) Southern California Society for Psychical Research, Inc., 170 South Beverly Drive, Room 314, Beverly Hills, California 90212.

The Naumov-Vilenskaya bibliography reflects the large rise of scientific publication on psi in the Soviet Union during the past few years. Some references to articles in popular magazines by scientists and others are also included. Interestingly, it's common for Soviet scientists generally to publish both professional papers and articles on their work in the popular media. In Russia, educating the public is considered a responsibility of the scientist. Such popular publications are more telling than they would be in the United States because the Soviet Press is censored and government controlled. As Arthur Koestler remarked in *The Roots of Coincidence*, "Since in the USSR all publications are state controlled, the sudden boom in parapsychology was obviously supported, or inspired, from higher quarters." Keeping an eye on how Soviet popular magazines treat such fields as psi research is a good method of determining the drift and sometimes the crosscurrents in government and political thinking about the subject. It's often pointed out by Sovietologists that frequently plans for new research in any area and the activities of more or less public research groups are only announced after a good deal of research has been accomplished by others behind the scenes.

Where to Find Slavic Publications

There are a variety of approaches and you may have to try more than one.

1. Check a volume called the *Union List of Serials* in your library to find the closest library, if any, to carry the publication you want.

2. Contact the Slavic section of the New York Public Library and the Library of Congress in Washington, D.C. In Canada, the University of Alberta has a good Slavic collection. Ask your librarian about special collections in your area, particularly universities, colleges, and institutes.

3. Much Soviet psi-related material appears in biology and medical journals. Medical and scientific libraries here often carry Soviet work. A problem that can come up if you are simply hunting through the literature is that the words "psychic," "psi," "parapsychology," may not appear. The Naumov-Vilenskaya bibliography should give some ideas of what to look for.

4. The National Technical Information Service, Springfield, Virginia, translates something in the order of 60,000 items into English each year. Many are Soviet; they may well have the article you seek. Current Joint Publications Research Service publications are announced in *US Government Research and Development Reports* issued semimonthly by the National Technical Information Service and are listed in the *Monthly Catalogue of US Government Publications*, issued by the Superintendent of Documents, US Government Printing Office, Washington, D.C. 20402.

5. If you draw a blanks with libraries, you can always try to buy the publication from a Soviet bookstore. Four Continent Book Corporation, 156 Fifth Avenue, New York, New York 10010. (They put out a catalogue and occasionally will come up with back issues of magazines.) In Canada, try Troika, 799A College Street, Toronto, Ontario.

6. If all else fails, try writing directly to the publication and asking for the desired back issue. We've sometimes had good results with this approach in Russia, Yugoslavia, Bulgaria. (It expedites matters to send three or four dollars to cover costs.)

7. A new collection in English of psi articles written by a wide variety of Communist researchers is entitled *ESP Papers*, ed. by Ostrander and Schroeder, Bantam, 1975.

Conferences

A good deal of information about current psi research in East

Europe and the Soviet Union has been presented at several international conferences, attended by substantial numbers of Americans.

1. *Symposium of Psychotronics, 1970, Prague.* Czech and Soviet papers published in Vol. 5, Nos. 1 and 2, *Journal of Paraphysics.* Additional information: "Symposium of Psychotronics, Part Three: Seminar on Bioplasma," Vol. 5, No. 4, *Journal of Paraphysics.*

2. *First International Symposium on Problems of Suggestology, Sofia & Varna, Bulgaria, 1971.* This conference included high-level representation from the Communist countries. Papers presented covered not only suggestology as a method of learning but also reports on relaxation, bioenergetics and the charting of human force fields. Proceedings in full, supposedly available by 1974 from the Institute of Suggestology, 9 Budapest Street, Sofia, Bulgaria.

3. *International Meeting on the Problem of Bioenergetics and Related Areas, Moscow,* 1972. Some Soviet papers, plus reports and interviews available. Vol. 6, No. 5, 1972, *Journal of Paraphysics.* Some added data and American papers in *The Journal of Paraphysics,* Vol. 7, No. 1, 1973.

4. *International Conference on Psychotronic Research, 1973, Prague.* Proceedings will be available in English. Keep an eye out for announcements in psi publications.

5. *A.R.E.—Soviet Meetings.* In the summer of 1971 members of this Edgar Cayce group including scientists, doctors, psychologists, and laymen exchanged information with various Soviet researchers and psychics. *The A.R.E. Journal,* March, 1972 (75¢), is entirely devoted to the report of their Russian findings. (See also September, 1972, *A.R.E. Journal* for more.)

Some "Soviets only" conferences of interest include:

Symposium on Telepathy by the Bioinformation Unit of the Scientific Technical Society for Radiotechnics and Electrocommunication, Moscow, 1970. For a short report, see "Russian Symposium," *Parapsychology Review,* January-February, 1972.

Seminar on the Biophysical Effect, Moscow, 1971. Well over a hundred researchers from across the USSR gathered to exchange information on "the biophysical effect," the Soviet term for dowsing. See "Dowsing in the USSR," *American Dowser,* summer, 1972. Also "Parapsychology Aids Geologists," *Parapsychology Review,* May-June, 1972.

All Union Conference on Astrobiology of the Moscow Society of Experimenters in Natural Sciences, 1968. For some information in English about papers at this conference see astrobiology section,

Natural Birth Control, Ostrander and Schroeder (Bantam, 1973).
Papers of 1968 and 1971 conferences in Russian, see *Sun, Electricity and Life* (Moscow: Moscow University Press), 1969; second
volume, 1972.

The Lozanov System—Where to Find Information

We briefly described the Lozanov educational system for jet-speed learning in Chapter 22 in *PDBIC*. This new teaching method,
developed by Georgi Lozanov, a Bulgarian medical doctor and
psychiatrist, is said to increase learning speed from five to fifty
times. This revolutionary speeding up of learning is accomplished
mainly through techniques of memory expansion and is based on
autogenics and a relaxation technique somewhat similar to that
outlined in Section Three, pages 139-40. The memory-expansion-relaxation part of the education method is fully coordinated with the
best elements of many other contemporary education methods. The
Lozanov system was first used in teaching languages because a
word count of new words learned per session provided a handy
progress index. The system enables people to learn a new language
in about twenty-four days.

Today, the Lozanov system, called suggestology, is organized
for use with most subjects in a school curriculum and has been used
very successfully in a regular public school in Bulgaria. Elementary
school pupils who were taught by the method in the 1972 school
year, completed their entire year's work in two and a half months
and devoted the remainder of the year to learning additional subjects.

Lozanov pioneered development of the system as his Institute for
Suggestology in Sofia, Bulgaria. The method is now in use in
institutes in many Soviet-bloc countries, including the prestigious
Moscow Foreign Languages Pedagogical Institute in the USSR and
the Etvos Lorand University in Budapest, Hungary.

North American rights to the Lozanov system have been acquired
by the Canadian government, and their teachers have been trained at
the institute in Sofia.

Tests of the Lozanov method have also been conducted at an
American university. Results surpassed expectations, according to
researchers. Students who had studied a Slavic language for some
360 class hours with an advanced Western teaching method were
compared to students who had been trained for only 120 hours using
the Lozanov method. On three written tests, the Lozanov-trained
students scored 95 to 100 percent, and in an oral proficiency test

based on an eight-point scale rating their performance was judged significantly higher than that of the students trained by the regular method. Researchers noted the students also had a strong feeling of enthusiasm and accomplishment with the Lozanov method.

Dr. Lozanov made a lecture tour of the US and Canada in 1971, and an International Symposium on the method was held in Bulgaria the same year.

Dr. W. Jane Bancroft, Associate Professor of French, University of Toronto at Scarborough, Ontario, Canada, has frequently traveled to Bulgaria and other Soviet-bloc countries, attended the 1971 symposium, and has written extensively about the Lozanov method and its application. For additional information about the system, see some of her articles in the *Educational Courier*: "The Psychology of Suggestopedia or Learning Without Stress," Vol. 42, No. 4, February, 1972. (Discusses the symposium and summarizes the basic theories behind the Lozanov methodology.) "Progressives and Pedagogues in the USSR," December/January, 1971. "Education for the Future or the Lozanov System Revisited," Vol. 43, No. 8, June, 1973. *The Lozanov Language Class* (pamphlet) $3.00.

The Educational Courier, Suite 315, 207 Queen's Quay, West, Toronto 1, Ontario, Canada. $1.00 per copy plus postage. (Mail service is very speedy.) The first article above was reprinted in Human Dimensions, Vol. 2, No. 1, 4380 Main Street, Buffalo, New York.

In the *Canadian Modern Language Review*, Dr. Bancroft describes class sessions with the Lozanov method in "Foreign Language Teaching in Bulgaria," Vol. XXVIII, No. 2, March, 1972, and new work in Hungary, "Civilization and Diversity—Foreign Language Teaching in Hungary," Vol. XXIX, No. 2, January, 1973. *Canadian Modern Language Review*, 194 Dawlish Avenue, Toronto, Ontario, Canada ($6.00 per year).

"A Word About Dr. Lozanov and His Method," Department of French News, University of Toronto, Scarborough, Ontario, Canada. Vol. 2, No. 22, March 4, 1971. *Michigan Foreign Language Newsletter*, January, 1972.

See also: "Learning Without Pain—Doctor Explains Suggestology," by Jo Carson, *Globe and Mail*, Toronto, March 9, 1971.

"Suggestion, Teachers and Doctors," Todor Tashev and Tanya Natan, *Bulgaria Today*, No. 9, 1966.

"Levitation, Yogis, and How Important It Is to Be a Skeptic. (Conversations with the Director of Sofia's Institute of Suggestology, G. Lozanov, About His Trip to India)," by V. Popovkin. Znaniye Sila, No. 7, 1968, pp. 47-48 (Moscow).

Dr. Lozanov's book describes the research on which his method is based and the various tests and applications of this teaching method. (The volume constituted his Ph.D. thesis for the University of Kharkov, in the USSR.) *Suggestology*, Georgi Lozanov, 1971 (p. 517), Nauka i Izkoustvo, 6 Russki Boulevard, Sofia, Bulgaria (4.59 Bulgarian leva). The book includes a summary of the text in English.

Proceedings of the First International Symposium on Suggestology in 1971 are available in English from: The Institute of Suggestology, 9 Budapest Street, Sofia, Bulgaria. *Suggestology and Suggestopedia Journal* (in English) $3.00, c/o Haemus Foreign Trade Co., 6 Russki Blvd., Sofia, Bulgaria. See also *The ESP Papers*, Ostrander and Schroeder, Bantam, 1975.

Additional information on American Research into Suggestology is available from Mankind Research Unlimited, Inc., 1143 New Hampshire Avenue, N.W., Washington, D.C. 20037.

More Information on Astrobiology

Astrobiology or cosmobiology, as the emerging new science is often called, is beginning to show that we are intimately connected to the universe—it might even be that the universe has a say in our conception. As information comes to light on the interplay between the human body and force fields and the body and fields of the universe, some believe we may have an alternative to the pill and other common forms of contraception. It may also aid those who have difficulty conceiving.

Sex selection, natural birth control, conception and birth defects—many people have queried us for more information about work in these areas by Czechoslovakia's Dr. Eugen Jonas and Hungary's Dr. Kurt Rechnitz. We have put together a book surveying all available material including commentary by various researchers on the Czech and Hungarian work. To put the investigations in context, the accumulating scientific research into astrobiology from the Soviet bloc and many other countries—France, Japan, the United States—is included. Relevant material on human force fields, such as the work of Dr. Harold Burr, is coordinated with the Czech findings in sex and conception. For the researcher there are how-to calculations for sex selection, birth control, and fertility.

Burr's recent publication—*Blueprint for Immortality, the*

Electric Patterns of Life, Neville Spearman, 1972—details decades of research done while he was professor of neuroanatomy at Yale. Exploring a detectable electric change that occurs at ovulation, Burr discovered that ovulation occurs outside of the normally recognized cycle. This appears to confirm the Jonas-Rechnitz clinical fdings and opens the way for verifiable methods of accurate natural birth control.

See *Natural Birth Control and How to Choose the Sex of Your Child,* Ostrander and Schroeder, Bantam, 1973 ($1.25). Available from Bantam Books, Inc., 414 East Golf Road, Des Plaines, Illinois 60016. In hardcover this book appears as *Astrological Birth Control,* Prentice-Hall, 1972 ($6.95); order from publisher, Englewood Cliffs, New Jersey 07632.

Art Rosenblum of the Aquarian Research Foundation has published a how-to booklet on the Jonas-Rechnitz method of birth control and sex selection. This work also discusses other unusual approaches to birth control uncovered by anthropologists. Computerized charts showing the position of the moon through the years, data needed for calculations, are included.

See *The Natural Birth Control Book,* Art Rosenblum and Leah Jackson; order from Aquarian Research Foundation, 5620 Morton Street, Philadelphia, Pennsylvania 19144 ($2.95).

ARF also publishes a newsletter with frequest updates on new developments in natural birth control, unorthodox medicine, items relevant to the commune movement, and some psi.

Further contacts: Birth Defect Research, PO Box 308, Giddings, Texas 78942; Bio-Dynamics Research, 2321 Colombia St., Palo Alto, California 94306.

Who's Who

If contacting or planning visits to scientists in foreign countries, you can sometimes glean professional addresses and background from such reference books as *Who's Who in the USSR,* available in many libraries. This sort of checking is a good idea because occasionally a visitor will be totally unaware he is talking to an expert in a relevant field. And because he doesn't know, pertinent questions never get asked.

Neither psi itself nor the study of it can be isolated from the culture in which it exists. In Soviet society particularly, there is a political aspect to all scientific and academic research. If journeying into Soviet research, it should really be remembered that this is not an open society; there is a communications curtain between East and West.

The Authors Guild of America, of which we are members, has continually protested against the viciously repressive treatment of writers in the Soviet-bloc countries. When these countries move toward détente in international policy, it is almost axiomatic that they become more hostile to freedom of thought and inquiry at home. In August, 1973, Nobel Prize winning author, Alexander Solzhenitsyn, banished from Moscow and still refused permission to publish, stated the Soviet government is "lacking in human or legal consideration." At the same time, Dr. Andrei Sakharov, father of the Soviet H bomb, is telling the world, "As far as the country's intellectual life is concerned, it actually does not exist. The isolation from the outside world, the lack of freedom to travel abroad and to return—this reflects on life here in a most destructive way. . . . It must be especially stressed that the role in society of the intelligentsia has been suppressed to an absurd degree." At this writing, Solzhenitsyn and Sakharov are frequently addressing statements to the international community—perhaps because they are about the only forthright objectors to certain aspects of Soviet society still at large—others who persisted in public commentary are either incarcerated in mental institutions, work camps, prisons, or on trial.

It is of prime importance to build bridges between psi investigation East and West. To do this, however, it is necessary to keep abreast of the shifting edicts of the powers that be in the USSR, in order not to become confused. For example, in 1971 yoga was in. Soviet scientists showed Western visitors films, papers, articles, on their decade-long research of yoga; films on the subject played in popular movie houses; experts spoke publicly of the bright future planned for yoga in the USSR as a method to improve health and intellect. By 1973 yoga was out. The official Sports Committee had degreed yoga "hostile to our society." It would be interesting, but out of place here, to speculate on why the officialdom suddenly decided it would be dangerous for the public to practice yoga.

It is understandable that Communist scientific investigators caught in this sort of on-again off-again crossfire make conflicting statements. If you want to be informed, major US newspapers, magazines, and many journals carry ample coverage of events and trends in the Soviet bloc.

Sources Closer to Home

Access to information on psi research and activities in America is easier to come by than a route to foreign information, but even here the path can get rugged. Libraries often do not carry psi journals. If yours doesn't, you might suggest that they subscribe to at least one of the recognized academic journals. Or if you want to be a philanthropist, pick out your favorite journal and give the library a subscription. Maybe enough people will become interested to prompt the library to continue subscribing in coming years.

Partial Listing of Journals and Newsletters

The American Dowser (quarterly). Scientific and personal accounts of dowsing, national and international. $6.00 per year. Danville, Vermont 05828.

The A.R.E. Journal (bimonthly). Edgar Cayce group publication, articles, reviews, some research and medical reports. $3.75 per year, A.R.E., Box 595, Virginia Beach, Virginia 23451.

ASPR Newsletter. Profiles, book reviews, news, and information on educational aspects of the parapsychology field. Also *The Journal of the ASPR* (quarterly). For the technical reader, scientific papers on current research. Both for $12.50 per year, the American Society for Psychical Research, 5 West 73rd Street, New York, New York 10023.

Human Dimensions (quarterly). Takes the "wholistic" view, includes news and articles on a variety of human dimensions—psi, meditation, frontier science, the arts, nutrition—plus one professional paper per issue. $3.50 per year, Human Dimensions Institute, 4380 Main Street, Buffalo, New York 14226.

The International Journal of Psychoenergetic Systems (quarterly). Scientific and technical papers from many countries "concentrating on the systemic properties of psychobiological systems." $19.50 per year, Gordon and Breach, Science Publishers, 1 Park Avenue, New York, New York 10016.

Journal of Paraphysics (bimonthly). Extensive translation and firsthand reports of psi-related work in the USSR and Czechoslovakia, as well as work of interest in England and on the Continent. Paraphysical Laboratories, Downton, Wiltshire, England.

The Journal of Parapsychology (quarterly). A long-established scientific journal dealing with ESP, PK, and related topics, published by J.B. Rhine's Foundation for Research on the Nature of Man. $8.00 per year. Also publishes the *FRNM Bulletin* (quarterly). $1.00 per year. Box 6847, College Station, Durham, North Carolina 27708.

Journal of the Society for Psychical Research (quarterly). Scientific reports, abstracts, and reviews from the world's oldest psychical research society, founded in 1882. The Society For Psychical Research, 1 Adam and Eve mews, London, W8, England.

Journal of the Spiritual Frontiers Fellowship (quarterly). Published by a nondemoninational group of clergy and lay people exploring parapsychology, healing, and mystical experience. Spiritual Frontiers Fellowship, 800 Custer Avenue, Evanston, Illinois 60202.

Journal of Transpersonal Psychology (quarterly). Often includes articles of interest to those concerned with the larger connotations of psi, research into peak experience and cosmic consciousness. PO Box 4437, Stanford, California 94305.

Frontiers of Science Newsletter (monthly). International coverage of parapsychological and parascientific research and news. Lists products, services, and seminars. Included with membership in Frontier of Science Association, $15.00 per year. Mankind Research Unlimited, 1143 New Hampshire Ave., NW, Washington, D.C. 20037.

New Horizon (published occasionally). Articles and research reports primarily from the Toronto Society for Psychical Research. $3.50 per issue, US; $3.00 in Canada. New Horizons Research Foundation, PO Box 427, Station F, Toronto, Ontario, Canada. (Toronto SPR headquarters, 10 North Sherbourne Street, Toronto 5, Ontario, Canada.)

Newsletter of the Institute of Noetic Sciences. A beginning publication put out by astronaut Edgar Mitchell's newly founded organization. The newsletter is available only to members, and Dr. Mitchell has invited people to write to him at the Institute for more information. 575 Middlefield Road, Palo Alto, California 94301.

Parapsychology Periodical. Articles, reprints, research reports, new and historic. California Parapsychology Foundation, 3580 Adams Avenue, San Diego, California 92116.

Parapsychology Review (bimonthly). Published by the Parapsychology Foundation (founded by the late Eileen Garrett), a well-written international clearinghouse for the

latest developments in the psychic dimension. News of
worldwide events, articles, and research reports. $4.00 per
year. Parapsychology Foundation, 29 West 57th Street, New
York, New York 10019.

Proceedings of the Parapsychological Institute of the State University of Utrecht (in English, published occasionally). Scientific reports, usually of work done by the distinguished
parapsychologist Professor W.H.C. Tenhaeff at the world's
first state-supported psi lab. Parapsychologisch Instituut der
Rijksuniversiteit, Springweg 5, Utrecht, Netherlands.

Psi Newsletter. Brief accounts of scientific research in India.
Department of Psychology and Parapsychology, Andhra University, Waltair, India.

Pursuit (quarterly). International in scope, reporting on enigmas
and anomalies of natural science from archaeology to UFO's.
$5.00 per year. Society for the Investigation of the Unexplained, Columbia, New Jersey 07832.

NOTE: *The International Journal of Parapsychology*, often referred
to in psi literature, was published by the Parapsychology Foundation from 1959-68. Contact the Foundation, 29 West 57th Street,
New York, New York 10019, for information on back issues.

Proceedings

Proceedings from professional conferences usually held annually
often contain valuable ideas and present new work.

The Academy of Parapsychology and Medicine—proceedings
from a variety of conferences are available: 314 Second Street, Los
Altos, California 94022.

The Academy of Psychical Research and Religion—proceedings
of academy's annual conference may be ordered from: 800 Custer
Avenue, Evanston, Illinois 60202.

Proceedings of the first symposium of the Parapsychological
Association presented at the 137th annual meeting of the American
Association for the Advancement of Science are available at $5.00.
Other issues of this series are planned. Order from PSI Communications Project, Suite 501 W, Newark College of Engineering,
323 High Street, Newark, New Jersey 07102. Also books featuring
psi research at Newark College of Engineering are available.

The Parapsychology Foundation—the foundation's annual conferences, held in Europe, bring together leaders in many different
areas of science and the humanities. Proceedings available from the

Parapsychology Foundation, 29 West 57th Street, New York, New York 10019

NOTE: This is a starter list. An increasing number of psi groups are coming out with journals and newsletters, some of which will no doubt prove excellent. Often these are announced in the publications listed. Fine psi journals exist in many foreign languages. Information and often copies can be found at the Parapsychology Foundation in New York.

Magazines

Popular magazines on things psychic have been coming and going at an almost supernormal pace lately. Two firmly rooted ones are:

Fate (monthly). The great-grandaddy of all popular magazines on the mysterious and unexplained. Stories and articles, first-person experiences, news of the psi and science scene included in the publisher's column and David Techter's books column. $4.50 per year, Clark Publishing Co., 500 Hyacinth Place, Highland Park, Illinois 60035.

Psychic (bimonthly). Slick, illustrated magazine, carrying news and well-annotated articles for the nonspecialist in all areas of psi; also interviews with leading personalities in the field. $5.50 per year, PO Box 26289, Custom House, San Francisco, California 94126.

Where Can I Find a Pyschic Group?

The perennial question—where to find a group of people who hare your slant on the psychic field. Most of the organizations publishing journals are open for public membership. Two national organizations exist, with chapters across the country. If these seem to be your cup of tea, to find the group nearest you, contact the national offices:

The Association for Research and Enlightenment (Edgar Cayce group), PO Box 595, Virginia Beach, Virginia 23451.

The Spiritual Frontier Fellowship, 800 Custer Avenue, Evanston, Illinois 60202.

Information on a wide variety of groups, courses, lectures, in various parts of the country, often appears in publication listings, particularly in *Parapsychology Review* and *Psychic*.

Apart from this, check events columns of newspapers, ask in psychic bookstores—there are thousands of groups, and we cannot begin to list them here.

See also: *Directory of the Occult*, Holzer, Regnery, 1974; *Psi, The Other World Catalogue*, Nicholas and June Regush, Putnam, 1974.

Educational Opportunities

For a ten-page directory entitled *Courses and Other Opportunities in Parapsychology*, send $1.00 and a self addressed Number 10 envelope to: Education Department, The American Society for Psychical Research, 5 West 73rd Street, New York, New York 10023.

Libraries

Many psi groups—Human Dimensions Institute in Buffalo, the Southern California SPR in Los Angeles, the Toronto SPR—to name just three—have libraries of varying sizes. Often they afford access to back issues of journals in the field. Probably the most extensive psi collection in the country is housed at the Eileen J. Garrett Library of the Parapsychology Foundation in New York City. This collection, well indexed and complete with a librarian, also includes items on psi-related subjects such as philosophy, drug research, humanistic psychology, as well as many foreign works and rare and antique books. Open to the public.

The American Society for Psychical Research also provides a good library in New York; members may borrow, the public may visit.

The A.R.E. in Virginia Beach has an excellent specialized modern library concentrating on the Cayce readings and related work, including extensive cross-indexing.

Supplies

If you do not have a hobby shop or electronics store near you to secure materials for experiments, a national mail-order company with a large selection of hard-to-find items is Edmund Scientific Co. Send for free catalogue, 300 Edscorp Building, Barrington, New Jersey 08007; in Canada, Scientific Products Co., 1947 Avenue Road, Toronto, Ontario. Canadian Catalog 25¢.

Books

If you can't find a particular book, write directly to the publisher. If it's out of print, there is still a good chance of locating it through a book-finders firm. They advertise in such spots as the *New York Times Book Review*. One California firm specializes in inexpensive reprints of works long out of print, such as some of the works of Baron von Reichenbach. They offer a gigantic list of titles for a small fee: Health Research, 70 Lafayette Street, Mokelumre Hill, California 95245.

A treasure-house for psychic, occult, and esoteric books is Samuel Weiser, Inc. They will answer questions about books available on a variety of topics. For catalog send 25¢ to 734 Broadway, New York, New York 10003.

Premonitions Registry Bureaus

To register a premonition about major national or international events:

Central Premonitions Registry, Box 482, Times Square Station, New York, New York

Premonitions Registry, Toronto Society for Psychical Research, 10 North Sherbourne Street, Toronto 5, Ontario, Canada

The Southern California SPR, send premonitions to: Carolyn Jones, 4325 East Broadway, Long Beach, California 90803.

Tapes

Tapes on various facets of psi are becoming available. Talks by each of the authors given at the 1971 national convention of the Association for Humanistic Psychology are on tape. These talks cover PK, acupuncture, telepathy, bioplasma, Kirlian photography, as well as a hypothesis to tie many of the phenomena together. Both talks available on a one-and-a-half-hour tape for $12.00. Order from Big Sur Recordings, 117 Mitchell Blvd., San Rafael, California 94903. (Indicate reel or cassette, mono or stereo.) "Parapsychology in Communist Countries," #647. Also from Big Sur other talks on psi related subjects. Send for list.

Psychology Today offers tapes on psychic phenomena. For the current list, see the magazine or write *Psychology Today*, Reader Service, PO Box 700, Del Mar, California 92014.

Apart from those listed on page 282, Science of Mind Symposium offers tapes on healing: "Meditation and Cancer," by O. Carl Simonton, M.D.; "Recollections of Things Spiritual," Gloria Swanson; "Scientific Studies of Unconventional Healing," Olga Worrall—$5.00 each from Science of Mind, PO Box 75127, Los Angeles, California 90075.

The Association for Research and Enlightenment has an extensive tape catalogue covering topics related to the work of Edgar Cayce, also meditation and psi. Send for listing: A.R.E. Tape Library, 2326 East Aldine, Phoenix, Arizona 85022.

UFOs

To report a UFO, contact Center for UFO Studies, PO Box 11, Northfield, Illinois 60093. Bulletins available.

FILMS

Inner Spaces and *The Ultimate Mystery* available from: Hartley Productions, Cat Rock Road, Cos Cob, Connecticut 06807.

ESP Film Festival, film lecture, Box 462, Station A, Vancouver, B.C., Canada.

Delving Deeper

The following publications, technical data, and suggestions, supplementing those in the text, are for people who wish to delve deeper into major topics covered in the handbook.

Points of Departure

For those interested in the forces that have helped bring in the new consciousness of psi, a few pertinent books are included here along with work mentioned in the chapter.

BAILEY, ALICE, *Esoteric Psychology*, New York: Lucis Paperback, 1971.

CASTANEDA, CARLOS, *Journey To Ixtlan*, New York: Simon and Schuster, 1972.

FARREN, D., *The Return of Magic*. New York: Harper and Row, 1972.

FREEDLAND, NAT, *The Occult Explosion*. New York: Berkley, 1972.

KOESTLER, ARTHUR, *The Roots of Coincidence*. London: Hutchinson, 1972.

KRISHNA, GOPI, *The Biological Basis of Religion and Genius*. New York: Harper and Row, 1972.

MUSES, C., and YOUNG, C., eds., *Consciousness and Reality*. New York: Outerbridge and Lazard, 1972.

OSTRANDER, S., and SCHROEDER, L., *Psychic Discoveries Behind the Iron Curtain*. Englewood Cliffs: Prentice-Hall, 1970; Bantam, 1971.

OSTRANDER, S., and SCHROEDER, L., *ESP Papers*. New York: Bantam, 1975.

PEARCE, JOSEPH, *The Crack in the Cosmic Egg*. New York: Pocket Books, 1973.

THOMPSON, W.I., *At the Edge of History*. New York: Harper Colophon, 1971.

WHITE, JOHN, ed., *The Highest State of Consciousness*. Garden City: Anchor Books, 1972.

Section One

For further data about plant reactions, apart from the sources listed here, check older libraries for the extensive but hard-to-find works of Sir Jagadis Chandra Bose.

ADAMENKO, V., "Living Detectors," *Technika Molodyezhi*, No. 8, 1970.

BACON, T., "The Man Who Reads Nature's Secret Signals," *National Wildlife*, February-March, 1969.

BOSE, J.C., *Plant Response as a Means of Physiological Investigation*. London: Longmans and Green, 1906.

———, "Awareness in Plants," *Consciousness and Reality* (C. Muses and C. Young, eds.). New York: Outerbridge and Lazard, 1972.

DAY, JOHN, "Music to Stimulate Plants," *Mind and Matter*, March, 1959.

DE LA WARR, G., "The Blessing of Plant Experiments," *Mind and Matter*, June, 1959.

———, "What Shall It Be?" *Mind and Matter*, September, 1959.

DE LA WARR, M., "Thought Transference to Plants," *Newsletter*, Radionic Centre Organization, Delawarr Labs, Oxford, England, autumn, 1969.

"ESP: More Science, Less Mysticism," *Medical World News*, March 21, 1969.

GRAD, B., "A Telekinetic Effect on Plant Growth," *International Journal of Parapsychology*, Vol. 5, spring, 1963.

———, "Some Biological Effects of the 'Laying on of Hands,' a Review of Experiments with Animals and Plants," *Journal of the American Society for Psychical Research*, Vol. 59, No. 2, 1965.

GRUZINOV, E., "Short Term Memory in Plants," *Evening Moscow*, September 20, 1969.

KUNZ, F.L., "Feeling in Plants," *Main Currents*, May-June, 1969.

LAWRENCE, L.G., "Electronics and the Living Plant," *Electronics World*, October, 1969.

————, "Electronics and Parapsychology," *Electronics World*, April, 1970.

————, "Biological Signals from Outer Space," *Human Dimensions*, summer, 1973.

LOEHR, FRANKLIN, *The Power of Prayer on Plants*. New York: New American Library, 1968.

MILLER, R.N., "The Positive Effect of Prayer on Plants," *Psychic*, March-April, 1972.

MUSES, C., "Communication of Consciousness Necessitates the Vacuum as Transducer," I. Konference O Vyzkumu Psychotroniky, Prague, 1973.

ROBBINS, J., and ROBBINS, C., "Startling New Research From the Man Who 'Talks' to Plants," *National Wildlife*, October-November, 1971.

RODALE, J.I., *Organic Gardening*, May, 1957.

ROMAN, A.S., INYUSHIN, V., "Some Data on Voluntary Influence on Electrobioluminescence," *Bioenergetics Questions*. Beverly Hills: Southern California Society for Psychical Research, 1972.

SCOTT, BRUCE, "Electricity in Plants," *Scientific American*, October, 1962.

"Solution to India's Food Shortage," *Newsletter of the Parapsychology Foundation*, January-February, 1970.

STUART, ARTHUR, "Plants That See, Feel and Think," *Popular Science Monthly*, Vol. 112, April, 1928.

TOMPKINS, P., and BIRD, C., "Love Among The Cabbages," *Harper's Magazine*, November, 1972.

————, *The Secret Life of Plants*. New York: Harper & Row, 1973.

WHITE, JOHN, "Plants, Polygraphs, and Paraphysics," *Psychic*, December, 1972.

Tapes

Cassette recordings of talks on their work by three investigators mentioned in the Plant Section are available at $5.00 each:

CLEVE BACKSTER, "Cellular Consciousness." A

ROBERT MILLER, "Scientific Evidence for the Effectiveness of Prayer." B

MARCEL VOGEL, "Thought and Molecular Structure." C

Designate by letter and order from: Science of Mind, PO Box

75127, Los Angeles, Califirnia 90075.

Section Two

Collections of Material on Kirlian Photography

Psychic Discoveries Behind the Iron Curtain, S. Ostrander and L. Schroeder, Chapters 16, 17, 18. Englewood Cliffs: Prentice-Hall, $8.95. Bantam, $1.25.

The Osteopathic Physician, October, 1972. Issue devoted to Kirlian photography. Includes data on "energy body" by Moss and Johnson; the aura as a diagnostic aid by J. R. Worsley, acupuncture expert; Kirlian photography as a new diagnostic tool by Amos, Hickman, and Krumsiek; evidence of psychic healing by Dean and DeLoach; material on psychotronics and eyeless sight. 733 Third Avenue, New York, New York 10017. $2.00.

A.R.E Journal, March, 1972. Whole issue on Russian psi research, includes general reports plus technical reports on psychoenergetic devices, key plans for Kirlian devices, diagrams, schematics, report by Dr. William Tiller. PO Box 595, Virginia Beach, Virginia 23451. 75¢.

Psychic, June, 1971. Special issue on ESP in the USSR, describes fact-finding trips to Russia by scientists, including Ullman and Moss; psychic enigmas and energies in the USSR by Ostrander and Schroeder; reports by researchers Rejdak and Raikov; and more. PO Box 26289, Custom House, San Francisco, California 94126. $1.00 for back issues.

Journal of Paraphysics. Has carried many articles and translations on Kirlian photography, among them, special issue: Prague Symposium of Psychotronics (1970), includes material by Inyushin, Sergeyev, Kulagin and work on relation of bioplasmic energies to hypnosis; Vol. 5, No. 4, 1971, reports from a seminar on bioplasma; Vol. 6, No. 1, 1972, devoted to material on the Kirlian effect and on living detectors and skin electricity; Vol. 6, No. 5, research by Inyushin relating to bioluminiscence and Kirlian photography; Vol. 7, No. 2, 1973, material on Kirlian photography reported at Moscow Conference on Bioenergetics, 1972. Paraphysics Laboratory, Downton, Wiltshire, England. $15.00 per year, $2.50 per issue (may fluctuate due to currency fluctuations).

Galaxies of Life (1973), p. 182. Includes thirteen papers from the First Western Hemisphere Conference on Kirlian Photography, Acupuncture and the Human Aura, edited by S.

Krippner and D. Rubin. Includes material by the Kirlians; new work by Moss and Johnson; Krippner; Dean; Tiller; Adamenko. Plans for making a device to detect acupuncture points also included. Profusely illustrated. Gordon and Breach Science Publishers, Inc., 1 Park Avenue, New York, New York 10016. $12.50.

Bioenergetics Questions. Translations into English of Soviet scientific papers presented at the 1969 Conference in Alma-Ata, USSR. Southern California Society for Psychical Research, 170 South Beverly Drive, Room 314, Beverly Hills, California 90212. $15 (tax deductible as a donation to this nonprofit society).

The Dimensions of Healing: A Symposium. Academy of Parapsychology and Medicine—1972 proceedings. Includes "Photographic Evidence of Healing Energies on Plants and People," Dr. Thelma Moss, and "Dimensions of Healing," Douglas Dean, plus many important papers from a wide range of researchers. 314 Second Street, Los Altos, California 94022. $10.00. For a popular account of the symposium, see *Fate*, June, July, 1973. 50¢.

On the Biological Essence of the Kirlian Effect, Inyushin, et al. (Forty-two-page booklet, in Russian.) Basic to research in Kirlian photography. Outlines Soviet scientists' theory of the nature of biological plasma, the energy visible in the Kirlian photos. Biology Faculty of the Kirov State University of Kazakhstan, 136 Kirova Street, Alma-Ata, Kazakhstan, USSR. 30 kopecks plus postage.

In the World of Miraculous Discharges, S. and V. Kirlian (1964), forty-page booklet, in Russian. How-to photography with high frequency electricity. Znanie, Tsentr, Novaya, D. 3/4, Moscow, USSR. 7 kopecks (about 10¢) plus postage.

"Kirlian" Electrophotography, Data Package A. 76 pages. How to photograph plus articles and schematics. Mankind Research Unlimited, Inc., 1143 New Hampshire Avenue, N.W., Washington, D.C. 20037. $4.75.

Some Helpful Articles on Kirlian Photography

"Radiation Field Photography," Moss and Johnson, *Psychic*, July, 1972. $1.00

"The Significance of Kirlian Photography," E. D. Dean. *Human Dimensions*, Vol. 2, No. 1, spring, 1973. 4380 Main Street, Buffalo, New York. $1.00

"Kirlian Photography: Photographing the Glow of Life," Natalie Canavor and Cheryl Weisenfeld. *Popular Photography*, February, 1973, Vol. 72, No. 2, 1 Park Avenue, New York, New York 10016. 75¢.

"Photography and Visual Observations by Means of High Frequency Currents," S. and V. Kirlian. *Journal of Scientific and Applied Photography*, Vol. 6, No. 6, 1961. Moscow. Translated by National Technical Information Service, Springfield, Virginia (No. FTD-TT-62-1549/ 1+2+4). $6.00. Also printed in *Galaxies of Life*.

"Electrography," S. Prat and J. Schlemmer. *Journal of the Biological Photographic Association*, Vol. 7, No. 4, June, 1939, pp. 145-48.

Other Material and Supplies

When we returned from Russia and East Europe in 1968, we brought back an enormous amount of published material on psi. The late Marjorie Kern, president of the Southern California Society for Psychical Research (then the affiliate of the American Society for Psychical Research), realized the importance of this information and graciously offered to help us make some of this data available to Western researchers through her organization. We turned over data to the Paraphysical Lab in England for distribution in the Commonwealth, and we turned over a fair number of Soviet and Czech scientific papers to be translated and distributed by the nonprofit SCSPR. A member of the SCSPR, George Schepak, a Russian émigré, began work on this mountain of technical translation.

In early 1971 we spoke on psi at a conference in Washington on Decision Making and Risk Analysis. Afterward we were approached by Carl Schleicher of Systems Consultants, Inc., a Washington-based seven-million-dollar-a-year engineering consulting firm specializing in government contracts. Like many people, Schleicher asked what had become of our scientific research material pertaining to *PDBIC*; and on learning we'd sent some of it to the SCSPR he suggested the translation might go faster if they had additional financing and an arrangement was worked out with Mrs. Kern. The data is now available in English.

To assess and explore practical applications of this and other psi data, SCI had set up a wholly owned subsidiary company, Mankind Research Unlimited, by February of 1972. Russian data became a cornerstone of this new business operation, and with proposals based on psi material, they were able to secure a number of US government contracts for research and feasability studies in "certain human engineering and psychosomatic evaluatory areas."

MRU also contracts to industry and foundations. Mankind Research Unlimited now has a staff of eighty-five scientific and technical consultants nationwide and a full-time staff of five involved in psi-related projects. As of 1973 the company became independent of SCI. MRU markets a number of psi items and data packages. For details contact Mankind Research Unlimited, Inc., 1143 New Hampshire Ave., NW, Washington, D.C. 20037.

Additional References (Section Two)

"Bacteria-Laden Halo Found," *Omen*, Vol. 1, and No. 2.

BARADUC, H. "The Human Soul, Its Movements, Its Lights." Paris: Librairie International de la Pensée Nouvelle, 1913.

BURR, H., *Blueprint for Immortality, The Electric Patterns of Life*. London, Neville Spearman, 1972.

———, *The Fields of Life*, New York, Ballantine, 1973.

FALLAH, S. "Research Notes on Current Activities in Selective Fields of Parapsychology." Washington: Cultural Information Analysis Center, May, 1969.

GULYAYEV, P.I., "The Electroauragram. The Electrical Field of Organisms as a New Biological Tie," Materials for the Symposium 'Physics and Biology,' Moscow, 1967, p. 19.

"Human Aura," editors of *Fate*. Evanston: Clark Publishing.

HUNT, I., and DRAPER, W., *Life Story of Nikola Tesla*. Denver: Sage Books, 1964.

KARAGULLA, S., *Breakthrough to Creativity*, Los Angeles: DeVorss, 1967.

KAZHINSKY, B.B., "Rays of Vision," in *Biological Radio Communication* (AD 415 676). Springfield, Virginia: Government Clearinghouse, April 1, 1963.

MILNER, D.R., and SMART, E.F., "There Are More Things," London: 1973.

MUGGERIDGE, MALCOLM, *Something Beautiful for God—Mother Teresa of Calcutta*. London: Collins, 1971.

NIPHER, F. E., *Transactions of the Academy of Sciences of St. Louis*, Vol. 10, pp. 151-66, plates xii-xvi, 1900.

OSTRANDER, S. and SCHROEDER, L., *Executive ESP*. Englewood Cliffs: Prentice-Hall, 1974.

PIERRAKOS, J., "Observations of the Energy Field (Aura) of Man in Health and Disease." *Newsletter*, Radionic Magnetic Centre Organization, Oxford. Winter, 1971.

PIETSCH, PAUL, "Shuffle Brain," *Harper's* Magazine. May, 1972.

POWELL, A. E., *The Etheric Double*. Wheaton: Theosophical Publishing House, 1973.

———, *The Astral Body*. Wheaton: Theosophical Publishing House, 1973.

PRAT, S., and SCHLEMMER, J., "Electrography." *Journal of the Biological Photographic Association*, Vol. 7, No. 4, Prague, June, 1939.

PRESMAN, A.S., *Electromagnetic Fields and Life*. New York: Plenum Press, 1970. (Originally, Moscow: Nauka Press, 1968.)

RUSSELL, E., *Design for Destiny*. London: Neville Spearman, 1971.

SCHWARZ, J., "The Human Aura—Paper for Fourth Conference on Voluntary Control of Internal States." Council Grove, Kansas, April, 1972.

SIVANANDA, SWAMI, *The Science of Pranayama*. Rishikesh, India: Yoga Vedanta Forest Academy Press, 1962.

The Lakhovsky MWO. Vista, California: BSR Foundation.

WORRALL, A., and WORRALL, O., *Explore Your Psychic World*. New York: Harper and Row, 1970.

ZABOTIN, V. I., "Aura Sensor for Contactless Recording of Biopotentials in the Air," *Bulletin of Leningrad University*, No. 21, Biology, Issue 4, 1968, pp. 99-103.

Luminescence

INYUSHIN, V. M., "The Problem of Bioplasma and Resonance Stimulation," *Problems of the Biodynamics and Bio-energetics of the Organism Under Normal Conditions and in Pathology*. Materials of the Republic Conference. Alma-Ata: May 11-13, 1971.

———, "Report No. 5," *Journal of Paraphysics* (in English). Vol. 6, No. 5, 1972. Downton, Wiltshire, England.

KAZNACHEEV, V. P. et. al., "On the Role of Superweak Luminescent Points in Biological Systems," *Bioenergetics and Biological Spectrophotometery*. Moscow: Nauka, 1967.

OSTROVSKIY, B., "Why Does A Cell Emit Light? On the Experiments of V. P. Kaznacheev." *Znaniye Sila*, No. 9, 1967, pp. 9-10.

Superweak Lumicescence in Biology, Materials of the Symposium Held in June, 1969. Moscow: Moscow State University, 1969.

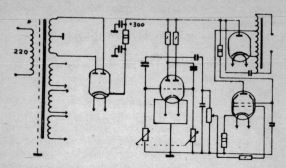

Schematic for high-frequency spark generator used in Kirlian research at the University of Moscow.

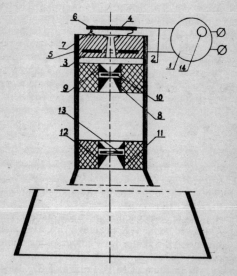

Soviet patent no. 118135 by S.D. Kirlian

TARUSOV, B. N., IVANOV, I.N., Petrusevich, Yu. M., *Superweak Luminescence of Biological Systems*. Moscow: Moscow State University, 1967.
ZHURAVLEV, A., *Living Light*. Moscow: Nauka, 1966.

Technical Section—Kirlian Photography

KIRLIAN PHOTOGRAPHY
  High-Frequency Spark Generator

University of Moscow scientists E. Ivanov, I. Shesterin, A. Tambiev, and M. Telitchenko describe in detail the Kirlian equipment and high-frequency generator they use in their research in their paper, "Design of a High-Frequency Generator for the Study of the Actions of Biological Objects in High-Frequency Field," published in *Scientific Reports of the University* [Moscow], Biological Sciences, No. 10, 1970, pp. 117-18, report No. 578 088 on Methods of Biological Research. The schematic for the high-frequency generator they use is included below. The high-frequency discharge is produced by use of a vacuum-type generator whose original construction was developed in collaboration with the electronics lab and biophysics department of the Moscow State University. The Moscow team reports that the generator operates at frequencies of twenty to one hundred twenty kilohertz and with potentials of zero to twenty kilovolts. It has a smooth-frequency tuning adjustment and a smooth regulation of the potential. The Moscow University scientists used the Kirlian system to study physiological characteristics of water organisms (plants, fish, worms) and invented a device for photographing biological objects in a moist medium. (See patent 264163.) Their paper, "Investigation of Various Water Organisms with the Kirlian Effect," is in *Bioenergetics Questions*, Alma-Ata, 1969.

Another type of high-frequency spark generator is described by scientists V.N. Lysikov, K.I. Krupenin, V.I. Chachulan, and P.L. Brik in "Simplified Generator for Photographing Biological Objects According to the S. D. Kirlian Method." Paper of Kishenevsky, s/h Institute of M.F. Frunze. T:37, 1964.

A simplified version of the Kirlian spark-generator circuit is included in the Kirlians' booklet, "In The World of Miraculous Discharges." Moscow: Knowledge, 1964.

The basic Kirlian patent is No. 106401, Class 57b, 1949. A Device for Photographing Various Kinds of Objects. It describes a method for obtaining photographs by means of high-frequency currents in which a high-frequency generator is connected to a conducting-capacitor electrode; and the object being examined constitutes the other electrode.

For the originals of any of the following patents, contact the Slavic division of the US Patent Office, Crystal City, Arlington, Virginia.

Soviet Patent No. 118135 (1950). Method of Taking Photographs of Different Kinds of Objects by S.D. Kirlian. In the original patent No. 106401, a plate of crystalline material is placed between the object and the photographic material in order to transmit images through a partition. The new method enables production of an enlarged image of the object. A diaphragm set in a vacuum tube with a hole covered by a plate of crystalline dielectric is placed between the object and photographic material. The second plate of the condenser is an electron-irradiated screen, which replaces the photographic material.

Soviet Patent No. 158205, Class 57b, 1962, by V.I. Mikhalevskii and K.Ya. Mikhalevskaya, is a device for photographing relief surfaces using high-frequency electrical fields. With this device the internal surfaces of cavities can be photographed. A small elastic balloon is used as the capacitor plate. The diagram shows a round metal disc (1), which holds a thin rubber elastic balloon (2). A conducting liquid is poured into the balloon through metal nipple (3) and closed by screw (4). The metal part (5) of the insulated handle (6) is screwed into the nipple and the unit is connected by a lead-in wire to the high-frequency spark generator. The photosensitive layer of a thin rubber film is pressed against the surface to be photographed by the pressure of the balloon. The high-frequency

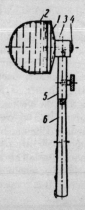

current is turned on to expose the film. A flat image of the cavity surface will be obtained on the film. Alternately, the balloon surface can be covered with a photosensitive layer and the balloon inflated after being placed inside the restricted cavity. After appropriate treatment of the photosensitive layer, the image is observed by reinflating the balloon with air or water.

Soviet Patent No. 1164905, 1963, by the Kirlians, is a device to permit photography with high-frequency currents in daylight. A regular camera (1) (generally 35 mm) can be used with the lens system removed. A cassette of roll film (2) is inserted in the camera and rolled from spool to spool with its photosensitive side facing outwards. The object to be photographed is pressed against the dielectric plate (3). The plate must fully cover a window cut in the front wall of the camera and fit into slots. The high-frequency generator is connected between the object and the metal conducting plate (5), which is mounted on an insulating dielectric plate (4) and pressed against the reverse side of the film. The time of exposure is determined by the shutter system in the camera.

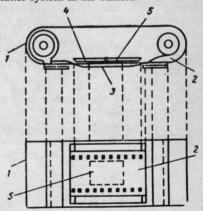

1. camera 2. film 3. dielectric plate 4. insulator 5. metal conducting plate

Soviet Patent No. 164906, class 21g, by Kirlian et. al. describes an Electrostatic Photography Apparatus. This device extends the range of application of the high-frequency technique by permitting visual examination or taking photographs of objects in difficult positions—e.g., cavities or holes. The electrode (1) has a shape corresponding to that of the object to be photographed and is made of a transparent conducting material. It is connected by a hinge to a concave mirror (2) whose frame is made of a dielectric. This frame is connected to a handle (3), which has a conductor (4) inside it to connect the electrode with the high-frequency generator. When the high-frequency current is turned on, a discharge occurs between the electrode and object, which is reflected into the magnifying mirror. Film placed on the working side of the electrode will permit photography of the object. The working side of the electrode should be covered with a dielectric grid to stabilize the discharge process.

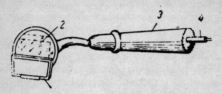

Soviet Patent No. 209968, 1966, by Victor Adamenko and S.D. Kirlian, is based on #164906 above and describes a method of producing high-frequency pictures of objects with complex irregular surfaces. This is done with the use of two transparent elastoplastic dielectrics divided by a thin textile layer. One dielectric is coated with a transparent conducting layer. The casing is placed in close contact with the complex surface being photographed or studied. Electrical current from the spark generator is supplied between the polarized dielectric and the conducting layer. A discharge takes place through the cells in the fabric and is two-dimensionally distributed according to the electrical condition of the object being observed or photographed. With this method any portion of the body can be photographed directly. A garment of silicon organic material can be used as the transparent electrode. It can be wrapped around the body and monitored photographically from a distance.

Soviet Patent 264163, Class 57b, 1968, by A. Tambiev, M. Telitchenko, I. Shesterin, is a high-frequency photography device that permits photographing biological objects in a moist medium and preserves the viability of the organisms investigated. The lower metallic plate is in the form of a mold which is filled with agar-agar solution. A hollow is made in the agar-agar gel, according to the form and size of the investigated object placed there, to photograph it within a drop of water or in a moist condition. With this method, organisms such as zooplankton preserve their viability during repeated photographs with high-frequency currents.

A host of other Kirlian patents deal with clamps and plates for photography. Patent 108088, 1950, condensor plates for contoured objects. No. 108090, 1950, condensor plates. No. 108092, 1950, device for photographing various kinds of objects. No. 108099, 1951, device for photographing various kinds of objects. No. 113807, 1955, device for photographing cylindrical metallic objects. No. 113837, 1955, device for photographing leaves of a plant. More details on these and other Soviet patents can be obtained from the US Patent Office.

Some of the Kirlian clamp devices include the following:

Photopincers. Capacitors put together in the form of tongs are used to photograph leaves of a plant. Flat metallic plates are used, strengthened by crosspieces made of a dielectric material. The interior surfaces are covered with celluloid with grooves for the film. The photopincers can be used for other flat objects as well. For photographing the crown of plants, one or both plates can be connected to the spark generator at a time to produce a variety of pictures.

Disc Plate. A circular plate on an insulated handle. With this device you can isolate certain areas of the object to be photographed, such as areas of the skin.

Elastic Device. Used to take pictures of cylindrical objects. A flexible spiral spring is attached to two handles made of dielectrical material. For photography of an object, the encased film is surrounded by the circumference of the device and with the aid of the handles squeezed together in the hands, is moved along the film. If the cylindrical object to be photographed varies in width, the spring, thanks to its elasticity, closely presses the film to the narrow parts so that the picture is uniform throughout. This device can be used for obaining images of rounded surfaces, such as hands and legs.

Roller Plate. For obtaining prints by rolling an object of unlimited length. Rollers can be interchangeable. Their width determines the dimensions of the photo.

Discharge-Optical Device. Can be attached to a microscope for direct observation of an object in a high-frequency field. 1. transitional nut; 2. threading; 3. upper half of device; 4. pin (bolt) for focusing; 5. threading; 6. lower half of device; 7. two holes (diameter 4 mm) arranged one in front of the other; 8. rubber washer; 9. contact; 10. metallic wire, precautionary circuit against a break through evaporation of the water; 11. lug in the form of a ring; 12. freely revolving contact nut; 13. ring; 14. threading; 15. traverse; 16. holes (diameter 5 mm); 17. floor of the traverse; 18. glass (thickness of 0.6–1 mm); 19. glass (thickness 0.13–0.14 mm); 20. chamber filled with water through hole 7; 21. 8 to 12 fold lenses (or objective); 22. brushing, which carries the lens (or objective); 23. threading (to match the threading of the tube of a microscope).

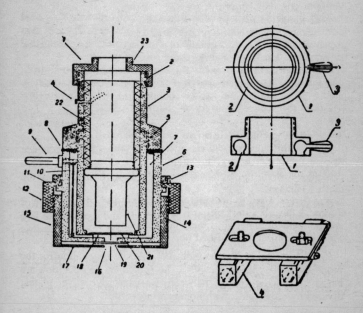

Discharge-optical plates to go with the discharge-optical device are designed to stretch the surface of the skin to make it ideally smooth for visual observation. (a) A wide ring (1) of dielectric material has a groove like a trench on one side. (2) The cavity is connected to a vacuum pump through (3).

(b) For stretching the skin in either direction, two bars with grooves (4) connected to a vacuum pump can be used.

For additional technical data on Kirlian photography see report by Dr. Tiller in *A.R.E. Journal*, March, 1972 (75¢). Box 595, Virginia Beach, Virginia 23451. See also *Galaxies of Life*.

A New Type of Detector to Register Physiological Functions
by
G.A. Sergeyev, G.D. Shushkev, E.G. Gryaznukhin
"The Sergeyev Detector"

We have developed a new type of detector that registers bio-plasmic processes in the human body. These highly sensitive detectors can register the physiological function of every area of the body.

The detector's operation is based on the following physical principle. The electrical-field activity of excited cells in the human organism can be regarded as turbulent low-temperature plasma that affects the dielectric properties of the environment.

Experimental investigations of low-temperature plasma structures of biological origin, together with computations performed by computer, brought us (Sergeyev, 1968) to the conclusion that the energetic processes in living organisms are subject to the formal requirements demanded by the thermodynamic systems with negative temperatures.

We established experimentally that the incidence of the sequence of processes of inversion of energetic levels is 7-9 hertz, which coincides with the mean fluctuation in frequency of intensity of the earth's magnetic field.

The maser effects in the living organism results in the emission of highly concentrated streams of free electrons and protons into free space, which may change the local properties of the dielectric conductivity of the air.

The above theoretical prerequisites laid the foundation for the proposed new type of detector. The principles of operation are based on a fixed voltage between two capacitive silver plates, divided by a dielectric with nonlinear properties.

Polarized barium titanate crystal (BaTiO₃) was used as a
dielectric. The voltae of the output of a barium titanate element is of
course determined by the formula:

$$\overline{\frac{4\Pi dE}{E(p)}} \quad \frac{\triangle l}{l}$$

where $E = 10^{12}$ dyne/cm²
at $t° = 10°C$ (Young's module)
             $d = 1.75 \cdot 10^{-6}$ (piezoelectric constant)

E(p) —dielectric constant depending on the P —the degree
of turbulence of the plasma field of biological origin.

hand on the values of the relative deformation $\frac{\triangle l}{l}$ (acoustical pressure) and on the other hand on the value of the dielectric constant
E(p).

During experimental testing, the detector was placed in an
acoustic screen and was used in a low-frequency range 0.1-30
hertz; within these boundaries it proved to be distorted relative to
the accoustical resonance point. But the voltages registered at the
output of the detectors reached tens of millivolts, in other words,
values that could not realistically be caused solely by the acoustical
pressure in any of the points of the body surface of the human
organism.

It follows from the examination of the formula that the changes of
the electric constant E(p) under the effect of the bioplasmic energy
field displace the value of the capacitive conductance in the gap
between the condensor plates.

Structurally the detectors are constructed in the form of flat
elements, which can be attached to any section of the human body
by elastic bands or placed at a distance (in accordance with specific
demands of the investigation). There is no direct contact between
detector and skin, since the elements are encapsulated in a rubber
sheath. The voltage of the detector output can be connected to the
input of any standard recording instrument (electroencephalograph,
electrocardiograph, vectorcardioscope, etc.). We have given the
recording curve the provisional name of "bioplasmagram."

The above translation was prepared by us and a Bulgarian
researcher. A "Sergeyev detector" was constructed in the early
1970's by a Czech émigré scientist, Jan Merta, while he was at
McGill University. Connecting the device to a stripchart recorder,
he was able to get some highly interesting results during psi

experiments. In Russia the detector has been used to chart field changes during PK (particularly with Nina Kulagina) and also to detect fields around a clinically dead body.

Section Three

Researchers have used many ingenious approaches to delve telepathy. Some of their findings are included in the sources listed. A few books are also mentioned for those interested in the subjective side of telepathy and in developing their own psi abilities.

BRAUD, W., and BRAUD, L., "Preliminary Explorations of Psi-Conducive States: Progressive Muscular Relaxation," *Journal of the American Society for Psychical Research*, Vol. 67, No. 1, 1973.

CAYCE, HUGH LYNN, *Venture Inward*. New York: Harper and Row (Harrow Paperback), 1972.

DEAN, E.D., "Non-Convential Communications," *Proceedings*, First Space Congress, Canaveral Council of Technology, 1964.

———, "Plethysmograph Recordings as ESP Responses," *International Journal of Neuropsychiatry*, Vol. 2, No. 5, 1966.

DUNNINGER, J., *The Art of Thought Reading*. Chicago: Clark, 1962.

EBON, M., *Test Your ESP*. New York: Signet, 1972.

———, Psychic Discoveries by the Russians. New York: Signet, 1971.

GARRETT, EILEEN, *Telepathy*. New York: Berkley, 1968.

———, *Awareness*. New York: Berkely, 1968.

———, *Many Voices*. New York: Dell, 1969.

HOY, D., *Psychic and Other ESP Party Games*. New York: Funk and Wagnalls, 1965.

KOGAN, I., "Is Telepathy Possible?" *Radio Engineering*, Vol. 22, pp. 75-81.

———, "Telepathy, Hypnosis and Observations," *Radio Engineering*, Vol. 22, pp. 141-44.

LEEK, SYBIL, *Telepathy*. New York: Collier, 1971.

LLOYD, D.H., "Objective Events in the Brain Correlating with Psychic Phenomena," *New Horizons*, summer, 1973.

MIHALASKY, J., and DEAN, D., "Bio-Communication," *Conference Record, 1969 IEEE International Conference on Communications*. Catalogue No. 69C29—Com.

OSTRANDER, S., and SCHROEDER, L. with DEAN, D., and
    MIHALASKY, J., *Executive ESP*. Englewood Cliffs: Prentice-
    Hall, 1974.

OWEN, A.R.G., "Editorial," *New Horizon*, summer, 1973.

PUHARICH, A., *Beyond Telepathy*. New York: Doubleday, 1962.

RHINE, LOUISA, *ESP in Life and Lab*. New York: MacMillan,
    1967.

RYZL, M., "A Method of Training in ESP," *International Journal
    of Parapsychology*, Vol. 8, 1966.

————, *How to Develop ESP in Yourself and Others*. San Jose,
    California: Ryzl Publication, Box 9459, Westgate Station.

SCHMEIDLER, G., "High ESP Scores After a Swami's Brief In-
    struction in Meditation and Breathing," *Journal of the
    American Society for Psychical Research*, Vol. 64, No. 1,
    1970.

SCHWARZ, B., *Parent-Child Telepathy*. New York: Garrett, 1971.

SERGEYEV, G., and KULAGIN, V., "The Interaction of Bioplasmic
    Fields of Living Organisms with Light Photon Sources,"
    Bioenergetics Questions. Beverly Hills: Southern California
    Society for Psychical Research, 1972.

SHERMAN, HAROLD, *How To Make ESP Work For You*. New
    York: Fawcett, 1969.

SINCLAIR, UPTON, *Mental Radio*. Springfield: Thomas, 1962.

TART, C., ed., *Altered States of Consciousness*. New York: Wiley,
    1969.

TENHAEFF, W.H.C., *Telepathy and Clairvoyance: Views of Some
    Little Investigated Capabilities of Man*. Springfield, Illinois:
    Charles Thomas, 1971. (Translated from Dutch.)

WHITE, R., "A Comparison of Old and New Methods of Response
    to Targets in ESP Experiments," *Journal of the American
    Society for Psychical Research*, Vol. 58, No. 1, 1964.

ULLMAN, M., "Can You Communicate with Others in Your
    Dreams?" *Family Circle*, August, 1971.

ULLMAN, L., and KRIPPNER, S., "An Experimental Approach to
    Dreams and Telepathy: II. Report of Three Studies," *The
    American Journal of Psychiatry*, Vol. 126, 1970.

————, "ESP in the Night," *Psychology Today*, Vol. 4, 1970.

WORRALL, A., and WORRALL, O., with OURSLER, W., *Explore
    Your Psychic World*. New York: Harper and Row, 1970.

Section Four

We weren't able to cover the increasing, intriguing research into

PK in this handbook. However, if you are trying to develop your ability, you might be interested in two recent reports on Nina Kulagina and Uri Geller, apparently outstanding PK talents who have attracted high-level scientific interest and research.

HERBERT, B., "Spring in Leningrad: Kulagina Revisited," *Parapsychology Review*, July-August, 1973.

VAUGHAN, A., "The Phenomena of Uri Geller," *Psychic*, June, 1973.

For information on Alla Vinogradova, who supposedly trained herself to do PK, see:

HERBERT, B., "Alla Vinogradova," *Journal of Paraphysics*, Vol. 6, No. 5, 1972.

TILLER, W., "A.R.E Fact Finding Trip to the Soviet Union," *A.R.E Journal*, Vol. 7, No. 2, 1972.

Further references to work mentioned in Section Four:

ALTER, A., "The Pyramid and Food Dehydration," *New Horizons*, summer, 1973.

BRUNLER, O., *Rays and Radiation*. Los Angeles: DeVorss, 1950.

FARRELL, T., "Secrets of the Great Pyramid Revealed," *Esquire*, April, 1973.

FLANAGAN, P., *The Pyramid and Its Relation to Biocosmic Energy*. Glendale: Pyramid Products, 1972.

GRAD, B., *Pastoral Psychology*, September, 1970.

————. *Journal of Pastoral Counseling*, fall-winter, 1971-72.

KARAGULLA, S., "Crystal-Magnets Have Energy Fields," *Breakthrough To Creativity*. Los Angeles: DeVorss, 1967.

KAZNACHEYEV, V., et. al., "The Role of Superweak Light Flows in Biological Systems," *Bioenergetika i Biologischeskaya Spektrofotometriyia*. Moscow: Nauka, 1967.

LAYNE, M., and CRABB, R., eds., *The Cameron Aurameter*. Vista: BSR Institute, 1970.

LONG, MAX FREEDOM, *The Secret Science at Work*, Los Angeles: DeVorss, 1953.

MRKVICKA, J., "Moscow Interview on 'Pyramids,' " *Journal of Paraphysics*, Vol. 6, No. 5, 1972.

OSTROVSKY, B., "Why Does a Cell Emit Light?" *Znayiye Sila*, No. 9, 1967.

OWEN, A.R.G., "The Shapes of Egyptian Pyramids," *New Horizons*, summer, 1973.

ROBINSON, L., *The Great Pyramid and Its Builders*. Virginia Beach: Edgar Cayce Publishing, 1958.

ROSS, S., "A Pyramid that Sharpens Razor Blades?" *En-Route*. Montreal: Air Canada, February 20-26, 1973.

SARYCHEV, S., and NIKANDROV, A., "Reciprocal Influences of Biological Generators Set in the Foci of Spherical Mirrors," *Problems of the Biodynamics and Bioenergetics of the Organism Under Normal Conditions and in Pathology*. Alma-Ata: Materials of the Republic Conference, 1971.

SIMMONS, D., "Experiments on the Alleged Sharpening of Razor Blades and the Preservation of Flowers by Pyramids," *New Horizons*, summer, 1973.

"Symposium of Psychotronics," *Journal of Paraphysics*, Vol. 5, Nos. 1 and 2, 1971.

Section Five

Arranged (hopefully) in order of helpfulness for the amateur experimenter.

1. *Breakthrough*, Konstantin Raudive (1971, 391 pages).
   Taplinger Publishing Co.
   200 Park Avenue South,
   New York, New York 10003. $10.00

   Lancer Books, Inc.
   1560 Broadway,
   New York, New York 10036. $1.75

2. *Breakthrough Record* (Catalogue No. VMS 100). Small LP record of sample voice phenomena recorded by Raudive. Very helpful in training the ear to hear the voices and includes samples of how they sound according to the different recording methods used.

   Vista Productions,
   64a Lansdowne Road,
   London W11 2LR England. $3.00
       (For speedy airmail service, add $2.00 postage.)

3. *Carry On Talking*, Peter Bander (1972, 167 pages).

Colin Smythe Ltd.
6 Station Road,
Gerrards Cross,
Buckinghamshire, SL9 8EL England. £1.90 plus postage.

4. "The Phenomena of Friedrich Jurgenson—An Analysis by Professor Hans Bender," *Journal of Paraphysics*, Vol. 6, #2, 1972.
Downton, Wiltshire, England. $15.00 per year.
(Same paper in German: *Zeitschrift für Parapsychologie*, University Institute of Freiburg, Vol. 12, No. 4.)

5. "Parapsychology in Germany," Hans Bender. *Parapsychology Review*, Vol. 3, No. 5, September-October, 1972.
29 West 57th Street, New York, New York. 85¢.

6. "About the Possibilities of Recognizing Sounds of Speech—Concerning the Usefulness of the Visible-Speech-Process and Other Methods in the Analysis of 'Voice Recordings' on Electromagnetic Tape" (in German), Jochem Sotscheck. *Zeitschrift für Parapsychologie und Grenzgebiete der Psychologie*, Vol. 12, No. 4.
University Institute of Freiburg,
Eichhalde 12, 78 Freiburg, Germany.

7. *Sprechfunk Mit Verstorbenen* (Radio-Link With the Beyond) (in German, 1967), Friedrich Jurgenson.
Verlag Hermann Bauer, KG,
78 Freiburg, Germany.

8. "Spirit Voices Tape-Recorded," Rolf Schaffranke, *Fate*, July, 1970. 50¢.
Clark Publishing Co.
500 Hyacinth Place, Highland Park, Illinois.

9. "Recording Voice Phenomena," *Newsletter*, No. 32, October 25, 1972.
Aquarian Research Foundation,
5620 Morton Street,
Philadelphia, Pennsylvania 19144. $1.00 ($10.00 per year.)

10. "Discussion re Voice Phenomena," *Light*, summer, 1971.
College of Psychic Studies,
16 Queensbury Place, London, SW 7, England.

References

BAILEY, ALICE, *Esoteric Psychology*. New York: Lucius, 1971.

CASSIRER, MANFRED, "Two Visits to Dr. Raudive," *Parapsychology Review*, Vol. 3, #2, March-April, 1972.

CAYCE, HUGH LYNN, *Venture Inward*. New York: Harrow Books, 1972.

EBON, MARTIN, *They Knew the Unknown*. New York: World, 1971.

FORD, ARTHUR, *Nothing So Strange*. New York: Paperback Library, 1968.

"From the European Press—Swiss Research on the 'Voices,' " *Parapsychology Review*, Vol. 3, No. 4, July-August, 1972.

GARRETT, EILEEN, "On Death," *Parapsychology Review*, Special Issue, October, 1970.

KING, PAUL, "Confess, Cousin, or the Sound of Your Voice Will Do It For You," *Canadian Magazine*, January 13, 1973.

MYERS, F.W.H., *Human Personality and Its Survival of Bodily Death*. Secaucus, N.J.: University Books, 1961.

ROBERTS, JANE, *The Seth Material*. Englewood Cliffs: Prentice-Hall, 1970.

———, *Seth Speaks*. Englewood Cliffs: Prentice-Hall, 1972.

SMITH, SUSY, *Life Is Forever*. New York: Putnam's, 1974.

TRECHTER, DAVID, "Review of *Carry On Talking*," *Parapsychology Review*, Vol. 3, No. 6, November-December, 1972.

UPHOFF, WALTER, "Review of *Breakthrough*," *Psychic*, October, 1971.

WHITE, STEWART EDWARD, *The Betty Book*. New York: Berkley, 1969.

———, *The Unobstructed Universe*. New York: Dutton, 1940.

Index

Index